Franchising and Licensing

Franchising and Licensing

Two Ways to Build Your Business

Andrew J. Sherman

amacom

American Management Association

This publication is designed to provide accurate and authoritative information in regard to the subject matter covered. It is sold with the understanding that the publisher is not engaged in rendering legal, accounting, or other professional service. If legal advice or other expert assistance is required, the services of a competent professional person should be sought.

Library of Congress Cataloging-in-Publication Data

Sherman, Andrew.
    Franchising and licensing : two ways to build your business / Andrew Sherman.
        p.   cm.
    Includes index.
    ISBN 0-8144-5024-5
    1. Franchises (Retail trade)—United States.   2. License agreements—United States.   I. Title.
HF5429.235.U5S54 1991   90-56193
658.8′708—dc20   CIP

Printing number

10 9 8 7 6 5 4 3 2 1

This book is dedicated with love
to my first franchisee,
Matthew Harris Sherman,
and to my wife,
Judy Joffe Sherman.

I thank them for their never-ending
support and patience.

Contents

Foreword

" **** " — four stars for Andrew Sherman's new book, *Franchising and Licensing: Two Ways To Build Your Business*. This book has been written from the vantage point of the practitioner. Andrew Sherman, who has been engaged in the business of franchising for the past dozen years, has seen the best and the worst sides of this business.

From this viewpoint, he has provided in these pages some excellent advice—do's and don'ts—for would-be franchisors. In addition, those who are currently in the business of franchising would do well to review their own development methods and practices in light of this fresh insight.

Although franchising has been called "the most significant innovation in business since the creation of the corporation over 200 years ago," and while it has been described by economists and experts as the "wave of the future," it is not for everyone; nor is it suited to every business development venture.

Franchising and Licensing clearly makes the case for carefully evaluating the advantages and disadvantages of this unique system of business development, and then after careful consideration and thorough planning, moving forward.

For those would-be entrepreneurs who are considering the formation of a franchise company and for many entrepreneurs who are engaged in the franchise business, I recommend Andrew Sherman's book for continuing education and enlightenment.

William B. Cherkasky
President, International
Franchise Association

Preface: Current Trends in Franchising

It would be difficult to imagine a day going by in either our personal or business lives during which we did not interact with a franchised business.

On a personal level, we can buy our home, cars, food, and our clothing from franchised stores and offices. We drop off our vehicles in the morning to franchised automobile service centers and our clothing for laundering at franchised dry cleaners. We plan our vacations with franchised travel agencies and enjoy our vacations and recreation at franchised entertainment facilities and health clubs. We can have our children tutored and our pets groomed at franchised offices nationwide.

At the business level, we can contract for temporary help, cleaning services, printing, accounting, computers, automobile rental, corporate travel, video production, interior design, coffee and tea, catering, courier services, and even rented mail boxes from franchised companies across the country. We can buy our business forms, business supplies, and even have our businesses sold by franchisors and franchisees.

The diversity of products and services offered by franchised businesses has enabled the contractual method of marketing and distribution known as franchising to become a powerful force in the United States economy. Franchised sales of goods and services at well over 525,000 locations across the country reached nearly $700 billion in 1990.

Franchised businesses now account for well over eight million jobs in nearly 100 different industries. From a global perspective, nearly 400 franchisors have sold franchises abroad, accounting for over 32,000 overseas locations in markets as diverse as Africa, Japan, Israel, France, and the Caribbean. Clearly, the men and women who make up the franchising community have a lot to be proud of.

How does all of this impact on you, the prospective franchisor, key staff member, advisor, investor, or lender of prospective franchisors and currently growing franchise companies? Maybe your thriving small business should think about franchising as a method of growth and expansion. Or, consider life as a subfranchisor, master licensee, or single-unit franchisee as a way to satisfy your entrepreneurial appetite. Or perhaps your role as a service provider or product supplier to franchisors and franchisees qualifies you for membership. But each requires a fundamental understanding of the business and legal issues affecting the franchise relationship. This knowledge is crucial to prosper in today's competitive marketplace. As you can see, there are many ways to become a member of this dynamic community.

What has made franchising so popular in the United States? From the perspective of the franchisor, franchising represents an efficient method of rapid market penetration and product distribution without the typical capital costs associated with internal expansion. From the perspective of the franchisee, franchising offers a method of owning a business, but with a mitigated chance of failure due to the initial and ongoing training and support services offered by the franchisor. From the perspective of the consumer, franchised outlets offer a wide range of products and services at a consistent level of quality and at affordable prices.

There are several trends, some good and some not so good, that will affect the growth of franchising in our economy as we approach the new century. Among the more positive developments in franchising are:

- A growing interest from the commercial banking and venture capital industries in franchising, which should lead to more loans and investments being made in franchisors and franchisees
- Franchisors joining forces, sometimes through master franchises or joint ventures and sometimes through domestic and international mergers and acquisitions, in order to offer combination franchises (for example, pizza and ice cream or mufflers and transmissions), operational and administrative efficiencies, and franchised mini-malls
- An increasing commitment from our nation's schools and universities to recognize franchising as a separate educational discipline
- An increased number of U.S.-based franchisors entering into international markets, which positively contributes to our trade deficit and the spirit of American innovation
- A deliberate effort by franchisors, subfrancisors, and state and local governments to expand the role of women and minority groups in franchising
- A growing commitment among existing franchisors to set up franchisee advisory councils, awards programs, regional and national meetings and seminars, and other programs to ensure that franchisees receive the support and recognition that they deserve
- The downsizing of corporate America coupled with a troubled economy is causing the layoffs of many well-trained executives who are candidates for franchises, leading to an even higher level of sophistication and financial strength of our nation's franchisees
- An increasing number of Fortune 500 companies entering the franchising area (such as Prudential Insurance Company, Merrill Lynch, Ashland Oil, S. C. Johnson, Union Carbide, First Interstate Bancorp), which in turn has resulted in new-unit and conversion franchising within new and often previously fragmented industries such as banking, real estate, insurance, and financial services

- Further growth predicted by the International Franchise Association within some of the franchising industries that have traditionally been the strongest, such as home improvement, cleaning services, businesses aids and services, fast food, automotive repair, lodging and leisure, equipment rental, convenience stores and educational services and unprecedented growth is expected in the franchising of health care services, child care services and food delivery services
- The maturation and growth of many of our nation's franchisors, forcing the entrepreneurial and free-wheeling management styles of the company's founders to the wayside, to be replaced by more seasoned corporate executives and management systems

Regrettably, there are also some disturbing trends, which, if not curbed, will surely negatively affect the future and growth of franchising. Among them are:

- Legal disputes between franchisors and franchisees cluttering our nation's courts, usually the result of some misunderstanding pertaining to the rights and obligations of the parties involved
- An explosion of companies in recent years offering "consulting services" to franchisors and franchisees; many of which are unqualified, and many urge the premature launch of a franchise program
- A growing number of franchisors who, either because they are undercapitalized or poorly counseled, place too great an emphasis on franchise sales rather than franchise support and services
- The U.S. Department of Commerce recently shutting down the only federal office that truly monitored the growth of franchising and its impact on the economy
- Capitol Hill's launching of a new round of hearings and Congressional inquiries in order to consider even more legislation on top of the existing web of federal and state regulations affecting franchising
- The International Franchise Association's prediction

that the number of franchisors could easily double to over 5,000 during the next ten years, creating many new opportunities, but also creating intense competition for qualified franchisees and experienced franchise executives in the areas of field operations, sales and marketing, corporate finance, and administration

In order to take advantage of the positive aspects of franchising, and to reverse these negative trends, current and prospective members of the franchising community need to be aware of—and respect—the key elements of the foundation of a successful franchising program.

A commitment to quality, fairness, and effective communication among franchisors and franchisees should go a long way in reducing disputes among franchisors and franchisees. Current and prospective franchisors must be committed to supporting and servicing the franchises they sell. Franchisors who develop strategic plans which focus on *quantity* of franchisees and expansion, rather than on *quality* of franchisees and training, are surely headed for disaster. These franchising management philosophies will be emphasized throughout the course of this book.

Franchising and Licensing has been written for two primary audiences: growing businesses considering franchising and companies already engaged in franchising. For the former, this book will explain the key management, operational, and legal issues that are involved in building a franchising program. For the latter, this book will examine certain issues that are of continuing concern for franchisors at all stages of development, including such topics as protection of intellectual property, litigation, international expansion, executive compensation, mergers and acquisitions, regulatory compliance, and field support.

This book, however, is not limited to these two audiences. Prospective franchisees and area developers should find this book helpful not only in gaining insight into the inner workings of a successful franchisor, but also in the evaluation of franchise offerings. Professional advisors of all types who work with franchisors and franchisees should find the material contained in this book useful and helpful in advising their clients.

Franchising and Licensing is divided into five primary parts. Each of the first four addresses the core management and legal issues that are critical in building and maintaining successful franchising programs: Management Systems focuses on the human resources, operations, and quality control concerns that are at the heart of a franchised business; Legal and Strategic Issues focuses on the regulatory and contractual issues that are of concern to the early-stage and growing franchisor, as well as protection of intellectual property, compliance systems, and dispute management, which are of special concern to the mature and established franchisor; Sales and Marketing Strategies focuses on domestic and international sales and marketing strategies; and Financial Strategies focuses on key issues for franchisors at all growth levels, such as capital formation and mergers and acquisitions.

Part Five of *Franchising and Licensing* explores the various alternatives to franchising, such as licensing, joint ventures, distributorships, and multi-level marketing structures, with special focus on the two primary types of licensing: technology licensing and merchandise licensing. Part Five is useful not only for licensing professionals, but also for prospective franchisors who are considering all of the alternative growth-oriented distribution strategies prior to jumping into franchising.

Andrew J. Sherman
Washington, D.C.

Acknowledgments

The concepts and issues discussed in this book are the result of over twelve years experience in franchising, from both a legal and business perspective. It would be impossible to thank all of the people with whom I have had the pleasure of working along the way. The support of the professional staff of the International Franchise Association and of my colleagues at Silver, Freedman & Taff deserve special mention.

There are certain individuals whose time, hard work, support and patience should be specially mentioned. I wish to thank Deborah Bouchoux for her assistance on Chapters 9 and 14, Melinda Rae for her assistance on Chapter 11, and especially Cheryl Costello for her assistance on Chapters 4 and 8. I owe special thanks to my secretary, Michele Lewis for her word processing magic, organizational skills and patience.

Once again, Andrea Pedolsky of AMACOM Books was there to provide moral support in pulling this entire project together. She is an excellent orchestrator.

Last, but certainly not least, I am grateful to my wife Judy and to my son Matthew, who once again sacrificed time with me so that I could complete this manuscript. I couldn't ask for a more supportive family.

Part One

Management Systems

1

The Foundation of Franchising

Over the last two decades, franchising has emerged as a popular expansion strategy for a variety of product and service companies, especially for smaller businesses that cannot afford to finance internal growth. Recent Department of Commerce statistics* demonstrate that retail sales from franchised outlets comprise nearly 40 percent of all retail sales in the United States, estimated at over $640 billion and employing some 7.3 million people in 1988. Notwithstanding these impressive figures, franchising as a method of marketing and distributing products and services is really only appropriate for certain kinds of companies. Despite the favorable media attention that franchising has received over the past few years as a method of business growth, it is not for everyone. There are a host of legal and business prerequisites that must be satisfied before any company can seriously consider franchising as an alternative for rapid expansion.

Many companies prematurely select franchising as a growth alternative and then haphazardly assemble and launch the program. Other companies are urged to franchise by unqualified consultants or advisors who may be more interested in professional fees that in the long-term success of the franchising program. This has caused financial distress and failure

*Franchising in the Economy 1986–1988, U.S. Department of Commerce, February 1988.

at both the franchisor and franchisee level and usually results in litigation. Current and future members of the franchising community must be urged to take a responsible view toward the creation and development of their franchising programs.

Reasons for Franchising

There are a wide variety of reasons cited by successful franchisors as to why franchising has been selected as a method of growth and distribution. Through franchising, they are able to:

- Obtain operating efficiencies and economies of scale
- Achieve more rapid market penetration at a lower capital cost
- Reach the targeted consumer more effectively through cooperative advertising and promotion
- Sell products and services to a dedicated distributor network
- Replace the need for internal personnel with motivated owner/operators
- Shift the primary responsibility for site selection, employee training and personnel management, local advertising, and other administrative concerns to the franchisee, licensee, or joint venture partner with the guidance or assistance of the franchisor

In the typical franchising relationship, the franchisee shares the risk of expanding the market share of the franchisor by committing its capital and resources to the development of satellite locations modeled after the proprietary business format of the franchisor. The risk of business failure of the franchisor is further reduced by the improvement in competitive position, reduced vulnerability to cyclical fluctuations, the existence of a captive market for the franchisor's proprietary products and services (due to the network of franchisees), and the reduced administrative and overhead costs enjoyed by a franchisor.

The Foundation of Franchising

Responsible franchising is the *only* way that franchisors and franchisees will be able to harmoniously co-exist in the twenty-first century. Responsible franchising requires a secure foundation from which the franchising program is launched. Any company considering franchising as a method of growth and distribution or any individual considering franchising as a method of getting into business must understand the key components of this foundation:

- *A proven prototype location* (or chain of stores) that will serve as a basis for the franchising program. The store or stores must have been tested, refined, and operated successfully and be consistently profitable. The success of the prototype should not be too dependent on the physical presence or specific expertise of the founders of the system.
- *A strong management team* made up of internal officers and directors (as well as qualified consultants) who understand both the particular industry in which the company operates and the legal and business aspects of franchising as a method of expansion
- *Sufficient capitalization to launch and sustain the franchising program* to ensure that capital is available for the franchisor to provide both initial as well as ongoing support and assistance to franchisees (a lack of well-written business plan and adequate capital structure is often the principal cause of demise of many franchisees).
- *A distinctive and protected trade identity* that includes federal and state registered trademarks as well as a uniform trade appearance, signage, slogans, trade dress, and overall image

- *Proprietary and proven methods of operation and management* that can be reduced to writing in a comprehensive operations manual, not be too easily duplicated by competitors, maintain their value to the franchisees over an extended period of time, and be enforced through clearly drafted and objective quality control standards
- *Comprehensive training programs for franchisees—* both at the company's headquarters and on-site at the franchisee's proposed location at the outset of the relationship and on an ongoing basis
- *Field support staff* who are skilled trainers and communicators and must be available to visit and periodically assist franchisees as well as monitor quality control standards
- *A set of comprehensive legal documents* that reflect the company's business strategies and operating policies. Offering documents must be prepared in accordance with applicable federal and state disclosure laws, and franchise agreements should strike a delicate balance between the rights and obligations of franchisor and franchisee.
- *A demonstrated market demand* for the products and services developed by the franchisor which will be distributed through the franchisees. The franchisor's products and services should meet certain minimum quality standards, not be subject to rapid shifts in consumer preferences (e.g., fads), and be proprietary in nature. Market research and analysis should be sensitive to trends in the economy and specific industry, the plans of direct and indirect competitors, and shifts in consumer preferences
- *A set of carefully developed uniform site selection criteria and architectural standards* that can be readily and affordably secured in today's competitive real estate market
- *A genuine understanding of the competition* (both direct and indirect) that the franchisor will face in marketing and selling franchises to prospective franchises

as well as the competition the franchisee will face when marketing products and services

- *Relationships* with suppliers, lenders, real estate developers, and related key resources as part of the operations manual and system
- *A franchisee profile and screening system* (as discussed in Chapter 10) in order to identify the minimum financial qualifications, business acumen, and understanding of the industry that will be required by a successful franchisee
- *An effective system of reporting and record keeping* to maintain the performance of the franchisees and ensure that royalties are reported accurately and paid promptly
- *Research and development capabilities* for the introduction of new products and services on an ongoing basis to consumers through the franchised network
- *A communication system* that facilitates a continuing and open dialogue with the franchisees and as a result reduces the chances for conflict and litigation within the franchise network
- *National, regional, and local advertising, marketing, and public relations programs* designed to recruit prospective franchisees as well as consumers to the sites operated by franchisees

Strategic Prerequisites to Launching a Franchising Program

The most important strategic prerequisite for the success of any business format franchise system is the operation and management of a successful prototype. This prototype location is where all operating problems must be resolved, recipes and new products tested, equipment and design decisions made, management and marketing techniques tested, a trade identity and goodwill established, and financial viability proven. It is not enough to have a prototype unit that is "somewhat similar" to the system and format that will be franchised. The franchisee's location must be an exact replica of the prototype. In short, the franchisor is selling a tried and tested package to a franchisee, and the contents of that package must be clearly identified prior to sale.

The concept of a system or prescribed business format that is operated according to a uniform and consistent trade identity and image is at the heart of a successful franchising program. Therefore, a prospective franchisor must be able to reduce all aspects of running the business to be franchised into an operations and training manual for use by franchisees in the day-to-day operation of their business. These systems must be adequately and clearly communicated in the initial and ongoing training program. If a company offers services that are highly personalized or a product that is difficult to reproduce, then franchising may not be the most viable alternative for growth because of the difficulty in replicating these systems or products in the operator's manual or in the training program. Similarly, if all the "kinks" in the system have not yet been worked out, it is probably premature to consider franchising.

There are a number of other important business and strategic factors that must be considered before franchising. First, franchising should not be viewed as a solution to undercapitalization or as a "get rich quick" scheme. While it is true that franchising is less capital-intensive than is construction of additional company-owned sites, the initial start-up costs for legal, accounting, and consulting fees can be extensive. Second, franchisors must view franchising as the establishment of a series of long-term relationships, and the ongoing success of the company as a franchisor will depend on the harmony of these relationships. A field support staff must be built to provide ongoing services to the existing franchisees, as well as to maintain quality control and uniformity throughout the system. New products and services must be developed so that the franchisee can continue to compete with others in its local market. Innovative sales and marketing strategies must be continually developed to attract new customers and retain existing patrons of the franchised outlet. If the franchisor expects the franchisee to continue to make its royalty payment on gross sales each week, then an array of valuable support services must be provided on an ongoing basis to meet the franchisee's changing needs.

Curbing the Failure Rate of Early-Stage Franchisors

One of the underlying premises of this book is that successful franchising requires proper planning, capital, and management. Our mission is to avoid the mistakes made by the hundreds of franchisors that have failed over the past few years. That's right, hundreds. Each year since 1986, between seventy-five to one hundred franchisors *went out of business.** This figure represents between 3 to 5 percent of all franchisors operating during those years. Figure 1-1 represents forty of the more common reasons why franchisors fail. *Read them carefully and read them often.* Make sure that your company does not meet the same fate in launching and building its franchising program.

Understanding the Franchisee of the 1990s

One way to avoid failure is to understand the profile of today's prospective franchisee. A wide variety of marketing, planning, operational, and strategic decisions can be made by the growing franchisor once certain basic premises are understood. As a general rule, franchisees in today's competitive markets are getting smarter, *not* dumber. The better educated, better capitalized franchisee is here to stay. As franchising has matured, prospective franchisees have more resources (seminars, media articles, trade shows, International Franchise Association programs, etc.) than ever before to turn to for information and due diligence. These new, sophisticated franchisees are very differ-

*Franchising in the Economy 1986–1988, U.S. Department of Commerce, February 1988.

Figure 1-1. Forty common reasons why franchisors fail.

- Lack of adequate control
- Difficulty attracting qualified franchisees
- Choice of the wrong consultants
- Lack of proper disclosure documents
- Failure to provide adequate support
- An unproven and unprofitable prototype
- Lack of franchise communications systems
- Premature launch into international markets
- Complex and inadequate operations manuals
- Inadequate site selection criteria
- Inability to compete against larger franchisors
- Lack of proper screening system for prospective franchisees
- Disregard for franchise registration and disclosure laws
- Lack of business and strategic planning
- Not joining the International Finance Association (IFA)
- Entering oversaturated markets
- Lack of quality control

- Unreasonable pressure to sell franchises
- Unworkable economic relationship with franchisees
- Lack of effective compliance systems
- Royalty underpayments/nonpayments by franchisees
- Operational systems that can be easily duplicated
- Lack of effective financial controls
- Lack of experienced management
- Unprotected trademarks
- Excessive litigation with franchisees
- Inadequate training program
- Decentralized advertising
- Lack of ongoing research and development
- Unbridled geographic expansion
- Choice of the wrong subfranchisors
- Unprofitable and unhappy franchisees
- Lack of public relations
- Unwillingness to enforce franchise agreement
- Inadequate relationships with key vendors
- Improper earnings claims

- Inexperienced lawyers and accountants
- Breakaway franchisees
- Premature termination of franchisees
- Lack of market research

---

ent from their "mom and pop" predecessors of the 1960s and 1970s. This prospect is better trained to ask "all the right questions" and hire "the right advisors" in the investigation and franchise agreement negotiation process. These new franchises are also better heeled and more likely to organize themselves into associations and take action if they are not receiving the required levels of support and assistance. As we will discuss in Chapter 10, those franchisors who fail to mold their sales and support systems around the characteristics of these new franchisees and continue to conduct business "the old-fashioned way" are headed on the road to disaster and litigation.

Our Hypothetical Start-Up Franchisor

From time to time throughout the course of this book, we will follow the plight of Richard Theoryman in his development and growth of the Prof-Finders franchising program. Here is his story:

After years of teaching at a prestigious Ivy League school in New England, with a vast array of accomplishments that included pioneering the school's Center for Franchise Development Studies, Richard Theoryman was ready for a change. Theoryman was well-known and liked by professors at business schools nationwide and was well-respected for his early commitment to franchise education. Frustrated by his attempts to locate a formidable successor for his position, he created Prof-Finders. Knowing that continued growth in the franchising of service businesses was predicted in the 1990s,

Theoryman was committed to the development of an executive placement and head-hunting organization for the academic community.

So enthused was Theoryman about his new concept, he approached his brother-in-law, Max Deeppocket, a Wall Street investment banker, and received a personal loan of $50,000 and an additional $20,000 in exchange for 10 percent of Prof-Finders Enterprises, Inc. (PEI). The Delaware corporation was formed for the development and operation of the prototype operations. From day one, it was Theoryman's intent to franchise the program, with an emphasis on marketing to other business professors having a midlife crisis, provided that the initial operations were successful *and* profitable.

Knowing that a company's trademarks and trade secrets are the cornerstone of a successful franchising program, Theoryman immediately began searching for, and found, qualified legal counsel to begin the long and tedious process of obtaining federal trademark registration for "Prof-Finders" and for his new slogan "Bringing the best minds to the best universities," as well as to prepare nondisclosure agreements for key employees and others who would come to be exposed to the proprietary features of the Prof-Finder programs and systems.

The initial site for the prototype office and national headquarters of PEI was selected as Boston, Massachusetts. Initial advertisements were placed in academic journals and university management publications and soon requests for additional information came rolling in. Total placement fees for the first full year of operations in fiscal year 1987 were moderately successful at $187,000 against expenses of $132,000 needed to maintain PEI's modest offices. It was not until the middle of the second year, when the newly hired director of marketing, Judy Bigidea, developed the "Two brains for the price of one" program did sales really take off. Under the "two brains" program, PEI would fill a second position, at no additional charge to the university, if PEI were retained for a placement. When the media took notice of the "two brains" program and the rapid growth of PEI, the requests for franchises began rolling in.

Naturally, Theoryman knew that he could not formally offer or sell franchises unless and until the appropriate franchise offering documents had been developed and properly registered. He also knew that comprehensive operations manuals and training manuals would need to be developed. He also knew that he was out of cash.

Impressed by PEI's growth, Deeppocket agreed to invest another $50,000, this time in exchange for an additional 20 percent of PEI. Rather than using care in the selection of the members of the management team and attempting to internally develop certain key components of the franchising program, Theoryman in his impatience hired a large West Coast franchise "packager" and turned the entire $50,000 over to this consulting firm. After six months of wheel spinning, lost franchise prospects, flat internal sales (because all of the time and resources were being devoted to the development of the franchise program), the near loss of Bigidea, and a general level of frustration, a set of unworkable franchise documents were delivered to PEI. Theoryman was outraged that the "final product" was filled with boilerplate language and policies that did not apply to the academic recruitment business. In fact, certain sections appeared to be "borrowed" from the operations manuals and franchise agreements of a chain of fast-food outlets, whose name appeared in the documents where the software appeared to have missed the "search and replace" feature.

Now what? With no capital left and a set of useless documents, Theoryman was ready to scrap the whole idea of franchising.

After two weeks of brooding and four weeks of refinancing the equity in his home, Theoryman was committed to the proper development of a franchising program. His work was definitely cut out for him. First, he needed to attract the right management team with franchising experience. Next, he had to fine tune and complete the proprietary operations manuals and training programs. Then, it was necessary to retain the appropriate lawyers and accountants to properly advise PEI as the business grows and changes. Finally, the sales and marketing programs designed to attract prospective franchisees needed to be refined and implemented.

Let's follow Richard in the development of the Prof-Finders franchising program.

2

Human Resources Issues

Beyond the need for a quality product and facility, franchisors rely on *people* for sales, training, development, and support of the franchise network. Attracting, training, compensating, and retaining these people is critical for the long-term growth and development of the franchise system. Yet the effective management of these human resources is an often neglected component in the planning of the franchise program.

When we envision the personal characteristics of the founders of many of this nation's top franchisors, certain traits come to mind: strong leadership, boundless energy, a commitment to training and operations, impeccable sales skills, eternal optimism, great communication skills, a fire in the belly, and a genuine vested interest in the franchisee's success. Although many of these traits do in fact personify the leader of many franchise companies, even the most talented entrepreneur learns that he or she simply can't do it all. Functional departments must be planned, established, and staffed in order to preserve the sanity of the founder as well as the ability of the company to grow.

In fact, the founder of a franchise system often only possesses one or two strong points that lead to the success of the initial prototype operation. For example, a creative salad chef may have the skills and talent to build a successful prototype that revolves around his many salad variations, but when the decision to franchise the business is made, a whole new set of skills will be required. *The chef is no longer in the restaurant business; he is now in the franchising business, and that will require a different set of skills and abilities.* Remember, great chefs did not build McDonald's; great franchise executives did!

The bottom line is that the founder of the franchisor, whose initial desire will naturally be to settle in as president of the company, should pick one or two functions that he or she does best and then begin the process of building a management structure.

Building a Management Structure

Naturally, the actual management structure, functional departments, and specific personnel needed by a franchising company will vary from industry to industry and from franchisor to franchisor (depending, in part, on the contractual obligations of the franchisor to the franchisees). For example, franchisors in the fast-food business may need considerably more staff in the field for supervising quality control, health, and sanitation standards than would our friends at Prof-Finders. Similarly, franchisors who provide a "turnkey facility" to the franchisee will require more resources in the real estate and construction field than would a franchisor who merely reserves the right to approve the sites secured and developed by the franchisee. A franchisor who directly sells a wide range of products to its franchisees will need a well-trained purchasing and distribution staff, whereas a franchisor who merely publishes quality control standards for franchisees to use when purchasing products from their own sources will not.

Regardless of the specifics of the franchise system, any company considering franchising will need the following management structure and operational departments:

• *Sales and marketing.* This department is responsible for identifying markets for the sale of franchises, developing profiles of prospective franchisees, developing the sales tools and advertising materials to attract and obtain new franchisees, presenting, following up and closing the prospective franchisee, and overall promoting of the franchise system. *The bottom line is that the sales department must possess the talent and ability to turn qualified leads into satisfied franchisees.* The sales team should have impeccable salesmanship and human relations skills, an excellent working knowledge of the terms of the franchise offering circular and the merits of the franchisor's overall system, and a sensitivity to the importance of legal compliance.

• *Training and preopening support.* The time period between execution of the franchise agreement and grand opening of the franchisee's facility is critical. Many franchisees during this stage experience a wide range of emotions including frustration, confusion, self-doubt, financial cold feet, a thirst for knowledge, and a need for attention. The training department must know how to deal with these emotions and meet these demands. *The principal role of this department is to get each franchisee off on the right foot through intensive training and education.* This includes the development of classroom and field training materials, programs, and renewals; the effective delivery of all technical and operational information that the franchisee will require to operate its facility; the mental conditioning and preparation of the franchisee to be an independent small business owner; and the development of special training programs for the introduction of new products and services. The focus of the overall training program should be on facility operations and management, *not* solely on marketing to attract clients and customers. Two of the less glamourous jobs of the training department include the training of the franchisor's internal staff on the mechanics of the franchise system (*everyone should be required to go through training*) and the screening out of troublesome or unqualified franchisees during the training program (Do yourself a favor and get rid of the deadwood well *before* the store is opened!).

• *Operations and field support.* Most franchisees on the grand opening day are well-trained and ecstatic. Someone must be concerned for keeping them that way, and such is the role of operations and field support. Often eventually viewed as a "spy" by the network of franchisees, the members of this department are responsible for ongoing support and assistance to the franchisees; the implementation of new programs, policies, products, and services; as well as maintenance of quality control standards and enforcement of the terms of the franchise agreement. Chapter 4 addresses the role of the field support officer in considerable detail.

• *Finance and collections.* The personnel of a growing franchisor is almost always stacked heavily in the areas of sales, a necessary concentration; however, the importance of a strong financial department is often overlooked. In fact, of the many franchisors I've represented over the years, finance is usually the weak point of the management of the company. It may be difficult for a young franchisor to attract a qualified chief financial officer who understands franchising as well as he or she understands corporate finance. The development of accounting systems, budgets, operating controls, cash flow management systems, capital formation strategies, royalty and fee collection procedures, accounts payable and vendor relations systems, federal and state tax planning, and the review of franchisee financial reports are all critical functions of the franchisor's finance and collections department.

• *Personnel and administration.* As in any organization, a growing franchisor will require a personnel and administration department to deal with recruitment, performance appraisal, and termination of its internal staff as well as to develop internal management systems to keep the franchise machine operating properly. *The personnel and administration department provides the glue that holds the franchisor's various functions together.* This is perhaps the only operational department that may not have much initial and ongoing communication with the franchisee network. Rather, the emphasis is on managing the franchisor's internal resources to ensure good franchisee relations and support.

• *Legal and compliance.* At a certain point in the franchisor's growth and development, an in-house legal and compliance staff may be developed in order to handle routine legal matters, monitor internal legal compliance, and serve as a liaison to outside legal counsel. The duties of the compliance staff are discussed in more detail in Chapter 5.

▪ *Real estate, design, and site approval.* One central component of any franchise system is the *uniformity* in the appearance, decor, and design of each franchisee's facility. The architecture, design, and fit out of each facility must be specified and approved by the franchisor. Not that each franchisor needs a disciple of Frank Lloyd Wright to be effective, but it *is* critical that architectural standards are properly developed and consistently enforced. This will require a site approval staff to ensure not only that the franchisee has selected a viable location from a marketing and demographics perspective, but also that the site is constructed in accordance with the franchisor's standards and specifications with respect to colors, layout, counters, displays, signage, decor, uniforms, inventory, storage, equipment, supplies, and personnel. The terms of the franchisee's lease as well as the "per-square-foot" costs of construction must also be reviewed and approved by the franchisor's real estate department. Most franchisors will provide the franchisee with a set of general specifications, allowing for some degree of design flexibility for the franchisee's specific site and/or the requirements of the commercial developer in the mall or shopping center where the site will be located. Zoning and sign restrictions may also play a role in the degree of flexibility that may be afforded. If the franchisor provides a "turnkey" location to the franchisee, then the real estate department takes on an entirely new dimension and responsibility: real estate development and construction management.

Depending on the rate of growth of the franchisor, as well as on the specifics of the services provided to franchisees, a franchisor may need to initially or eventually establish departments in the areas of research and development; equipment leasing; franchisee financing; product purchasing, warehousing, and distribution; customer service and relations; franchisee relations and support; public relations and communications; data processing; and printing and mail handling.

Recruiting a Management Team

It is difficult for any company to recruit key executives who are qualified, talented, aggressive, and able to fit into the culture and environment of the business. It is especially difficult for franchisors, because only a handful of our nation's colleges and universities offer courses in franchising. This lack of educational opportunities has caused franchisors to actively recruit from within the franchise community; the result is a fierce competition for well-trained franchise veterans. In fact, the competition has become so fierce that a cottage industry, franchise executive recruitment firms, has developed. The pioneer in this field has been Jerry Wilkerson, a former International Franchise Association executive who founded Franchise Recruiters Ltd. ("FRL") in the early 1980s. FRL is a matchmaker between growing franchisors and franchising professionals. Firms like FRL will match the needs of the franchisor in the areas of training, finance, operations, administration, and sales with qualified individuals who meet the franchisor's profile with respect to compensation, experience, personality, work ethic, attitude, goals, and objectives. Because fees under certain circumstances can be costly, franchisors should develop their own detailed position descriptions and hiring criteria that should be reviewed and discussed with the recruiter before the search commences. Be prepared to pay a premium for a genuine franchising veteran. Consider the following sample advertisements from a recent FRL newsletter:

> MARKETING VICE PRESIDENT
>
> We need a top-quality individual from a major franchisor for this challenging opportunity. Compensation will be above $100K. If your marketing, advertising, and sales skills

to attract franchisees are strong and seasoned, then you could be the one for this international franchise company, third largest in the industry and willing to negotiate an attractive compensation package including corporate bonus and executive benefits.

SR. VP FRANCHISE
MARKETING/DEVELOPMENT

$150K BASE+ +. We have been retained to find the top franchise executive in the country for this midwest franchisor with explosive growth and profits. Must understand all aspects of franchising, especially marketing, sales, operations, and have management skills to run the entire company.

SR. VP OPERATIONS

$200,000.00+ We have been retained to conduct a search for a Senior Vice-President/Operations. Only the very best will be considered for this prestigious, industry-leading international company. This individual must absolutely have experience in all aspects of franchising. In other words, you must be responsible for running a company or division. Should have skills and ability to eventually assume the responsibility of the president of the company. Company has great story and is still developing with more than 2,200 units operating.

The Use of an Outside Sales Force

As you can see, talent does not come cheap. FRL publishes an annual compensation survey of franchise executives, with recent average base salaries, bonuses, deferred compensation, and other perquisites reaching nearly $100,000. [A copy of this report can be obtained by contacting FRL at 800-334-6257.] As a result, some early-stage franchisors rely on independent sales and marketing organizations to offer and sell their franchises. In fact, Judy Bigidea had suggested that Prof-Finders hire an independent franchise sales broker. Such a strategy may be a viable solution to a pressing personnel or budgetary problem, but it should by no means be considered a long-term strategy or solution. These outside brokers and sales agents can end up costing Prof-Finders a whole lot more than a commission if they are unqualified and have no regard for legal compliance. Bigidea must understand that many of these individuals care far more for franchise commissions than they do about finding qualified candidates for her company, which could lead to unqualified franchisees and eventual litigation.

Remember that the franchise sales and marketing staff serve as the "arms and legs" of the franchise organization. These individuals are the first people that a prospective franchisee will meet on behalf of the franchisor, and if the salesperson is not carefully selected, they will also be the last. The initial impression that a prospect will have of the franchisor is riding on the presentation, professionalism, and skill of the franchise sales representative. Therefore, it may be very dangerous to entrust such a key task to an independent franchise broker, whose divided loyalty could result in lost sales, claims of misrepresentation, and an inability to attract truly qualified prospective franchisees.

Despite the existence of a few reputable independent franchise brokers within the franchise community, there is simply no substitute for the loyalty of a full-time employed salesperson. The difficulty of "serving more than one master" becomes apparent to even the best franchise broker when faced with a prospective franchisee that is willing to consider a wide range of different businesses, often resulting in an inherent conflict of interest for the broker representing multiple franchisors.

From a legal perspective, the independent franchise broker is more difficult to control and monitor. The franchise broker will not typically possess extensive knowledge of the franchisor's programs and policies, which increases the chance of misunderstanding as to the costs of the franchise, the franchisor's initial and ongoing obligations to the franchisee, or the franchisor's willingness to negotiate the terms and conditions of the franchise agreement. All too often our nation's courts award monetary damages to disgruntled franchisees who relied on promises made by the sales representative at the outset of the relationship that served as an inducement for signing the franchise agreement, even though such promises are nowhere to be found in the franchisor's offering documents. Many of these risks can be alleviated with the development of a franchise sales compliance program, as discussed in Chapter 6, which is far easier to implement and enforce if an internal sales staff is hired and closely monitored.

The use of an additional intermediary between the franchisor and franchisee also increases the chances that a prospect will not be adequately evaluated and reviewed before being accepted and approved as a franchisee. The time to learn that a prospective franchisee lacks the experience or the capital to own and operate the franchise is not two weeks after the franchise agreement has been signed.

Given the investment that most franchisors make in the development of their franchise programs, it seems "pennywise and pound-foolish" to fill the most important gap in the management team with independent franchise brokers. The recruitment and training of an internal sales staff is an asset likely to pay for itself many times over for the emerging franchisor.

The Importance of Employment Agreements for the Growing Franchisor

The employment agreement serves as an important and cost-effective manner of both safeguarding confidential business information and preserving valuable human resources. These agreements, when combined with a well-developed compensation plan, provide both an economic and legal foundation for long-term employee loyalty to the franchisor.

There are many other reasons why employment agreements may be fundamental to a franchisor's existence and growth. For example, venture capital investors will often insist on employment agreements between the company and its founders/key employees in order to protect their investment. Second, individuals with special management or technical expertise may insist on employment agreements as a condition to joining the franchisor. Finally, they serve as an important human resources management tool in terms of description of duties, the basis for reward, and the grounds for termination.

Franchisors should nevertheless carefully consider the long-term implications of the terms and conditions contained in the employment agreement. Once these promises are made to an employee in written form, the expectation is created that any special benefits will be available throughout the term of the agreement. Failure to meet these obligations on a continuing basis will expose the franchisor to the risk of litigation for breach of contract.

The key provisions of an employment agreement with a key employee include:

- Duration
- Statement of duties
- Compensation arrangements
- Grounds for rewards/bonuses
- Provisions for reimbursement of expenses, vacations, and benefits
- Nondisclosure clauses
- Restrictive covenants against competition
- Provisions defining rights to intellectual property inventions and "shop rights"
- Arrangements in the event of illness, disability, or death
- Grounds for termination, including the employee's obligations upon departure

Protecting Intellectual Property and Restrictive Covenants in the Employment Agreement

At the heart of any franchise program are the proprietary systems and manuals that are licensed by the franchisee. Therefore, it is especially critical that the franchisor's key employees are bound to covenants of nondisclosure and noncompetition in their employment agreements. There are four key categories of covenants that must be included in the employment agreement:

1. *Covenants of nondisclosure.* Trade secrets owned by the franchisor may be protected with covenants in the employment agreement which impose obligations on the employee not to disclose, in any form and to any unauthorized party, any information that the company regards as confidential and proprietary. This includes, but is not limited to, recipes, operations manuals, computer systems, franchisee prospect lists, financial and sales data, agreements with key suppliers, business and strategic plans, marketing strategies and advertising materials, or anything else that gives the franchisor an advantage over its competitors. This covenant should apply to pre-employment (interview or training period) during the term of the agreement and post-termination. The scope, conditions regarding use and disclosure, sources and forms of information, and geographic limitations described in the covenant should be broadly in favor of the employer; however, the covenant will only be enforceable to the extent necessary to reasonably protect the nature of the intellectual property that is at stake.

2. *Covenants against competition.* Naturally, an early-stage franchisor such as Prof-Finders would like to be able to impose a restriction on its team of key employees that should any one of them ever leave the company, they will be absolutely prohibited from working for a competitor in any way, shape, or manner. Courts, however, have not looked favorably on such attempts to deprive individuals of their livelihood

and as a result have required that any covenants against competition be reasonable as to scope, time, territory, and remedy for noncompliance. An unreasonable restriction runs the risk of being completely set aside by the court, unless the jurisdiction applies the "blue pencil" rule under which only the offensive and unreasonable language is removed by the judge.

The type of covenants against competition that will be tolerated by the courts vary from state to state and from industry to industry, but they must always be reasonable under the circumstances. It is crucial that an attorney with a background in this area be consulted when you draft these provisions of the employment agreement. To be enforceable, the covenant against competition must be supported by consideration. An offer of paid employment will usually suffice; however, additional consideration might be necessary to support an unusually long period of time or large territory under which the employee agrees not to compete after the term of the agreement. The covenant should be no broader than is necessary to protect the legitimate business interests of the employer, and its terms should be reasonable as to duration, territory, activity, remedy, and its relation to other provisions in the employment agreement.

3. *Covenants regarding ownership of inventions.* Suppose that an employee of the franchisor's research and development staff discovers a new recipe for the seasoning of fast-food broiled chicken. Must the employee disclose the discovery to the company's management? Who will own the rights to the recipe? Must the franchisor pay the employee a fee or royalty upon the subsequent commercial exploitation of the discovery? Is the employee entitled to share in the proceeds if the recipe is eventually used throughout the franchise network?

All of these questions must be expressly addressed in the employment agreement; otherwise basic common-law rules regarding ownership of an employee's ideas, inventions, and discoveries will govern. These rules do not necessarily favor the employer, especially if the discovery was made outside the scope of the employment or if the employee did not utilize the employer's resources in connection with the invention. For example, the common law principle of "shop rights" dictates that if an invention is made by an employee that is outside the scope of the employment but utilizes the resources of the employer, then ownership is vested in the employee, subject to a nonexclusive, royalty-free, irrevocable license to the employer.

A sample clause for such a situation is:

> *Work Made for Hire.* If any inventions or discoveries of the employee are protectable by definition of "work made for hire," as such term is defined in 17 U.S.C. Section 101, such work shall be considered a "work made for hire," the copyright of which shall be owned solely, completely, and exclusively by Franchisor. If any one or more of the aforementioned items are protectable by copyright and are not considered to be included in the categories of work covered by the "work made for hire" definition contained in 17 U.S.C. Section 101, such items shall be deemed to be assigned and transferred completely and exclusively to Employer by virtue of the execution of this Agreement.

A franchisor can limit the reward for an invention to the employee's basic salary if express provisions regarding ownership of inventions were included in his employment agreement. Naturally, this clause must be balanced against business considerations such as the ability of the franchisor to attract and retain key employees with such a limited reward for innovation. The provision should insist on prompt and full disclosure of any inventions as well as full cooperation in any subsequent attempt by the company to obtain a patent, copyright, or trademark on the discovery.

4. *Covenants to protect intellectual property upon termination.* When a key employee leaves the franchisor, the obligations of nondisclosure and noncompetition should be reaffirmed with an exit interview. The applicable provisions of

the employment agreement should be reviewed with the departing employee with at least one witness present. The franchisor should apprise the employee of the continuing duty to preserve the confidentiality of trade secrets and reiterate what information is regarded as confidential. The franchisor should obtain assurances and evidence (including a written acknowledgment) that all confidential and proprietary documents have been returned and no copies retained. The name of the new employer or future activity should be obtained and, under certain circumstances, even notified of the prior employment relationship and its scope. This will put the new employer/competitor "on notice" and prevent it from claiming that it was unaware that its new employee had revealed trade secrets. Finally, the employer should insist that the employee covenant not to hire co-workers, with a document such as:

> *Covenants Not to Hire Employees.* It is recognized and understood by the parties hereto that the employees of Franchisor are an integral part of Franchisor's business and that it is extremely import for Franchisor to use its maximum efforts to prevent Franchisor from losing such employees. It is, therefore, understood and agreed by the parties hereto that, because of the nature of the business of Franchisor, it is necessary to afford fair protection to Franchisor from the loss of any such employees. Consequently, as a material inducement to Franchisor to employ (or to continue to employ) Employee, Employee covenants and agrees that, for the period commencing on the date of Employee's termination of employment for any reason whatsoever and ending two (2) years after Employee's termination of employment with Franchisor, Employee shall not, directly or indirectly, hire or engage or attempt to hire or engage any individual who shall have been an employee of Franchisor at any time during the one (1)-year period prior to the date of Employee's termination of employment with Franchisor,

whether for or on behalf of Employee or for any entity in which Employee shall have a direct or indirect interest (or any subsidiary or affiliate of any
such entity), whether as a proprietor, partner, co-
venturer, financier, investor or stockholder, director,
officer, employer, employee, servant, agent, representative, or otherwise.

Compensation and Employee Stock Ownership Strategies

The competition for qualified franchise executives is quite
fierce. Franchisors in this new decade will need to consider
aggressive and creative compensation and benefit strategies in
order to attract and retain necessary personnel. A flat salary
for a CFO or straight commission plan for a sales representative simply isn't enough anymore. Early-stage and growing
franchisors such as Prof-Finders may wish to consider executive stock option or ownership plans as part of the overall
compensation strategy. The mechanics and key issues in establishing these plans are discussed in the sections that
follow.

Stock Option Plans: An Overview

Selecting the appropriate benefit program for any given organization depends largely upon a realistic assessment of the
company's stage of business development. Franchisors at a
mature stage of development usually have base salaries that
are strongly competitive in the market place and hence find
short-term incentives and perks to be more cost-efficient over
the long run. Franchisors who are in a growth stage still find
use for long-term incentive plans to bolster continued growth
and stability. Long-term incentives are, however, the foundation for the compensation programs of early-stage franchisors.
    Young franchisors in the early stage find numerous stra-
tegic advantages to the adoption of long-term incentive plans,

including (1) the ability to attract high-quality employees while offering lower base salaries but providing long-range financial rewards for taking a "risk on the company," (2) encouragement of executives to improve the long-term value and productivity of the company, and (3) delay of large cash payments until a later date when cash flow may be less restricted.

The following discussion of stock options and executive compensation plans will focus almost exclusively upon long-term incentives. Long-term incentive plans can be divided roughly into three categories: (1) equity participation plans, (2) deferred compensation plans, and (3) qualified retirement plans.

Equity Participation Plans. Equity participation plans include nonqualified stock options, incentive stock options, restricted stock plans, and performance stock plans. A nonqualified stock option plan (NSO) allows an employee to purchase shares of the franchisor's stock for a specified period of time at a predetermined price. This "option price" is usually equal to the then-current market value of the stock, and participants will benefit only if the price of the stock rises over time. Once the option is exercised, an employee will recognize ordinary income only to the extent that the market value of the stock when the option is exercised exceeds the stated option price. The employer is then entitled to a deduction in the amount that the executive has been taxed.

Since the repeal of the favorable capital gain rates, the primary advantage of incentive stock option (ISO) programs is the option for executives to defer taxation on the stock's appreciation until such time as plan shares are sold. The employer, however, is not entitled to a deduction under an ISO plan. This, in part, has caused many companies in recent years to consider converting ISOs to NSOs in order to produce tax deductions for the company.

Finally, under a restricted stock option plan (RSO), an employee is awarded stock that is not immediately transferable. Under the terms and conditions of the typical RSO, the employee will generally be required to remain with the franchisor for a specified period of time. All or part of the shares will generally be forfeited should the employee leave before the restricted period elapses. Recognition for tax purposes can, however, be deferred until the restrictive period is over. The franchisor receives a deduction concurrent with the employee's deduction. The employee under this plan does have an option to elect to be taxed on the difference between their cost and the value of the stock shares at the time of purchase, which defers a potentially excessive tax liability when the restrictions expire.

Deferred Compensation Plans. Deferred compensation plans, which permit employees to postpone part of their present compensation to future years, provide two key benefits:

1. An executive's tax rate may be lower in the year when compensation is eventually paid out (usually after retirement).
2. A larger amount can be invested on behalf of the employee up front, because pretax dollars are invested and the deferred portion is not immediately taxable.

An executive's decision to participate in these types of programs will depend in large part on whether the individual actually anticipates having lower marginal rates in the future. Potential overall tax rate increases may make such plans of questionable utility to some highly paid executives, especially to young executives who may be many years away from retirement.

Qualified Retirement Plans. Qualified retirement plans offer certain strategic advantages to a growing franchisor. Among these advantages are (1) an ability to deduct the franchisor's contributions within certain defined limits, (2) income deferral permitted for employees participating in the program until benefits have been actually distributed, (3) permitted accumulation and compounding of earnings on a tax-deferred basis, and (4) favorable tax treatment for employees receiving certain specific lump-sum distributions.

To constitute a "qualified plan" as defined by the Internal Revenue Code of 1986 (as amended), a plan must meet the following general requirements:

- The plan must be written and communicated to employees.
- It must be intended to be permanent.
- It must be available to employees on a nondiscriminatory basis, (that is, not discriminate in favor of highly compensated employees).
- It must provide contributions or benefits that also do not discriminate in favor of highly compensated employees.
- It must be funded (pay-as-you-go arrangements will not qualify).
- It must satisfy certain standards concerning age and length-of-service requirements (generally an employee who has attained age 21 and completed one year of service must be eligible to participate).
- It must benefit either certain specified percentages of all employees or all employees who qualify under a classification that does not discriminate in favor of officer, shareholders, or highly paid employees.
- It must satisfy accrual and vesting rules that require benefits to accrue and become nonforfeitable according to certain specified schedules (plans that provide more than 60 percent of accrued benefits to "key" employees face more stringent rules with respect to minimum benefits and vesting for nonkey employees).
- It must satisfy restrictions on maximum contributions and benefits that limit amounts that individuals may defer.
- It must satisfy minimum distribution rules.

Once a plan is designated as a "qualified plan," it will fall into one of two categories, either (1) a defined contribution plan or (2) a defined benefit plan. A defined contribution plan does not guarantee a set level of benefits at retirement; instead the company itself contributes a designated amount each year to an individual account for each participant. The ultimate level of retirement benefits depends upon the plan investment manager's ability to achieve a higher-than-average return on investment (ROI). Defined contribution plans tend to be more effective if the employees are younger and have more years to potentially contribute to the plan. In addition, these plans are generally more easily communicated to and understood by employees than are defined benefit plans.

If a defined contribution plan is selected, it may be structured as a money purchase pension plan or a profit-sharing plan. A money purchase pension plan generally provides for contribution based upon a set formula, such as a percentage of each participant's compensation. A profit-sharing plan, on the other hand, permits employees to make discretionary annual contributions so long as the contributions are allocated to employee accounts on a nondiscriminatory basis. Profit-sharing plans tend to work well for growing companies with sporadic cash flows, primarily because contributions, if any, can vary from year to year. Money purchase pension plans allow larger deferrals and are attractive if cash flow is relatively certain and the owners are mostly young. Another unique feature of profit-sharing plans is that distributions may be made to active employees, as opposed to money purchase pension plan provisions, which do not allow preretirement distributions to be made to active employees.

A profit-sharing plan may also be designed with a cash-or-deferred feature (a so-called 401(K) plan), whereby employees voluntarily agree to take a reduction in pay and have the amount contributed to the plan. Because the amount contributed will not be reportable income for the year, the effect is the same as if it were deductible by the employee. A 401(K) plan must also meet special nondiscrimination tests, which in effect prohibit highly compensated employees from deferring compensation unless lower-paid employees also elect to do so. To encourage participation in 401(K) plans, franchisors often make matching contributions that must also meet special nondiscrimination tests.

Defined benefit plans provide for benefits that are determined in advance through the use of a preestablished formula. The formula is generally based in some fashion upon the length of the employee's service and his/her overall compensation. A plan might, by way of example, provide for an annual retirement benefit after age 65 that is equal to 1.5 percent of the individual's base pay for each year of service. The company is then committed to make contributions based upon actuarial computed amounts that will provide for a sufficiently large fund. Unlike the defined contribution plan, the investment risks and rewards under this scheme are borne by the employer. An improved ROI will make it possible to reduce future contributions.

The Use of Employee Stock Ownership Plans (ESOPs) by a Growing Franchisor

An employee stock ownership plan ("ESOP") is a tax-qualified plan of deferred compensation under Section 401(a) of the Internal Revenue Code of 1986, as amended (the "Code"). The primary objective of an ESOP is to provide stock ownership of the employer's securities to the employees. Two general categories of ESOPs are:

1. *Leveraged ESOP.* Uses borrowed funds (either directly from the company or from a third-party lender based on the guaranty of the company as well as the actual securities of the employer as collateral) to acquire the employer's securities. The loan will be repaid by the ESOP from employer and employee contributions, as well as any dividends that may be paid on the employer's securities.
2. *Nonleveraged ESOP.* A stock bonus plan (or contribution stock bonus plan with a money purchase pension plan) that purchases the employer's securities with funds that *were not* provided by a third-party lender.

Figure 2-1. Structuring the stock option plan.

In structuring and establishing any stock option program, a careful analysis should be undertaken by the franchisor to ensure that the chosen scheme meets the following standards: (1) It will provide at a minimum an adequate level of retirement income for employees, (2) it will satisfy the tax deferral needs of owner-managers, and (3) the program as designed will not put undue strain on the employer's financial resources. Once a decision has been made that adequately reflects these considerations, the plan will be established utilizing two fundamental documents: (1) the Stock Option Plan (the "Plan") and (2) the Stock Option Agreement (the "Agreement").

(*I*) The Plan

Regardless of the exact type of plan selected, a Stock Option Plan should generally include the following key provisions:

(1) *Purpose.*The plan sets out the rationale behind the company's decision to adopt a plan, generally citing the promotion of the company's financial success and overall growth.

(2) *Method of administration.* The Plan indicates whether it is to be overseen by the board of directors or an independent trustee. Among other administrative functions, the administrative entity shall have the power to interpret the Plan as well as amending and rescinding rules and regulations relating to the actions necessary for the implementation of the Plan.

(3) *Eligibility.* This section indicates which employees qualify for the Plan and the criteria used to select eligible employees.

(4) *Types of awards and shares subject to the Plan.* This section sets forth the award contemplated, i.e., whether incentive- or performance-based, as

Figure 2-1. continued

well as the number and classes of shares available for use under the plan.

(5) *Terms of the options.* This section sets forth in detail how an award of an option will be communicated to the recipient, how the option price is to be determined for each individual award, and the time limit for acceptance of the option. A description of the necessary steps to be taken to exercise an option, and any limitations that may apply as to frequency of exercise as well as provisions addressing the prompt payment of any and all tax liabilities due upon exercise are also included.

(6) *Termination of employee relationships.* Provisions are made herein to transfer any accumulated options to the estate of a deceased employee. The estate is then generally constrained by the same time limits and terms of exercise as is the deceased employee. Employees terminated by the company for good cause usually lose any and all rights to accrued options.

(7) *Restrictions on transfer.* The Plan indicates what if any restrictions will be placed on the subsequent sale or transfer of shares purchased pursuant to the Plan.

(8) *Amendment, modification, and termination of the Plan.* This section sets forth which amendments and modifications will require stock-holder approval and which may be accomplished solely through an action of the administrative body. This section also sets forth employee rights in the event of Plan termination.

(II) The Agreement

This document constitutes the actual contract between the franchisor and its executive/qualified employees with respect to the terms and conditions of the plan.

Among the issues to be addressed by the Agreement are:

(1) Number of shares offered to the employee under the plan
(2) Price of the optioned shares
(3) Time period for exercise of the option
(4) Procedures for exercise of the option
(5) Effect of termination of the employment relationship (note that cause for termination may trigger different types of results)
(6) Employer's rights of first refusal on transfer of the option or the optioned shares
(7) Restrictions on transfer of the options and the optioned shares

General Legal Considerations in Structuring an ESOP

ESOPs, like all types of deferred compensation plans, must meet certain minimum requirements set forth in Section 401(a) of the Code. Failure to meet these requirements will result in the contributions by the sponsoring employer not being deductible, which thereby defeats many of the tax advantages of the ESOP. *These Code requirements include the following:*

1. A *trust* must be established by the plan sponsor in order to make contributions. The trust must be for the exclusive benefit of the participants and their beneficiaries.

2. The overall ESOP structure (as well as the allocation of assets and income distribution) *must not discriminate* in favor of officers, major shareholders, or highly compensated employees. At least *70 percent of all lower-paid compensated employees must be covered* by the plan ("coverage test") or any other coverage test set forth in Section 410 of the Code. (*Note:* Certain part-time employees, employees under the age of 21, and employees with *less* than one year of service may be excluded when you calculate the coverage test.)

3. The plan must benefit no fewer than fifty employees or 40 percent or more of the employees of the plan sponsor, whichever number is less.

4. The ESOP must *invest primarily in the securities of the sponsoring employer.* Although there are no strict guidelines, it is assumed that the ESOP portfolio should include at least 50–60 percent of the employer's securities at any given time. Control and dilution issues should be balanced against productivity improvement considerations. Remaining assets of the ESOP trust should be invested in prudent securities that offer liquidity and diversification of the portfolio.

5. The ESOP structure must meet one of the minimum vesting schedules set forth in Section 411 of the Code. The plan must adopt either the five-year "cliff" vesting (employee must be vested after five years of service but need not be vested at all before that time) or seven-year "scheduled" vesting (20 percent vesting after three years, increasing 20 percent per year until 100 percent vesting is reached after seven years).

6. The ESOP structure must meet the *voting* requirements of Section 409 of the Code (where applicable). Under the Code, voting rights may be vested in the trust's fiduciary, except under certain circumstances where rights must be "passed through" to the plan's participants. Generally, passing through becomes an issue when the vote will involve mergers, consolidations, reorganizations, recapitalizations, liquidations, major asset sales, and the like. Voting rights "in toto" may be passed through to employees, however, at the discretion of the employer in structuring the plan. Failure to fully "pass through" these rights may raise personnel and productivity problems (if the employees do not feel like true owners and as a result are cynical about the ESOP), thereby defeating a major incentive for adopting the ESOP.

7. Distribution of ESOP benefits/assets must be made in compliance with Section 409 of the Code. The plan must provide for a prompt (within one year) distribution of benefits to the participant following *retirement, disability,* or *death.* The nature and specific timing of the distribution depends in part

on the *cause* for separation from service with the company as well as whether the sponsoring employer is closely held as opposed to being publicly traded.

8. Contributions to an ESOP may be based on a specific percentage of payroll, such as a money purchase pension plan, or contributions may be based on some other formula, such as a percentage of profits, as is the case with some profit-sharing plans. This form provides for maximum flexibility in that contributions depend completely on the discretion of the employer. Each year the employer simply makes a determination of the appropriate amount of contribution. The plan provides for a minimum contribution to allow payment of any principal and interest due from a loan used to acquire employer securities. The employers' contribution may be made in cash or other property, including employer's securities. In the event that the employer contributes its own securities, it may obtain a so-called "cashless deduction." The employer is entitled to deduct the fair market value of the securities so contributed (subject to the general limitations of Section 404 of the Code), and the contribution involves no cash outlay by the employer.

9. Closely held franchisors must include a "put option" on stock distributed from the ESOP. This provides a terminated employee with the opportunity to "cash out." Transfer restrictions may also be placed on the shares in order to vest a "right of first refusal" in the company or the ESOP *before* the participating employee may sell the shares to a third party. If the stock is to be purchased back by the company or the ESOP on an *installment basis*, then the price terms must: (1) be spread over a period not exceeding five years, (2) be substantially equal payments, (3) begin not more than thirty days after the exercise of the put, (4) have adequate collateral available to secure the payments, and (5) pay a reasonable rate of interest. Put options are not required if the franchisor's stock is publicly traded.

10. Because "adequate consideration" must always be provided in connection with the purchase of employer stock in an ESOP, some method for valuation of the shares must be

available. For publicly traded companies, this is generally not a problem because the prevailing market price is a sufficient indication of value. For privately held franchisors, however, value must be determined by the fiduciaries of the plan acting in good faith. This will generally require an *independent appraisal*, initially upon the establishment of the ESOP, and at least annually thereafter. The appraisal firm *and* the methods used must meet the standards of both the Code and the Department of Labor. (The *cost* and *impact* of such an appraisal on a closely held company should be considered before adoption of an ESOP plan.)

Key Legal Documents in the Establishment of an ESOP

There are a wide variety of legal documents that must be prepared in connection with the organization and implementation of an ESOP by a franchisor. These documents must be prepared by counsel, however, only after input has been received by all key members of the company's ESOP team (e.g., financial and human resources staff, accountants, investment bankers, commercial lenders, the designated trustee, the designated appraisal firm). The preliminary analysis that should be conducted *prior to* the preparation of the documents should include (1) impact on dilution, ownership, control, and earnings of the company; (2) type of securities to be issued (common vs. preferred); (3) tax deductibility of contributions and related tax issues; (4) registration of the securities, where required, under federal and state securities laws; (5) employee motivation and productivity improvement analysis; (6) current and future capital requirements and growth plans of the company; (7) interplay of the ESOP with other current or planned employee benefit plans within the company, and (8) timetable for planning, organization, and implementation of the ESOP.

Once these and other factors have been considered and strategic decisions made, counsel may be instructed to prepare the necessary documentation. In a leveraged ESOP, the documents may include (1) ESOP Plan, (2) ESOP Trust Agreement (which may be combined with the plan), (3) ESOP Loan

Figure 2-2. Key issues to address in the ESOP plan and ESOP stock purchase agreement.

The primary issues to be addressed by each of these documents are as follows:

1. *The ESOP Plan (where trust agreement is self-contained)*
   - Designation of a name for the ESOP
   - Definition of key terms (e.g., *participant, year of Service, trustee*)
   - Eligibility to participate (standards and requirements)
   - Contributions by employer (designated amount or formula; discretionary)
   - Investment of trust assets (primarily in employer securities, plans for diversification of the portfolio, purchase price for the stock, rules for borrowing by the ESOP)
   - Procedures for release of the shares from encumbrances (formula as ESOP obligations are paid down)
   - Voting rights (rights vested in trustee; special matters triggering employee voting rights)
   - Duties of the trustee(s) (accounting, administrative, appraisal, asset management, record keeping, voting obligations, preparation of annual reports, allocation and distribution of dividends)
   - Removal of trustee(s)
   - Effect of retirement, disability, death, and severance of employment
   - Terms of the put option (for closely held companies)
   - Rights of first refusal upon transfer
   - Vesting schedules

2. *ESOP Stock Purchase Agreement*
   - Appropriate recitals
   - Purchase terms for the securities

Figure 2-2. continued

- Conditions to closing
- Representations and warranties of the seller
- Representations and warranties of the buyer
- Obligatons prior to and following the closing
- Termination
- Opinion of counsel
- Exhibits, attachments and schedules

Documentation (e.g., loan agreement, note guaranty; the initial set of documents may be from the commercial lender to the sponsoring employer, with a "mirror image" loan being made by the employer to the ESOP), (4) ESOP Stock Purchase Agreement (where stock is purchased from the employer or its principal shareholders), (5) Corporate Charter Amendments and Related Board Resolutions, and (6) Legal Opinion and Valuation Reports.

3

Developing an Effective and Comprehensive Operations Manual

At the heart of any successful franchising program is a prescribed *system* that ensures quality control and consistency throughout the franchise network. In most franchised businesses, the key elements of this system have been developed and fine-tuned in the operation of the franchisor's prototype location. The administration of this system requires effective and comprehensive *documentation* that must be provided to each franchise, both at the inception of the relationship and on an ongoing basis.

The documentation required to properly administer the franchise system includes:

- Statement of corporate philosophy, policies, and general rules of operations
- Confidential operations and procedures manual
- Local sales, marketing, and public relations kit
- Site selection, architectural, interior design, signage, equipment, and inventory specifications
- Guidelines for financial record keeping and reporting
- Quality control and inspection reports
- Special manuals for subfranchisors and area developers (where applicable)

Depending on the nature of the franchisor's business, many of the required items listed above may be combined into a single confidential operations manual ("the manual"). The manual is the heart and soul of the franchising program, designed to be a resource for the franchisee when the franchisor can't be there. Despite the importance of the manual to the long-term success of the franchising program, many early-stage franchisors experience great difficulty in their attempts to prepare a proper manual. Yet a franchisor unable to properly document and communicate the critical steps of successfully operating the business (often in painstaking detail) is doomed for failure and really has no business getting into franchising in the first place. Remember *that*, so the success of your prototype location(s) will *articulate* how and why you achieved success.

Guidelines for Preparation of the Manual

Before sitting down to prepare your operations manual, keep in mind the following basic principles and guidelines:

1. The operations manual is a living, breathing document. Its contents will develop and change as your franchise system develops and changes. Be sure to reserve this level of flexibility in your franchise agreement.

2. Because it is inevitable that your franchise system will evolve, prepare the manual in a format that is user-friendly and easy to update. For example, a series of three-ring notebooks with tabs for each major heading will make section or page replacements and additions quick and easy.

3. *Assume nothing* about the skills and experience of your typical franchise. The text of the manual should be written at a high school reading level of comprehension and should anticipate that your franchisee is likely to be a complete novice in your industry. Dry,

Figure 3-1. The relationship between the franchise offering circular and the manual.

It is the modern practice of many franchise lawyers to be rather vague in the preparation of Franchise Offering Circulars and Franchise Agreements, with common references to information contained in the manual. The rationale here is that amending a manual is far less complicated than amending a registered disclosure document or binding legal agreement. Although I generally advocate this practice, be careful. If the document is too vague, then it will be challenged by the examiners in the registration states. Similarly, if the franchisor attempts to introduce a significant new program, operating procedure, or policy, this may trigger a "material change" that *will* require amendment of the offering circular and perhaps even the franchise agreement itself. See Chapter 6 for a more detailed discussion of the "material change" regulations.

technical, and difficult-to-use manuals *will* be ignored by franchisees, and this will cause a breakdown of quality control throughout the system.

4. No detail should remain unaddressed in the manual. Do not leave any operating discretion in the hands of the franchisee. Everything ranging from preopening procedures to preparation of products to employee discipline must be included. Remember that comprehensiveness in the preparation of your manual provides a certain level of legal protection. Franchisees will not be able to claim, "They never told me how to _____" in any subsequent litigation *if* all details are addressed.

5. The manual must be comprehensive (yet generic) enough to be followed by all franchisees that must run their businesses in a range of different markets and operating conditions. For example, if procedures are different for long stand-alone facilities (as opposed to kiosks within a regional mall), then these expected differences must be included and discussed. If advertis-

ing strategies differ in a rural area (as opposed to an inner-city location), then these differences must be anticipated and included within the manual.

6. The manual should anticipate and answer some of the questions most commonly asked by your franchisees. The more often they need to call you for assistance, the larger the administrative staff (and thus overhead) you need to maintain.

7. Remember that the manual is confidential and proprietary. As such, it should be treated as a trade secret under the law of intellectual property. Procedures must be developed for protection and care of the manual by each franchisee and its employees. Access should be restricted to those with a "need to know" basis. Remember that the manual is *licensed, not sold* to a franchisee. It remains the property of the franchisor at all times. Special receipts should be developed for providing the manual to franchisees and special forms prepared for ordering replacement manuals.

8. The manual should at all times be consistent with the representations made in the Franchise Offering Circular (FOC), the disclosure document that must be delivered to prospective franchisees under federal and state law, as well as with the specific obligations contained in the franchise agreement. One easy way to find yourself in litigation with your franchisees is through inconsistencies between promises made in the FOC and actual obligations contained in the manual.

Suggested Outline for the Operations Manual of a Franchisor

An operations manual should encompass virtually every aspect of the business to be operated by the franchisee, from prior to grand opening to the ongoing day-to-day operating procedures and techniques. The following is an outline that has been designed for a typical franchisor in the services business, such as Prof-Finders.

Section A: Introduction

1. Foreword/Notice of Proprietary and Confidential Information
2. Acknowledgment
3. History of the Franchisor
4. The Franchisor's Management Team
5. The Franchisor's Obligations to the Franchisees (an overview)
6. The Franchisee's Obligations to the Franchisor and the System (an overview)

Section B: Timetables for Opening the Franchised Office

A comprehensive timetable that the franchisee is to follow, beginning the date that the franchise agreement is signed to the first date that business will be conducted and beyond.

Section C: Preopening Obligations and Procedures

1. Architectural, Engineering, Interior Design, and Site Construction Specifications
2. Minimum Requirements for Utilities, Ventilation, etc.
3. Signage

   a. General Information
   b. Description and Explanation of Signs to Be Used, Interior and Exterior
   c. Dimensions, Specifications, etc.

4. Ordering and Receiving Fixtures, Supplies, Equipment, and Inventory
5. Building the Management Team: Managers, Employees, and Professional Advisors
6. Application for Licenses, Permits, Utilities, Insurance, and Bonding
7. Lease Review and Negotiations

8. Community Involvement, Trade Groups, Charities, Chambers of Commerce, etc. (pre- and postopening)
9. Recommended Reference Books on Small Business Management

Section D: Office Policies

1. Image, Decor, and Theme
2. Quality Standards of Services
3. Pricing Policies and Fee Structure
4. Service and Courtesy to Clients
5. Handling Typical Complaints and Problems
6. Employee Appearance (uniforms) and Hygiene
7. Hours of Operation

Section E: Office Operation and Maintenance

1. General Housekeeping
2. Basic Duties of Personnel: Office Manager, Sales Staff, Employees, etc.
3. Daily Office: Opening Procedure, Checklists
4. Daily Office: Closing Procedure
5. Daily, Weekly, and Monthly Reports
6. Self-Inspection
7. Health and Safety Standards
8. Rest Rooms
9. Pest Control
10. Parking Lot Care and Management (Where Applicable)
11. Alarms, Locks, and Keys
12. Emergency Procedures

Section F: Equipment, Computer System, Inventory, and Supplies

1. Equipment, Inventory, and Supply List for a Typical Franchised Office

        a. Specifications
        b. Approved Vendors
        c. Repair and Maintenance (Equipment Only)

2. Operation and Management of the Franchisor's Proprietary Database
3. Approved Vendors for Equipment, Inventory, and Supplies

Section G: Administration

1. Personnel: job chart, position descriptions, hiring, qualifications and interviewing, application form; checking references, hours, shifts, timekeeping, vacancies, sick pay, time off, training, payroll taxes, law concerning employees, rules of conduct for employees, bulletin boards, and required notices
2. Record Keeping and Accounting
3. Collections and Accounts Receivable Management
4. Managing Accounts Payable
5. Recruitment and Training
6. Quality Control
7. Group Insurance Policies

Section H: Sales Promotion

1. Grand-Opening Promotion Plans (With Timetable)
2. General Ongoing Promotion: Newspaper, Radio, Direct Mail, Advertising Cooperatives, Community Groups
3. Special Promotions: Franchisee Referral Programs, Customer Referral Premiums, etc.
4. Public Relations
5. Use of Public Figures
6. Use of Coupons and Direct-Marketing Mailers
7. Group Discounts and Promotions
8. Maintaining High Visibility in the Community
9. Understanding and Analyzing Local Demographic Statistics and Trends

Section I: Protection of Trademarks and Trade Secrets

1. Trademark Usage and Guidelines
2. Examples of Trademark Misuse
3. Care and Protection of Trade Secrets
4. Use and Care of the Operations Manual
5. Key Employee Nondisclosure Agreements
6. Protection of Proprietary Computer Software and Manuals

Section J: Preparation of Reports to the Franchisor

1. Guidelines and Requirements
2. Examples of Forms

Section K: Guidelines for Transfer of a Franchise

1. Requirements
2. Sample Forms and Notices

Section L: Financing and Corporate Structure

1. Required Corporate Structure
2. The Franchisor and Franchisee as Independent Parties
3. Financing and Loan Applications
4. Financing Alternatives

Drafting the Operations Manual: Selected Topics

The preparation of a comprehensive operations manual is truly an art. No level of attention or detail may be ignored. For example, most franchisors might (and for good reason) assume that a typical franchisee would know how to prepare a peanut butter and jelly sandwich. Yet there are many levels of details that need to be addressed if the old-fashioned "PB&J" sandwich were a staple on the franchisor's menu, such as:

- What type of peanut butter? Chunky or smooth? Any particular brand?
- What flavor jelly? Grape? Apricot? Strawberry? May a customer choose?
- How many ounces of peanut butter per sandwich? Of jelly?
- What type of bread should be used? White? Wheat? Rye? May a customer choose?
- The bread served toasted or untoasted? Toasted using what type of oven? How long should the bread be in the oven?
- The sandwich served with condiments? Pickles? Potato chips? Coleslaw? How much of each condiment?
- How is the sandwich to be served? What type of packaging?
- What are the suggested price ranges for the sandwich? Does the condiment selected affect the price? What other products should be recommended to the customer when the sandwich is ordered?

Now multiply the answers to these questions by the number of issues that must be addressed in order for the franchisee to properly operate the specific franchised business, and you begin to get a feel for the level of detail required.

For example, the Prof-Finders' operations manual will emphasize hiring and recruiting techniques, sales training, interviewing and screening methods, development of referrals, fee structure, use and protection of the proprietary computer system and database, public relations, and administrative management.

The specific organization and content of each manual will vary from franchisor to franchisor and from industry to industry. Naturally, the manual of a fast-food operation may have a more detailed section on sewage, plumbing, and lavatory facilities than would that of our friends at Prof-Finders.

Consider the level of detail contained in these sample provisions in Figure 3-2 dealing with garbage, refuse, and rodent control for a fast-food franchisor.

(Text continues on page 56.)

Figure 3-2. Sample operations manual provisions concerning garbage and refuse.

Containers

(1) Garbage and refuse shall be kept in durable, easily cleanable, insect-proof and rodent-proof containers that do not leak and do not absorb liquids. Plastic bags and wet-strength paper bags may be used to line these containers, and they may be used for storage inside the food service establishment.

(2) Containers used in food preparation and utensil washing areas shall be kept covered after they are filled.

(3) Containers stored outside the establishment, and dumpsters, compactors, and compactor systems shall be easily cleanable; provided with tight-fitting lids, doors, or covers; and shall be kept covered when not in actual use. In containers designed with drains, drain plugs shall be in place at all times, except during cleaning.

(4) There shall be a sufficient number of containers to hold all the garbage and refuse that accumulates.

(5) Soiled containers shall be cleaned at a frequency to prevent insect and rodent attraction. Each container shall be thoroughly cleaned on the inside and outside in a way that does not contaminate food, equipment, or utensils, and detergent or steam shall be provided and used for washing containers. Liquid waste from compacting or cleaning operations shall be disposed of as sewage.

Storage

(1) Garbage and refuse in the premises shall be stored in a manner to make them inaccessible to insects and rodents. Outside storage of unprotected plastic bags or wet-strength paper bags or baled units containing garbage or refuse is prohibited. Cardboard or other packaging material not containing garbage or food wastes need not be stored in covered containers.

(2) Garbage or refuse storage rooms, if used, shall be con-

structed of easily cleanable, nonabsorbent, washable materials, shall be kept clean, shall be insect-proof and rodent-proof, and shall be large enough to store the garbage and refuse containers that accumulate.

(3) Outside storage areas or enclosures shall be large enough to store the garbage and refuse containers that accumulate and shall be kept clean. Garbage and refuse containers, dumpsters, and compactor systems located outside shall be stored on or above a smooth surface of nonabsorbent material such as concrete or machine-laid asphalt that is kept clean and maintained in good repair.

Disposal

(1) Garbage and refuse shall be disposed of often enough to prevent the development of odor and the attraction of insects and rodents.

(2) Where garbage or refuse is burned on the premises, it shall be done by controlled incineration that prevents the escape of particulate matter in accordance with law. Areas around incineration facilities shall be clean and orderly.

Reasoning

Proper storage and disposal of garbage and refuse is necessary to minimize the development of odors, to prevent such waste from becoming an attraction and harborage or breeding place for insects and rodents, and to prevent the soiling of food preparation and food service areas. Improperly handled garbage creates nuisance conditions, makes housekeeping difficult, and may be a possible source of contamination of food, equipment, and utensils.

Examples of violations

— Garbage stored in unprotected plastic bags outside of building

Figure 3-2. continued

— Lid on outside garbage storage container left open
— Refuse containers not cleaned frequently
— Drain plugs missing on dumpster-type storage units
— Outside refuse area not kept clean and neat
— Outside garbage cans and dumpster-type storage unit
  set on unpaved area

Discussion

Complying with each section of the manual makes compliance with other sections much less a task. An excellent example of this interrelationship are the requirements of this section easing compliance with the following sections on insect and rodent control.

Note some of the specific requirements of these paragraphs:

— Storage of garbage and refuse in plastic bags is approved for inside the restaurant building, but not outside.
— Provide hot water, detergent, or steam for washing containers.
— Dumpsters or containers must be located on a nonabsorbent slab of concrete or blacktop; and preferably, some distance away from the establishment doors so as not to entice vermin into the establishment.
— Indoor garbage and refuse storage rooms must be insect and rodent proof.
— Cardboard or other packaging material not containing garbage or food wastes need not be stored in covered containers.

INSECT AND RODENT CONTROL

General Requirements

Effective measures intended to minimize the presence of rodents, flies, cockroaches, and other insects on the premises shall be utilized. The premises shall be kept in such condition as to prevent the harborage or feeding of insects or rodents.

Openings

Openings to the outside shall be effectively protected against the entrance of rodents. Outside openings shall be protected against the entrance of insects by tight-fitting, self-closing doors; closed windows; screening; controlled air currents; or other means. Screen doors shall be self-closing, and screens for windows, doors, skylights, transoms, intake and exhaust air ducts, and other openings to the outside shall be tight-fitting and free of breaks. Screening material shall not be less than sixteen mesh to the inch.

Reasoning

Insects and rodents are capable of transmitting diseases to humans by contamination of food and food-contact surfaces. Because insects require food, water, and shelter, action must be taken to deprive them of these necessities.

Examples of violations

- Front/back door of restaurant propped open for prolonged period
- Screening on doors and windows in poor repair
- Evidence of recent rodent activity
- Outside doors not self-closing or tight-fitting

Discussion

A restaurant cannot keep both pests and customers. One or the other must go. And there can be no doubt as to which is more expendable. There is no place for pests in the facility. Your pest control measures may include:

- Mechanical means such as the use of screen and screening materials, traps, electric screens, and even "air curtains."
- Chemical means such as the use of sprays, repellents, baits, and other insecticides.
- Preventive measures such as cleanup campaigns, proper storage techniques, and other measures related to sanitation and good housekeeping.

Figure 3-2. continued

A proper warning: Prevent contamination by pests without introducing contamination by pesticide. A number of federal regulations cover the handling, use, storage, and disposal of pesticide. Be aware of these regulations if you are conducting your own control program.

If you select a pest control company, be certain it is knowledgeable and competent. The following guidelines are offered in choosing a reliable pest control company and ensuring quality service:

— Reach a complete understanding with a company before work starts or a contract is signed. Find out what the pests are, what will be done, over how long a period of time, and what results can be expected at what cost.
— Be sure you know what is and isn't guaranteed. Be sure the company will back up its work.
— Ask about how the technician who will serve your food service operation has been trained. There are numerous home study courses as well as frequent seminars and training courses run by associations and universities.
— Ask your fellow operators for the name of the company they are currently using or may have used in the past. Find out if they were happy and satisfied with the service.
— Seek value from the pest control company you hire. Don't just look at the price.
— Pests of concern to the food service operation may generally be placed in three classes:

  1. Insect pests, including roaches, ants, flies, and pantry pests
  2. Rodent pests, including mice and rats
  3. Pest birds, including pigeons, starlings, and sparrows

Another critical area for a fast-food operation, which must be addressed in a detailed manner, is the management of relationships with vendors. Franchisees in the fast-food business are likely to have daily contact with food suppliers and sundry vendors; weekly contact with uniform and linen supply companies, equipment maintenance and service companies, trash collectors, vending machine dealers, and pest control companies; and periodic contact with insurance agents, sign makers, security system installers, locksmiths, plumbers, and cash register equipment companies. It is incumbent on the franchisor to develop quality-control criteria and specifications for the selection and approval of these vendors. The mechanics of the vendor approval process should be reviewed by legal counsel in order to consider all applicable principals of antitrust law. Qualification standards must be carefully developed, clearly communicated, and reasonably enforced throughout the franchise system. Nepotism, greed, and the failure to approve qualified suppliers are a cause of constant conflict between franchisors and franchisees, as discussed in Chapter 4.

4
Ensuring Quality Control

Many owners of growing companies fear that the decision to franchise will result in the loss of quality control over the operations and management of their business. In reality, there are a variety of vehicles available to the franchisor for maintaining the level of quality that they and their consumers have come to expect. A well-planned franchising or licensing program will include operational and training methods and manuals to establish quality control guidelines as well as a carefully assembled field support staff to educate franchisees and enforce the franchisor's quality control guidelines.

To succeed, a franchise system demands quality control. A system that does not maintain and enforce an effective quality control strategy is not likely to survive in the competitive marketplace. The licensor of a trademark has an obligation under federal trademark laws to control the quality of the products and services offered in connection with the trademark. Thus, by establishing and enforcing quality control standards, a franchisor not only assures uniformity of quality but also satisfies an obligation imposed by law upon the owner of a trademark. Failure to monitor and control the operations of a franchisee/licensee could result in a "statutory abandonment" of the franchisor's rights in the trademark, because it may no longer distinguish a particular product or service from those offered by others in the market. Therefore, the trademark laws provide a *justification* and basis for the implementation of reasonable controls over franchisees/licensees in all aspects of the business format.

Developing and Enforcing System Standards

The glue holding the typical franchise system together consists of the uniform policies, procedures, and specifications that must be followed by all franchisees. These rules and regulations, typically found in the operations manual, must be (1) *carefully planned* and developed by the franchisor; (2) *clearly articulated* by the franchisor to the franchisees both initially and on an ongoing basis; (3) *accepted* by the network of franchisees as being understood and reasonable; (4) *consistently applied*; and (5) *rigidly enforced* by the franchisor, typically through its field support staff. Obviously, the development of uniform standards is of little utility unless there are systems in place for monitoring and enforcing these standards, as well as penalties for noncompliance with the standards, which are typically found in the franchise agreement.

Compliance with quality control standards requires mutual respect by and among the franchisor and all of its franchisees. The franchisor must be reasonable and resist the temptation to "go hogwild" in the development and enforcement of system standards. The franchisee must understand that reasonable standards are in the best interests of all franchisees in the network. Franchisees typically have a "love-hate" relationship with system standards. On the one hand, they love reasonable standards that result in happy consumers and "weed out" noncomplying franchisees. On the other hand, they detest standards that are unattainable, vaguely communicated, and arbitrarily or too rigidly enforced.

Methods for Enforcing Quality Control and System Standards

There are many methods a franchisor may use to ensure certain levels of quality are maintained that help distinguish the franchisor's products and services from those of its competitors. This chapter examines the use of (1) the franchise agreement; (2) operations manuals; (3) initial and ongoing training programs; (4) tying arrangements; (5) approved supplier programs; and (6) field support personnel to establish, ensure, and maintain quality control. The limitations imposed by law with respect to the controls that may be imposed upon a franchisee/licensee are also explored.

Field Support Staff and Quality Control

Many franchisors view their field support personnel as necessary for providing franchisees the ongoing support and assistance the franchisor is obligated to provide under its franchise agreement. While ongoing support is an important component of the role of field support personnel, franchisors may overlook the important role a well-assembled field support staff can play in ensuring that franchisees maintain the franchisor's quality control and uniform system standards. These two components of the role of field support staff should be carefully considered by current and prospective franchisors.

For the early-stage franchisor, it is not difficult to make periodic visits to each franchisee for the purpose of providing support and assistance, ensuring compliance with quality control guidelines, and listening to franchisees' questions and concerns. This becomes more of a challenge as the franchisor's network of franchisees continues to grow and spread throughout the country, which makes it impossible for the franchisor to offer the same level of tender love and care (TLC) to its franchisees. This growth could have an adverse impact on the quality of the products and services offered by the franchise system. Developing and training a field support staff that can continue to provide TLC and ensure compliance with quality control standards when there are five hundred franchisees, at the same level provided when the franchisor had five franchisees, will help the franchisor's system succeed and prosper.

Ongoing Support and Assistance. Most franchisors undertake to provide franchisees some level of ongoing support and assistance. A field support staff is generally assembled for this purpose. A franchisor's ability to duplicate the level of success and quality offered by its prototype facility is in the hands of the field support staff.

For this reason, field support personnel should be carefully selected and trained. To ensure consistency, each member of the field support team should receive *exactly the same types and levels of training*. They should know the intricacies of the franchise business, be sensitive to the needs and concerns of franchisees, and be diplomatic in their dealings with franchisees. The information provided to the franchisees should be accurate and consistent. If there are differences in the interpretation of a particular standard or role among various members of the field support staff nationwide, then the standard itself may be considered waived or even abandoned. If there is no consistency in the enforcement and communication of standards, then they will be viewed as not being standards at all, and this will lose consumer goodwill, dilute the franchisor's trademarks and proprietary system, and occasion litigation and lowered franchisee morale.

It is important for field support personnel to be able to recognize and satisfy the ongoing needs of franchisees, using a positive management philosophy, motivation techniques, good communication, and innovative franchisee programs. If field support personnel are successful in maintaining good relationships with franchisees, franchisees will be motivated to comply with the necessary controls established by the franchisor for the operation of the business. Maintaining a good relationship with franchisees is accomplished through conducting regular regional and national meetings, providing retraining programs and periodic seminars that focus on various areas of interest to franchisees, offering management consulting services, and maintaining routine telephone and personal contact.

▪ *Meetings and seminars.* Regional and national meetings should be used, among other things, as a forum for franchisees to voice their concerns and questions. The franchisor should take all franchisee questions, concerns, and criticisms seriously and directly address each by (1) offering immediate comfort and suggestions at the meeting, (2) addressing problems raised in newsletters or follow-up bulletins after the meeting, and (3) conducting interviews one-on-one with the franchisee(s) who raised such concerns. The ability of the franchisor's field support personnel to address such concerns and offer franchisees comfort and/or solutions is critical to the viability of the franchisor's system. The franchisor must, at all times, be perceived by its network as sensitive to the needs and concerns of its franchisees and capable of providing meaningful, realistic, and practical solutions.

Seminars that focus on a particular aspect of the operation of the franchise business should be conducted on a regular basis. The franchisor's field support staff should play an important role in developing these seminars. Through personal contacts with franchisees, they can offer insight into appropriate topics for seminars and identify essential issues that franchisees would find beneficial. Seminars can be excellent tools to both educate and motivate franchisees.

■ *Training and retraining programs.* The franchisor must carefully develop a training program that covers all of the topics of concern to franchisees. The initial training program must be comprehensive and informative, covering topics such as management and operation of a business, preparation of products and/or provision of services, quality control, managing personnel, advertising and marketing, bookkeeping and reporting, use of trademarks, maintaining the confidential nature of trade secrets, legal obligations, and customer relations. In developing an initial training program, franchisors must be mindful that many franchisees have never owned or operated a business. For this reason adequate initial training and ongoing assistance and support is crucial to the success of the franchisees and the franchisor. Marketing topics should *not* predominate the training session. Franchisees must be taught not only how to bring in the business, but also *how to deliver* the products and services once the customer is in the door.

Franchisors should also consider implementing retraining programs for franchisees who need continuous reinforcement of the franchisor's business format, standards, and guidelines. Retraining should be recommended (or required) for franchisees who continuously fail in one or more identifiable areas of the operation of the franchise business. *For example:* A franchisee has continuously failed to provide the franchisor with all of the required monthly, quarterly, and annual reports mandated by the franchise agreement. The franchisor's field support personnel have worked with the franchisee several times to correct the deficiency; however, the problem has not been resolved. Field support personnel report to the franchisor that the franchisee is (1) unfamiliar with the reporting requirements and forms, (2) not accustomed to the computer-generated accounting system, and (3) willing to learn and comply but *slow.* This franchisee may have good intentions but may just need some additional training and attention in learning the financial aspects of the business. He or she should, therefore, be allowed (or required) to attend a retraining program that focuses on accounting, reporting, record keeping, and other financial matters. If the franchisor's field support personnel continuously report the same franchisee deficiencies for a group of franchisees, then the franchisor may want to reevaluate that portion of its training program to determine its overall effectiveness. The field support visit to the franchisee's site should be viewed as a quality control enforcement check *as well as* a tutoring and assistance session for troubled franchisees.

▪ *Management consulting services.* Some franchisees have problems that cannot be resolved with the periodic assistance of field support personnel. For this reason, some franchisors offer management consulting services to franchisees at an hourly rate. While this is a more costly means of resolving a franchisee's problems, it may be the only way to identify and deal with them. If a consultant (usually someone who is part of the field support staff) is on-site for one to two weeks, the franchisee's deficiencies will be more quickly and accurately identified. Once problems are identified, the consultant can suggest methods and techniques for resolving them, assist in the implementation, and, to a certain extent, monitor the results. Management consulting services should be offered to franchisees only if the franchisor truly has the personnel and expertise to provide meaningful services. Additionally, the rates charged for consulting services should be reasonable so as not to be perceived by the franchisee as merely a money-making vehicle for the franchisor.

■ *Personal and telephone contact.* Field support personnel are notorious for their regular monthly visits to the franchise location, inspections, unexpected visits, and telephone calls. These are the traditional and most effective methods for providing on-site field support and quality control inspections of franchisees. If, however, a visit by the field support staff is viewed as an intrusion (or even as spying) on the franchisee's ability to operate his business independently, then the franchisor has not succeeded in establishing a good relationship with its franchisees. It is difficult to balance the franchisee's desire for independence with the franchisor's need for quality control. If an appropriate balance is not found, franchisees may become resentful and resist the franchisor's necessary controls, thus creating an unnecessarily tense and hostile relationship. The field support staff is primarily responsible for striking the appropriate balance between the interests of the franchisees and those of the franchisor. It is, therefore, critical that the franchisor use care in the hiring and training of its field support personnel.

The personal visit to a franchisee's operating location by a field support person offers the best opportunity for establishing the appropriate relationship and striking that balance of interests. The franchisor should put together a staff large enough to cover the entire network on a regular basis, such as once per month. If the staff is "spread too thin," it will not be able to conduct timely follow-up visits to check on the franchisee's progress with certain problems. Additionally, if a field support person is responsible for visiting too many franchisees, he or she is less likely to remember each franchisee's problems and concerns, which may make it more difficult to establish and maintain the necessary rapport between the franchisor's staff and the franchisee.

The field support representative should set aside enough time to prepare for each visit (see Figure 4-1) and time to summarize the meeting soon afterward. These details may be overlooked if the franchisor's field support staff is overloaded. A franchisee will recognize an unprepared representative and certainly won't appreciate the inconvenience and waste of time this is likely to create. Each field support person typically develops his or her own style and each franchisee has different needs, but this is no excuse for straying from the uniform system standards that must be continuously communicated to the franchisees.

The visit itself should be carefully orchestrated and always include (1) follow-up on goals set during last meeting, (2) walk-through inspection, (3) training (usually in an area of weakness or a newly introduced service, product, method, or technique), (4) identification of the franchisee's successes and weaknesses, (5) establishment of goals to be met by the next

Figure 4-1. Preparing for site visit.

- Send confirmation of visit, including an agenda of things franchisee should have prepared (unless the visit is intended to be a random "surprise" for enforcement and monitoring purposes).
- Contact franchisee to get input for developing the agenda.
- Identify staff members needed for meetings and secure time for them during the visit.
- Evaluate franchisee's sales data and reports.
- Review report from last visit.
- Check on timeliness of royalty and other payments to franchisor.
- Develop goals for visit.

visit, (6) identification of franchisee's needs and concerns, (7) talk with employees and customers, and (8) reinforcement of quality control guidelines.

Inspections of the franchisee's facility should be conducted in accordance with a standardized checklist developed by the franchisor. A point-scoring method is typically used for such evaluations. Field support personnel should be required to report the results of these evaluations to the franchisor within a specified time frame. All reports should note both deficient and outstanding-quality performance.

Except for certain major infractions, which there is no effective means of correcting (these typically result in immediate notice of termination under the franchise agreement), franchisees should be given the opportunity to cure or correct defaults or deficiencies. The field representative should be responsible for (1) offering guidance to the franchisees on ways to correct the cited deficiencies and (2) following up with franchisees to see that deficiencies have been corrected. Typically a franchisee is given thirty days to correct deficiencies unless the deficiency cannot be corrected within this time period.

• *Unannounced visits and test customers.* Field visits and inspections should occur on a regular basis. A 1985 study conducted by the International Franchise Association indicates that most franchisors conduct monthly field calls and that a large number of franchisors also conduct such calls on a quarterly, bimonthly, or semiannual basis. In addition to regularly scheduled visits, field personnel should conduct periodic surprise/unannounced visits and inspections. Many franchisees may be put off by unannounced inspections, viewing them as an infringement on their independence. For this reason, the field personnel should carefully orchestrate surprise inspections. Franchisees should be informed from the start that an imminent inspection should have no effect on the standards, service, products, cleanliness, or other aspects of its business operation. The field person should be viewed as "just another customer," grading and judging the same way customers do. The difference is that the field person will go behind the scenes to check aspects of the business that create the product and service. The inspection is designed to help the franchisee improve its performance. An unsatisfied customer won't return; the field person, on the other hand, will help the franchisee identify and correct any problems.

Franchisors often discover that adjacent franchisees establish a network to inform other franchisees that the field support person is in the area. As a franchise system grows, the communication network makes it more and more difficult to conduct "truly" surprise visits. Nonetheless, such visits should continue to be used as part of the franchisor's quality control program.

Test customers can be used as an alternative or supplement to surprise visits by field personnel. Generally the franchisor will hire people unfamiliar to its franchisees to act as customers for the purpose of evaluating the franchisee's performance in the areas of customer relations, product and service quality, and cleanliness. To achieve the best results, test customers should not identify themselves as such and should report to the field person with detailed observations. Later, the field support person who usually deals with the franchisee should make an announced visit for the purpose of discussing the observations of the test customer. Maintaining the anonymity of test customers (1) prevents franchisees from alerting other area franchisees that a surprise inspection is likely and (2) puts the franchisee on notice that any customer could in fact be a "test customer" sent by the franchisor.

The Development of Enforcement Systems

As a general rule, the franchisor has an obligation to develop system standards and procedures that are reasonable and attainable. Once developed, the standards and procedures should be clearly communicated and uniformly enforced. The enforcement must be neither too loose nor too rigid. If the penalties for noncompliance are too loose, the franchisor will be viewed as a toothless lion who neither intends nor has the power to insist on compliance. If the enforcement is too rigid, the standards will be resented and disregarded, resulting in litigation and poor franchisee morale throughout the network.

Many times, the enforcement strategy adopted depends on the franchisor's own stage of growth. For example, a gentle rap on the knuckles (in lieu of an actual termination) may be more prudent early on in the franchisor's own development because of the impact of a dispute at this stage. The costs of litigation, the perception of actual and prospective franchisees, and the nature of the infraction should all be considered. If a "quasi-acquiescence" policy of enforcement is adopted by the younger franchisor, then issues of waiver and laches should be discussed with legal counsel. As the franchisor grows and matures, it becomes easier to rigidly enforce system standards and apply significant penalties for noncompliance because the threat of termination becomes a more powerful deterrent.

The franchisor should consider the following general factors in determining how to proceed against a franchisee in noncompliance with system standards: (1) whether the franchisee in question has a "high profile" within the system, (2) the exact nature of the franchisee's infraction(s), (3) the current condition and stability of the franchisor's industry, (4) the availability of a replacement franchisee for this specific site, (5) the quality of the training program and operations manual in the area where the infractions have incurred, (6) the existence of any potential counterclaims by the franchisee, (7) the quality of the evidence gathered by the field support personnel to prove the incidents of noncompliance, (8) the reaction of the other franchisees within the system to the enforcement action, and (9) the geographic location of the franchisee in question. The penalties that may be applied by the franchisor to the noncomplying franchisee include a formal warning, a written notice of default, a threat of termination, actual termination, damages or fines, a forced sale or transfer, or a denial of a benefit, such as eligibility for participation in a new program. Support for those penalties must be found in the franchise agreement or must be separately negotiated.

Other Methods of Enforcing Quality Control Standards in a Franchise System

Operations Manuals and Training Programs. The franchisor usually provides the franchisee with a comprehensive operations manual, which is generally reviewed for the first time at the initial training session for owners and managers of the franchise business. These manuals and training programs instruct the franchisee on all aspects of operating and managing the business within the quality control standards established by the franchisor. The operations manual should set forth in a clear and concise fashion the minimum levels of quality to be maintained in all aspects of the business, from cleanliness to customer service to recipes to employee relations. These standards should be taught and reinforced throughout the training program.

Architectural/Engineering Plans and Drawings. In most types of franchised businesses, uniformity of physical appearance is imperative. The franchisor often provides detailed architectural drawings and engineering plans both as a service to franchisees and as a method of protecting quality control. These plans reinforce the importance of a consistent image in the minds of consumers, who may be looking for the "golden arches" or "orange roof" in their search for a familiar place to eat along the highway. Plans may include specifications for signage, counter design, display racks, paint colors, HVAC systems, lighting, interior decoration, or special building features.

Site Selection Assistance. The top three priorities for the success of a franchisee's business have often been cited as "location, location, and location." Many franchisors assist franchisees in selecting a proper site for their franchise business and even assist in lease negotiations and supervision of construction. Such efforts not only help to ensure the franchisee's success, but also provide an additional basis for maintaining quality control in terms of minimum parking requirements, traffic patterns, minimum/maximum square footage, demographics of the local market, and prevention of market saturation.

National or Uniform Advertising Programs. Advertising and promotion of the franchise business on a local and national level is an essential part of virtually all franchise systems. If the franchisees are left on their own to develop advertising and promotional materials for local television, radio, and newspapers, the system will not be sending out a uniform message about the products and/or services offered by the franchise network. Additionally, franchisors will not have control over the quality and content of the advertising materials used by franchisees. Franchisees may not be knowledgeable of the laws prohibiting unfair or deceptive advertising and trade practices. Thus, without the franchisor's guidelines, they are more likely to stumble into trouble, diminishing the goodwill the franchisor has worked hard to build.

For this reason, a centralized advertising program, engineered by the franchisor's in-house staff or an outside advertising agency, develops newspaper, television, and radio advertisements for use by franchisees in their local markets, helping the franchisor maintain a certain minimum level of quality in advertising. Moreover, this centralized advertising program should include a franchisor review and approval process for advertisements developed by franchisees.

Approved Supplier Program. The franchisee will need a wide variety of raw materials, office and business supplies, equipment, foodstuff, and services in order to operate the franchise business. The level of control that the franchisor is entitled to exercise over the acquisition of these supplies and materials will vary, depending on the nature of the franchise business and the extent to which such goods are proprietary. Franchisors may be prohibited, under certain circumstances, from forcing a franchisee to buy all equipment and supplies from them or their designated sources.

The franchisor does, however, have a right to establish objective performance standards and specifications to which alternate suppliers and their products or services must adhere. Such standards are justifiable for the purpose of ensuring a certain minimum standard of quality.

In establishing an approved supplier or vendor certification program, the franchisor should carefully develop procedures for the suggestion and evaluation of alternative suppliers proposed by the franchisee. The standards by which a prospective supplier is evaluated should be clearly defined and reasonable. This evaluation should be based upon:

1. Ability to produce the products or services in accordance with the franchisor's standards and specifications for quality and uniformity
2. Production and delivery capabilities and ability to meet supply commitments
3. Integrity of ownership (to assure that association with the franchisor would not be inconsistent with the franchisor's image or damage its goodwill)
4. Financial stability
5. Familiarity of the proposed supplier with the franchise business
6. Negotiation of a satisfactory license agreement to protect the franchisor's trademarks

The franchisor should always reserve the right to disapprove any proposed supplier who does not meet these standards. In addition, an approved supplier should be removed from the list of suppliers if, at any time, it fails to maintain these standards. Other reasonable standards, applicable in the franchisor's industry, may also be adopted.

Special Legal Issues Affecting Exclusive Supplier and Vendor Certification Programs

For certain highly proprietary aspects of the franchise business such as the "secret sauce," the franchisor typically has the authority to require the franchisee to purchase those prod-

ucts *exclusively* from the franchisor or from a supplier designated and approved by the franchisor. This is known as a tying
arrangement. Not all tying arrangements are permitted under
applicable antitrust laws. Proposed tying programs continue
to be one of the greatest sources of conflict and litigation between franchisors and franchisees. This section discusses how
and when a franchisor can legally require its franchisees to
purchase products solely from the franchisor (or a specific
supplier, which may or may not be affiliated with the franchisor). It also examines the limitations on the franchisor's right
to impose a tying arrangement and discusses other limitations
on the franchisor's controls over franchisees.

Federal antitrust law identifies a *tying arrangement* as an
arrangement whereby a seller refuses to sell one product (the
tying product, franchise) unless the buyer also purchases another product (tied product, food products or ingredients, for
example). Such arrangements are perceived as posing an unacceptable risk of "stifling competition" and as a general matter are not favored by the courts.

One of the critical factors examined by the courts in determining whether a particular transaction or set of purchase
terms constitutes an unlawful tying arrangement is a tie-in between *two separate and distinct products* or services which
are readily distinguishable in the eyes of the consumer
whereby the availability of the tying product is conditioned
on the purchase of the tied product.

For example, in a case involving Kentucky Fried Chicken
Corp. (KFC), the court discussed the distinction between two
separate products unlawfully tied together by a seller and two
interrelated products which are justifiably tied together.
In that case Marion-Kay, a manufacturer and distributor of
chicken seasoning, counterclaimed against KFC, alleging unlawful tying of its KFC franchises to the purchase of its own
special KFC seasoning exclusively from two designated distributors. The court found that the alleged tying product (the
KFC franchise) and the alleged tied product (the chicken seasoning) were not two separate products tied together unlawfully. Rather, the court stated that the use of the KFC

trademarks and service marks by franchisees is *so* interrelated with the KFC chicken seasoning that *no person could reasonably find that the franchise and the seasoning are two separate products.*

In the Kentucky Fried Chicken case, the court recognized *the need* and *the right* of a franchisor to require its franchisees to purchase certain products from the franchisor directly or from *its* designated sources *if* those products are *so* intimately related to the intellectual property licensed to the franchisee as to be necessary for the purpose of maintaining the quality of the product identified by the trademark. The crucial inquiry is into the relationship between the trademark and the product allegedly tied to it. In a similar case involving Baskin-Robbins franchisees, the court found that the trademark licensed to the Baskin-Robbins franchisees was inseparable from the ice cream itself and concluded that the trademark was therefore utterly dependent upon the perceived quality of the product it represented. If the trademark serves *only* to identify the tied product, there can be no illegal tie-in, because the trademark and the quality of the product it represents are so inextricably interrelated in the mind of the consumer as to preclude any finding that the trademark is a separate product.

The crucial distinction is between a *product-driven franchise* system (distribution system), where the trademark represents the end product marketed by the system and a *business format system* in which there is generally only a remote connection between the trademark and the products the franchisees are compelled to purchase. In a product-driven system, a tying arrangement is more likely to be upheld because the products being tied to the purchase of the franchise are an integral part of the franchisor's system and are intimately related to the trademarks being licensed to the franchisee.

A *business format franchise* is usually created merely to implement a particular business system under a common tradename. The franchise outlet itself is generally responsible for the production and preparation of the system's end product or service. The franchisor merely provides the trademark and, in some cases, also provides the supplies used in operating the franchised outlet and producing the system's products. Under a distribution system, the franchised outlet serves merely as a conduit through which the trademarked goods of the franchisor flow to the ultimate consumer. Generally, these goods are manufactured by the franchisor or by its licensees according to detailed specifications.

In a related case involving the Chicken Delight franchise system, the tied products imposed on the franchisees were commonplace paper products and packaging goods neither manufactured by the franchisor nor uniquely suited to the franchised business. Under the business format franchise system, the connection between the trademark and the products the franchisees are compelled to purchase were remote enough that the trademark, which simply reflects the goodwill and quality standards of the enterprise it identifies, *may be considered as separate* from the commonplace items that are tied more closely to the trademark's actual use.

Therefore, in order for tying arrangements to be looked upon favorably, the court must find that the tied products are uniquely related to the franchise system and *intimately related to the trademarks being licensed to franchisees.* Thus, the purchase of certain products, which are sold by franchisees under the franchisor's trademarks and are highly proprietary and an integral part of the system, may be restricted by designating certain suppliers (even if that supplier is the franchisor) and maintaining strict product specifications.

On the other hand, it is unlikely that restrictions on the purchase of supplies such as forms, service contracts, business cards, and signage would be upheld as a valid tie-in because these items, although an integral part of the system, are not uniquely suited to the system or intimately related to the trademarks licensed to the franchisees. Furthermore, as more fully discussed below, a restriction on the purchase of these supplies could not be justified if less restrictive alterntives are available that would yield the same level of quality control. In the case of these "commonplace" supplies, a court could find that providing strict specifications for the quality and uniformity of supplies and allowing franchisees to obtain the approval of other suppliers for these items would be less restrictive and thus the favored method of ensuring quality and uniformity.

Justification for Certain Types of Tying Arrangements. An otherwise illegal tying arrangement may, under appropriate circumstances, be justified by a franchisor and upheld by a court. One such justification recognized by the courts is a tying arrangement necessary to preserve the distinctiveness, uniformity, and quality of a franchisor's products in connection with the license of the franchisor's trademarks.

In the case of a franchisor who grants a license to its franchisees to use its trademarks, the franchisor (licensor) owes an affirmative duty to the public to ensure that in the hands of the licensee the trademark continues to represent what it purports to represent. If a licensor relaxes quality control standards by permitting inferior products under a licensed mark, this may well constitute a misuse or even statutory abandonment of the mark. Courts have qualified what would appear to be a level of absolute discretion being vested in the franchisor by stating that *not all* means of achieving and maintaining quality control are justified. Rather, they have held that a restraint of trade can be justified only in the absence of less restrictive alternatives.

If specifications of the type and quality of the products to be used by the franchisee are sufficient to ensure the high standards of quality and uniformity the franchisor desires to maintain, then this less restrictive alternative must be utilized in lieu of requiring the franchisee to purchase those products only from the franchisor. If specifications for a substitute would require such detail that they could not be supplied (i.e., they would divulge trade secrets or be unreasonably burdensome), then protection of the trademarks may warrant the use of what would otherwise be an illegal tying arrangement.

More recently, several courts have again recognized the business justification standard as an appropriate defense to an allegation that a franchisor is involved in an illegal tying arrangement. In 1987, the U.S. Court of Appeals held that a

United States importer of German automobiles was justified in requiring its dealers to purchase all of their replacement parts from the importer as a condition of their securing a franchise to sell the automobiles in order to secure quality control, to protect goodwill, and to combat "free-riding" dealers. The court was satisfied with the substantial evidence to support the importer's assertion that the tie-in was used to assure quality control in view of the fact that the importer purchased 80 percent of its parts from German manufacturers and subjected parts purchased from other manufacturers to an *elaborate and rigorous inspection procedure.*

Whether a legally recognizable justification exists to warrant a tying arrangement will ultimately depend on (1) the licensor's legitimate need to ensure quality control, (2) the availability of "less restrictive means" to achieve protection of the quality control, and (3) whether the alleged "tied product" is truly proprietary in nature. The relationship between the trademark and the product must be sufficiently intimate to justify the tie-in on grounds of quality control, uniformity, and protection of goodwill. More importantly, a tie-in otherwise justified in the name of quality control will not be upheld if less restrictive means are available for assuring quality and uniformity.

There is a continuous struggle between the antitrust laws that generally disfavor tying arrangements and the trademark laws that impose a duty upon the owner of a trademark to monitor the use of the mark by licensees to ensure that the licensor's standards of quality are maintained and that the licensee's use of the mark is consistent with the licensor's intentions.

Quality Control and the Field Staff

The franchisor's quality control program that is, for the most part, administered by the field support staff, is the front line of defense for the franchisor's trademarks. Field support personnel are responsible for enforcing the franchisor's quality control standards and for reporting field conditions to the franchisor. Quality control strategies developed by top management may be misguided if the information gathered and reported by field support personnel is not accurate. The franchisor should, therefore, closely monitor its field support personnel and replace those who are lenient, arbitrary, or inconsistent.

In a large system, the field support staff is typically the only contact the franchisee will have with the franchisor. It is, therefore, essential that all members of the field support staff possess those qualities necessary to create and maintain a good relationship with franchisees while at the same time reinforcing the franchisor's necessary standards. A properly administered quality control program provides the franchisor with a method for policing franchisees that achieves positive results and uniformity throughout the franchise system. By establishing, maintaining, and enforcing high standards of quality, all parties, including the franchisee, will benefit. Thus, the importance of quality control should be properly explained to franchisees (initially at training) and reinforced on an ongoing and consistent basis by field support personnel.

The role of field support staff does not end with the enforcement of quality control standards. Often, field personnel act as troubleshooters in helping franchisees improve their business. In emergency situations, they may even step in as operating manager. For this reason, the franchisor's field personnel should be well educated in the intricacies of operating the franchise business. They should be able to handle any situation that may arise. They will be looked to as leaders and should be comfortable in that role. Above all, field support personnel should be good listeners and communicators.

Part Two
Legal and Strategic Issues

5

The Regulatory Framework of Franchising

The offer and sale of a franchise is regulated at both the federal and state level. At the federal level, the Federal Trade Commission (FTC) in 1979 adopted its trade regulation rule 436 (the "FTC Rule") which specifies the minimum amount of disclosure that must be made to a prospective franchisee in any of the fifty states. In addition to the FTC Rule, over a dozen states have adopted their own rules and regulations for the offer and sale of franchises within their borders. Known as the registration states, they include most of the nation's largest commercial marketplaces, such as California, New York, and Illinois. These states generally follow a more detailed disclosure format, known as the Uniform Franchise Offering Circular (the UFOC).

The UFOC was originally developed by the Midwest Securities Commissioners Association in 1975. The monitoring of and revisions to the UFOC are now under the authority of the North American Securities Administrators Association (NASAA). Each of the registration states has developed and adopted its own statutory version of the UFOC. The differences among the states should be checked carefully by both current and prospective franchisors and their counsel, as well as individuals considering the purchase of a franchise opportunity.

Brief History of Franchise Registration

The laws governing the offer and sale of franchises began in 1970, when the state of California adopted its Franchise Investment Law. Shortly thereafter, the FTC commenced its hearings to begin the development of the federal law governing franchising. After seven years of public comment and debate, the FTC adopted its trade regulation rule that is formally titled "Disclosure Requirements and Prohibitions Concerning Franchising and Business Opportunity Ventures" on December 21, 1978, to be effective October 21, 1979. Many states followed the lead of California, and there are now fifteen states that regulate franchise offers and sales.

The states that require registration of a franchise offering prior to the "offering" or selling of a franchise are California, Illinois, Indiana, Maryland, Minnesota, New York, North Dakota, Rhode Island, South Dakota, Virginia, Wisconsin, and Washington.

Other states that regulate franchise offers include Hawaii, which requires filing of an offering circular with the state authorities and delivery of an offering circular to prospective franchisees; Michigan, which requires filing of a "Notice of Intent to Offer and Sell Franchises"; Oregon, which requires only that presale disclosure be delivered to prospective investors; and Texas, which requires the filing of a notice of exemption with the appropriate state authorities under the Texas Business Opportunity Act.

Among other things, the FTC Rule requires that every franchisor offering franchises in the United States deliver an offering circular (containing certain specified disclosure items) to all prospective franchisees (within certain specified time requirements). The FTC has adopted and enforced its rule pursuant to its power and authority to regulate unfair and deceptive trade practices. The FTC Rule sets forth the minimum level of protection that shall be afforded to prospective franchisees. To the extent that a "registration state" offers its citizens a greater level of protection, the FTC Rule *will not preempt state law.* There is no private right of action under the FTC Rule; however, the FTC itself may bring an enforcement action against a franchisor that does not meet its requirements. Penalties for noncompliance have included asset impoundments, cease and desist rders, injunctions, consent orders, mandated rescission or restitution for injured franchisees, and civil fines of up to $10,000 per violation.

The FTC Rule regulates two types of offerings: (1) package and product franchises and (2) business opportunity ventures.

The first type involves three characteristics: (1) The franchisee sells goods or services that meet the franchisor's quality standards (in cases where the franchisee operates under the franchisor's trademark, service mark, trade name, advertising, or other commercial symbol designating the franchisor ("Mark") that are identified by the franchisor's Mark, (2) the franchisor exercises significant assistance in the franchisee's method of operation, and (3) the franchisee is required to make payment of $500 or more to the franchisor or a person affiliated with the franchisor at any time before to within six months after the business opens.

The second type also involves three characteristics: (1) The franchisee sells goods or services that are supplied by the franchisor or a person affiliated with the franchisor; (2) the franchisor assists the franchisee in any way with respect to securing accounts for the franchisee, or securing locations or sites for vending machines or rack displays, or providing the services of a person able to do either; and (3) the franchisee is required to make payment of $500 or more to the franchisor or a person affiliated with the franchisor at any time before to within six months after the business opens.

Relationships covered by the rule include those within the definition of a "franchise" and those represented as being within the definition when the relationship is entered into, regardless of whether, in fact, they are within the definition. The FTC Rule exempts (1) fractional franchises, (2) leased department arrangements, and (3) purely verbal agreements. The Rule excludes (1) relationships between employer/employees and among general business partners, (2) membership in retailer-owned cooperatives, (3) certification and testing services, and (4) single trademark licenses.

The disclosure document required by the FTC Rule must include information on the twenty subjects listed in Figure 5-1.

The information must be current as of the completion of the franchisor's most recent fiscal year. In addition, a revision to the document must be promptly prepared whenever there has been a material change in the information contained in the document. The disclosure document must be given to a prospective franchisee at the earlier of either (1) the prospective franchisee's first personal meeting with the franchisor or (2) ten days prior to the execution of a contract or payment of money relating to the franchise relationship. In addition to the disclosure document, the franchisee must receive a copy of all agreements that it will be asked to sign at least five days prior to the execution of the agreements.

The FTC Rule requires that an offering circular be provided to the prospective franchisee at the earliest of the following: (1) the *first personal meeting* or (2) *ten business days* before the signing of the franchise agreement or any other binding agreement by the prospective franchisee, or (3) *ten business days* before the acceptance of any payment from the prospective franchisee.

The FTC Rule also requires that a completed franchise agreement and related agreements be provided to the prospective franchisee *five business days* before the agreements are executed. A business day is any day other than Saturday, Sunday, or the following national holidays: New Year's Day, Washington's Birthday, Memorial Day, Independence Day, Labor Day, Columbus Day, Veteran's Day, Thanksgiving, and Christmas.

The timing requirements described above apply nationwide and preempt any lesser timing requirements contained in state laws. The ten-day and five-day disclosure periods may

Figure 5-1. Topics to address in the FTC disclosure document.

1. Identifying information about the franchisor
2. Business experience of the franchisor's directors and key executives
3. The franchisor's business experience
4. Litigation history of the franchisor and its directors and key executives
5. Bankruptcy history of the franchisor and its directors and key executives
6. Description of the franchise
7. Money required to be paid by the franchisee to obtain or commence the franchise operation
8. Continuing expenses to the franchisee in operating the franchise business that are payable in whole or in part to the franchisor
9. A list of persons, including the franchisor and any of its affiliates, with whom the franchisee is required or advised to do business
10. Realty, personalty, services, and so on that the franchisee is required to purchase, lease, or rent and a list of any person with whom such transactions must be made
11. Description of consideration paid (such as royalties, commissions, etc.) by third parties to the franchisor or any of its affiliates as a result of franchisee purchases from such third parties
12. Description of any franchisor assistance in financing the purchase of a franchise
13. Restrictions placed on a franchisee's conduct of its business
14. Required personal participation by the franchisee
15. Termination, cancellation, and renewal of the franchise
16. Statistical information about the number of franchises and their rate of termination
17. Franchisor's right to select or approve a site for the franchise
18. Training programs for the franchisee
19. Celebrity involvement with the franchise
20. Financial information about the franchisor

run concurrently, and sales contacts with the prospective franchisee may continue during those periods.

It is an unfair or deceptive act or practice within the meaning of Section 5 of the FTC Act for any franchisor or franchise broker:

1. To fail to furnish prospective franchisees, within the time frame established by the Rule, with a disclosure document containing information on twenty different subjects relating to the franchisor, the franchise business, and the terms of the franchise agreement
2. To make any representations about the actual or potential sales, income, or profits of existing or prospective franchisees except in the manner set forth in the rule
4. To fail to furnish prospective franchisees, within the time frame established by the rule, with copies of the franchisor's standard form of franchise agreement and copies of the final agreements to be signed by the parties
5. To fail to return to prospective franchisees any funds or deposits (such as down payments) identified as refundable in the disclosure document

State Franchise Laws

The goal of the FTC Rule is to create a minimum federal standard of disclosure applicable to all franchisor offerings and to permit states to provide additional protection as they see fit. Thus, while the FTC Rule has the force and effect of federal law and, like other federal substantive regulations, preempts state and local laws to the extent that these laws conflict, the FTC has determined that the rule will not preempt state or local laws and regulations that either are consistent with the rule or, even if inconsistent, would provide protection to prospective franchisees equal to or greater than that imposed by the rule.

Examples of state laws or regulations that would not be preempted by the Rule include state provisions requiring the registration of franchisors and franchise salespersons, state requirements for escrow or bonding arrangements, and state-required disclosure obligations set forth in the Rule. Moreover, the Rule does not affect state laws or regulations that regulate the franchisor/franchisee relationship, such as termination practices, contract provisions, and financing arrangements.

Definitions Under State Law

Each state franchise disclosure statute has its own definition of a "franchise," which is similar to, but not the same as, the definition set forth in the FTC Rule.

There are three major types of state definitions of a franchise or business opportunity. They consist of:

A. **Majority State Definition.** In the states of California, Illinois, Indiana, Maryland, Michigan, North Dakota, Oregon, Rhode Island, and Wisconsin, a franchise is defined as having three essential elements:

1. A franchisee is granted the right to engage in the business of offering, selling, or distributing goods or services under a marketing plan or system prescribed in substantial part by a franchisor.
2. The operation of the franchisee's business ... is substantially associated with the franchisor's trademark or other commercial symbol designating the franchisor or its affiliate.
3. The franchisee is required to pay a fee.

B. **Minority State Definition.** The states of Hawaii, Minnesota, South Dakota, and Washington have adopted a somewhat broader definition of *franchise*. In these states, a franchise is defined as having the following three essential elements:

1. A franchisee is granted the right to engage in the business of offering or distributing goods or services using the franchisor's trade name or other commercial symbol or related characteristics.

2. The franchisor and franchisee have a common interest in the marketing of goods or services.
3. The franchisee pays a fee.

C. **New York Definition.**The state of New York has a unique definition. Under its law a franchisee is defined by these guidelines:

1. The franchisor is paid a fee by the franchisee.
2. Either the franchisee's business is substantially associated with the franchisor's trademark or the franchisee operates under a marketing plan or system prescribed in substantial part by the franchisor.

D. **Virginia Definition.**The Commonwealth of Virginia also has its own definition of a franchise, which stipulates that:

1. A franchisee is granted the right to engage in the business of offering or distributing goods or services at retail under a marketing plan or system prescribed in substantial part by a franchisor.
2. The franchisee's business is substantially associated with the franchisor's trademark.

Virginia and New York have definitions that are broad in certain respects. Virginia does not have a "fee" element to its definition. New York requires a fee, but specifies *either* association with franchisor's trademark *or* a marketing plan prescribed by the franchisor. Therefore, in New York no trademark license is required for a franchise relationship to exist. However, the regulations in New York exclude from the definition of a franchise any relationship in which a franchisor does not provide significant assistance to or exert significant controls over a franchisee.

Preparing the Disclosure Document: Choosing the Appropriate Format

In many ways, the choice of the appropriate format for the franchisor's franchise offering circular is difficult and complex, because the requirements of the FTC Rule, the UFOC guidelines, and the particular state laws must all be coordinated. The format selection process is a decision regarding the form in which the disclosure is made but is not a choice of which law shall govern. Even if the UFOC format is selected, the federal laws governing the timing of the delivery of the disclosure document, the restrictions on the use of earnings claims, and the penalties available to the FTC for noncompliance still apply.

Depending on the targeted markets selected by the company, most franchisors have elected to adopt the UFOC format in the preparation of their disclosure documents. Because many registration states do not accept the FTC Rule format (even though the FTC has endorsed the UFOC format), it is simply more cost-effective to have only one primary document for use in connection with franchise offers and sales. If the franchisor will be limiting its marketing activities to states that do not have registration statutes, then the FTC Rule format may offer certain advantages. For example, the FTC Rule format generally requires less information than the UFOC format does in the areas of training and personnel of the franchisor, the litigation history of the franchisor (FTC Rule requires a seven-year history while the UFOC format requires a ten-year history), history of termination and nonrenewals (FTC, one year; UFOC, three years), bankruptcy history (FTC, seven years; UFOC, fifteen years), sanctions under Canadian law (required by UFOC but not FTC) and requires less stringent disclosure regarding the refundability of payments made by the franchisee.

The FTC Rule format may also be easier for the early-stage franchisor to satisfy, because it allows for a three-year phase-in period for the use of audited financials. Under the UFOC format, audited financials are required from the onset and if the financial condition of the franchisor is weak, then many state administrators will impose costly escrow and bonding procedures or require personal (or parent company for a subsidiary) guaranties of performance. In some registration states, a financially weak franchisor will be denied registration until its condition improves. Early-stage franchisors that are grossly undercapitalized, have a negative net worth, or may have suffered significant recent operating losses should be prepared for an uphill battle with the state franchise examiners before approval will be granted.

Preparing the Disclosure Document Under UFOC Guidelines

The UFOC format of franchise disclosure consists of twenty-three categories of information that must be provided by the franchisor to the prospective franchisee at least ten business days prior to the execution of the franchise agreement. Because this format has been adopted by many states as a matter of law, franchisors may not change the order in which information is presented, nor may any of the disclosure items be omitted in the document. In addition, many sections of the UFOC must be a mirror image of the actual franchise agreement (and related documents) that the franchisee will be expected to sign. There should be no factual or legal inconsistencies between the UFOC and the franchise agreement.

A description of the information required by each disclosure item of the UFOC is as follows:

1. *The franchisor and any predecessors.* This first section of the UFOC is designed to inform the franchisee as to the historical background of the franchisor and any of its predecessors. The franchisor's corporate and trade name, form of doing business, principal headquarters, state and date of incorporation, prior business experience, and current business activities all must be disclosed in this section. The franchisor must also disclose the nature of the franchise being offered and its qualifications for offering this type of business. This includes a general description of the business operations to be conducted by the franchisee, the length of time that the franchisor has offered franchises for such businesses, and a discussion of the comptition that the franchisee will face in similar lines of business.

2. *Identity and business experience of persons affiliated with the franchisor; franchise brokers.* This section requires disclosure of the identity of each director, trustee, general partner (where applicable) and officer or manager of the franchisor who will have significant responsibility in connection with the operation of the franchisor's business or in the support services to be provided to franchisees. The principal occupation of each person listed in item 2 for the past five years must be disclosed, including dates of employment, nature of the position,and the identity of the employer. The identity and background of each franchise broker (if any) authorized to represent the franchisor must also be disclosed in this item.

3. *Litigation.* A full and frank discussion of any litigation, arbitration, or administrative hearings affecting the franchisor, its officers, directors, or sales representatives over the past ten years should be included in this section. The formal case name, location of the dispute, nature of the claim, and the current status of each action must be disclosed. Item 3 does not require disclosure of *all* types of litigation but rather focuses on specific allegations and proceedings that would be of particular concern to the prospective franchisee.

4. *Bankruptcy.* This section requires the franchisor to disclose whether the company or any of its predecessors, officers, or general partners, have during the past fifteen years been adjudged bankrupt or reorganized due to insolvency. The court in which the bankruptcy or reorganization proceeding occurred, the formal case title, and any material facts and circumstances surrounding the proceeding must be disclosed.

5. *Franchisee's initial franchise fee or other initial payment.* The initial franchise fee and related payments to the franchisor upon execution of the franchise agreement must be disclosed in this section. The manner in which the payments are made, the use of the proceeds by the franchisor, and whether or not the fee is refundable in whole or in part must be disclosed.

6. *Other fees.* Any other initial or recurring fee payable by the franchisee to the franchisor or any affiliate must be dis-

closed and the nature of each fee fully discussed, including but not limited to royalty payments, training fees, audit fees, public offering review fees, advertising contributions, mandatory insurance requirements, transfer fees, renewal fees, lease negotiation fees, and any consulting fees charged by the franchisor or an affiliate for special services. The amount, time of the payment, and refundability of each type of payment should be disclosed.

7. *Franchisee's initial investment.* Each component of the franchisee's initial investment that the franchise is required to expend in order to open the franchised business must be estimated in this section, usually in chart form, regardless of whether such payments are made directly to the franchisor. Real estate, equipment, fixtures, security deposits, inventory, construction costs, working capital, accounting and legal fees, license and permit fees, and any other costs and expenditures should be disclosed. The disclosure should include to whom such payments are made, under what general terms and conditions, and what portion, if any, is refundable. The following statement must appear at the end of Item 7: "There are no other direct or indirect payments in conjunction with the purchase of the franchise."

8. *Obligations of the franchisee to purchase or lease from designated sources.* Any obligation of the franchisee to purchase goods, services, supplies, fixtures, equipment, or inventory that relates to the establishment or operation of the franchised business from a source designated by the franchisor should be disclosed. The terms of the purchase or lease as well as any minimum-volume purchasing requirements must be disclosed. If the franchisor will or may derive direct or indirect income based on these purchases from required sources, then the nature and amount of such income must be fully disclosed. *Remember that such obligations must be able to withstand the scrutiny of the antitrust laws.*

9. *Obligations of the franchisee to purchase or lease in accordance with specifications or from approved suppliers.* All quality control standards, equipment specifications, and

approved supplier programs that have been developed by the franchisor and must be followed by the franchisee must be disclosed under this item. The criteria applied by the franchisor for approving or designating a particular supplier or vendor must be included. A detailed discussion of these standards and specifications need not be actually set forth in the UFOC; rather, a summary discussion of the programs with reference to exhibits or confidential operations manuals is sufficient. Finally, any income derived by the franchisor in connection with the designation of an approved supplier, or as a result of an approved supplier being an affiliated corporation, must be disclosed.

10. *Financing arrangements.* In this section, the franchisor must disclose the terms and conditions of any financing arrangements offered to franchisees either by the franchisor or any of its affiliates. The exact terms of any direct or indirect debt financing, equipment or real estate leasing programs, operating lines of credit, or inventory financing must be disclosed. If any of these financing programs is offered by an affiliate, then the exact relationship between the franchisor and the affiliate must be disclosed. Terms that may be detrimental to the franchisee upon default, such as a confession of judgment, waiver of defenses, or acceleration clauses, must be disclosed in this item of the UFOC.

11. *Obligations of the franchisor; other supervision, assistance, or services.* This section is one of the most important to the prospective franchisee because it discusses the initial and ongoing support and services provided by the franchisor. Each obligation of the franchisor to provide assistance must be cross-referenced to the specific paragraph of the franchise agreement where the corresponding contractual provision may be found. Most services offered by the franchisor fall into one of two categories: initial or continuing services. *Initial-support* includes all services offered by the franchisor prior to the opening of the franchised business, such as the provision of architectural or engineering plans, construction supervision, personnel recruitment, site selection, preopening pro-

motion, and acquisition of initial inventory. The location, duration, content, and qualifications of the franchisor's staff responsible for conducting the training program offered by the franchisor must be discussed in some detail. Any assistance provided by the franchisor that it is not contractually bound to provide must also be disclosed in item 11. Similar disclosures should be made for the *continuing services* to be offered by the franchisor once the business has opened, such as ongoing training, advertising, and promotion; bookkeeping; inventory control; and any products to be sold by the franchisor to the franchisee.

12. *Exclusive area or territory.* The exact territory or exclusive area, if any, to be granted by the franchisor to the franchisee should be disclosed, as well as the right to adjust the size of this territory in the event that certain contractual conditions are not met, such as the failure to achieve certain performance quotas. The right of the franchisor to establish company-owned units or to grant franchises to others within the territory must be disclosed. A detailed description and/or map of the franchisee's territory should be included as an exhibit to the franchise agreement.

13. *Trademarks, service marks, trade names, logotypes, and commercial symbols.* It has often been said that the trademark is at the heart of a franchising program. Therefore, the extent to which the franchisor's trade identity (trademarks, logos, slogans, etc.) have been protected should be disclosed, including whether or not these marks are registered at either the federal or state level, or whether there are any limitations or infringement disputes involving the marks or related aspects of the trade identity. The rights and obligations of the franchisor and franchisee in the event of a trademark dispute with a third party must also be disclosed.

14. *Patents and copyrights.* Any rights in patents or copyrights that are material to the operation and management of the franchised business should be described in the same detail as required by item 13.

15. *Obligation of the franchisee to participate in the actual operation of the franchised business.* The franchisor must

disclose in this item whether or not absentee ownership and management will be permitted in connection with the operation of the franchised business. If direct participation is required by the franchisee, then the extent of such participation must be disclosed. If the franchisee may hire a manager to operate the franchised business, then the franchisor must disclose any mandatory employment terms or equity ownership requirements.

16. *Restrictions on goods and services offered by franchisee.* In this section the franchisor must disclose any special contractual provisions or other circumstances that limit either the types of products and services the franchisee may offer or the types or location of the customers to whom the products and services may be offered.

17. *Renewal, termination, repurchase, modification, and assignment of the franchise agreement and related information.* This item is typically the longest section of the UFOC and also of great importance to the prospective franchisee. The term of the franchise agreement, the conditions to renewal, the grounds upon which the franchise agreement may be terminated, the conditions under which the franchise agreement may be assigned, and the rights of the heirs of the franchisee upon death must all be disclosed in this section. Specific events of default, as well as any notice provisions and opportunities to cure defaults that will be provided by the franchisor to the franchisee, must be defined. Obligations of the franchisee following termination, such as covenants against competition or against the use of proprietary information, must be disclosed. Finally, the conditions under which the franchise agreement may be modified either by the franchisor or franchisee must be discussed in this item.

18. *Arrangements with public figures.* Any compensation or benefit given to a public figure in return for an endorsement of the franchise and/or products and services offered by the franchisee must be disclosed. The extent to which the public figure owns or is involved in the management of the franchisor must also be disclosed. The right of the franchisee to use the name of the public figure in its local promotional campaign

and the material terms of the agreement between the franchisor and the public figure must also be included in this item.

19. *Actual, average, projected, or forecasted franchise sales, profits, or earnings.* If the franchisor is willing to provide the prospective franchisee with sample earnings claims or projections, they must be discussed in item 19. See Figure 5-2.

20. *Information regarding franchises of the franchisor.* A full summary of the number of franchises sold, number of operational units, and number of company-owned units must be broken down in item 20 usually in tabular form, including an estimate of franchise sales for the upcoming fiscal year that are broken down by state. The names, addresses, and telephone

Figure 5-2. Use of earnings claims.

In 1986 NASAA adopted new regulations for the use and content of earnings claims by franchisors. These new guidelines were adopted as the exclusive form of earnings claims permitted by the FTC as of January 1, 1989. Under the new rules, any earnings claim made in connection with the offer of a franchise must be included in the UFOC. If no earnings claim is made, then the following statement must appear:

> Franchisor does not furnish or authorize its salespersons to furnish any oral or written information concerning the actual or potential sales, costs, income, or profits of (*franchised business name*). Actual results vary from unit to unit and franchisor cannot estimate the results of any particular franchise.

If the franchisor does elect to make an earnings claim, then it must (1) have a reasonable basis at the time the claim is made, (2) include a description of the factual basis for the claim, and (3) include and overview of the material assumptions underlying the claim.

numbers of franchisees should be included in this item. In addition, the number of franchisees terminated or not renewed (voluntary and involuntary), and the cause of termination or nonrenewal must be broken down for the previous three years of operations.

21. *Financial statements.* A full set of financial statements prepared in accordance with generally accepted accounting principles must be included in item 21 as part of the disclosure package to be provided to a franchisee. Most registration states require that the statements be audited, with limited exceptions for start-up franchisors. The balance sheet provided should have been prepared as of a date within ninety days prior to the date that the registration application is filed. Unaudited statements may be used for interim periods. Franchisors with weak financial statements may be required to make special arrangements with the franchise administrator in each state for the protection of prospective franchisees.

22. *Franchise agreement and related contracts.* A copy of the franchise agreement as well as any other related documents to be signed by the franchisee in connection with the ownership and operation of the franchised business must be attached as exhibits to the UFOC.

23. *Acknowledgment of receipt by a prospective franchisee.* The last page of the UFOC is a detachable document that is executed by the prospective franchisee acknowledging receipt of the offering circular. See Figure 5-3.

The Mechanics of the Registration Process

Each of the registration states has slightly different procedures and requirements for the approval of a franchisor prior to offers and sales being authorized. In all cases, however, the package of disclosure documents is assembled, consisting of an offering circular, franchise agreement, supplemental agreements, financial statements, franchise roster, mandated cover pages, acknowledgment of receipt, and the special forms that are required by each state, such as corporation verification

Figure 5-3. Sample acknowledgment of receipt.

ACKNOWLEDGMENT OF RECEIPT

I hereby acknowledge receipt of the Franchise Offering Circular provided by_____, on this ____ day of _____, 19__, including all exhibits attached thereto, to wit:

Exhibit A - Financial Statements

Exhibit B - Form of Franchise Agreement

Exhibit C - Form of Area Development Agreement

Exhibit D - Deposit Agreement

Exhibit E - Inventory Purchase Agreement

Exhibit F - Option for Assignment of Lease

Exhibit G - Mandatory Addendum to Lease

Exhibit H - Advertising Submission Agreement

Exhibit I - Roster of Franchisees

_____

Prospective Franchisee

statements, salesperson disclosure forms, and consent to service of process documents. The specific requirements of each state should be checked carefully by the franchisor and its counsel. Initial filing fees range from $250 to $500, with renewal filings usually ranging between $100 to $250.

The first step is for counsel to "custom tailor" the UFOC format to meet the special requirements or additional disclosures required under the particular state's regulations. Once the documents are ready and all signatures have been obtained, the package is filed with the state franchise administrator and a specific franchise examiner (usually an attorney) is assigned to the franchisor. The level of scrutiny applied by the examiner in reviewing the offering materials will vary from state to state and from franchisor to franchisor. The sales history, financial strength, litigation record, reputation of legal counsel, time pressures and workload of the examiner, geographic desirability of the state, and the general reputation of the franchisor will have an impact on the level of review and the timetable for approval. Franchisors should expect to see at least one "comment letter" from the examiner requesting certain changes or additional information as a condition of approval and registration. The procedure can go as quickly as six weeks or as slowly as six months, depending on the concerns of the examiner and the skills and experience of legal counsel.

The initial and ongoing reporting and disclosure requirements vary from state to state. For example, the filing of an amendment to the offering circular is required in the event of a "material change" (discussed in greater detail in Chapter 6); however, each state has different regulations as to the definition of a *material change*. Similarly, although *all* registration states require the annual filing of a renewal application or annual report, only Maryland and Wisconsin require that quarterly reports be filed. When advertising materials are developed for use in attracting franchisees, they must be approved in advance by *all* registration states, *except* Virginia and Hawaii. (See discussion of advertising material requirements in Chapter 6). All franchise registration states except Virginia require the filing of salesperson disclosure forms. California, New York, Illinois, and Washington require their own special forms. It is critical that the franchisor's legal compliance officer stay abreast of all of these special filing requirements.

6

Building a Franchise Compliance Program

The development of an in-house legal compliance program and the designation of a legal compliance officer *is a necessity, not a luxury* for the growing franchisor operating in today's litigious society. In all likelihood, the compliance staff will be "pitted against" the sales and marketing staff, with ongoing conflict and tension between the need to market aggressively and the need to market legally. An attitude and a philosophy of teamwork must be fostered early on in order to avoid such tension within the company. There must be a commitment from day one to only sell franchises within the bounds of the law and to maintain complete and comprehensive compliance files. (See Figure 6-1 for contents of a typical compliance file). The compliance file should contain information about the initial meeting with the prospect to the execution of the franchise agreement to the termination of the relationship and beyond. These record-keeping requirements will often seem burdensome but will also go a long way in protecting the company in the event of a subsequent dispute with the franchisee or in connection with a federal or state regulatory investigation.

A compliance program means more than careful record keeping. A well-planned compliance system will require initial and ongoing training for the franchisor's sales and marketing personnel, the development of special forms and checklists, a management philosophy and compensation

Figure 6-1. Developing a typical compliance file.

The contents of a typical compliance file that must be established and maintained by the compliance staff are listed here.

1. Acknowledgment of receipt of offering circular
2. Completed applicant questionnaire
3. Executed deposit agreement (if used)
4. Copy of the check for initial deposit
5. Copy of executed franchise agreement
6. Area development agreement (where applicable)
7. Inventory purchase agreement (where applicable)
8. Option for assignment of lease
9. Mandatory addendum to lease
10. Receipt for manuals
11. Written consent of board of directors of franchisee
12. Proof of insurance
13. Franchisor's written approval of site
14. Franchisee's certification of receipt of all licenses, permits, and bonds
15. Franchisee's written notice of commencement of construction
16. Franchisor's approval of the opening of the franchised business
17. Copy of franchisee's lease
18. Certification of completion of basic training
19. All ongoing correspondence between franchisor and franchisee (postopening)
20. Inspection reports
21. Notices of default

structure that rewards compliance and discourages noncompliance, a system for monitoring all registration and renewal dates, custom-tailored verbal scripts and video presentations that must be used and strictly followed by the sales personnel, the development of a compliance manual and periodic policy statements, special approval and renewal process for the award of new franchises, and a periodic random and "unannounced" inspection of the franchise sales and compliance files in order to ensure that procedures are being followed. The success of the compliance program should not be made dependent on outside legal counsel, but should rather be a priority for the franchisor's management team.

No compliance system is 100 percent perfect in preventing franchise law violations. Human nature forces a franchise sales representative to "stretch the truth a little" if he or she has not had a sale in months and faces the loss of a job or a home. Human error may result in a Maryland resident being disclosed with a New York offering document because the wrong package was hastily pulled off the shelf. The franchisor's ability to devote sufficient resources for the compliance program, select the right person as the compliance officer, and foster a positive attitude toward compliance among the sales staff will all affect the success or failure of the compliance program.

The franchise compliance officer must be selected carefully and charged with the responsibility of implementing the compliance program and enforcing its procedures. The officer serves as the in-house clearinghouse for franchise files and information, as well as the liaison with outside legal counsel. The compliance officer must gain (and maintain) the respect of the sales and marketing personnel or the system will fail. This will only be achieved if a senior executive within the company assumes responsibility for disciplining those who have an apathy toward compliance.

Special Topics in Compliance: Earnings Claims

One classic catch-22 in franchising is the desire of a prospective franchisee to know what it is likely to earn as a franchise owner and the strict rules governing the use of "earnings claims" in a sales presentation to a prospect. In the early days of franchising, there was much abuse in this area, with salespersons jotting down projections "on the back of a hotel cocktail napkin" in order to induce the prospect to buy a franchise. Eventually, federal and state regulators caught on to these potentially deceptive practices and developed strict regulations for the use of an earnings claim.

An earnings claim is defined under the law as any information given to a prospective franchisee by, on behalf of, or at the direction of a franchisor or its agent, from which a specific level or range of actual or potential sales, costs, income, or profit from franchised or nonfranchised units may be easily ascertained. Earnings claims may include a chart, table, or mathematical calculation presented to demonstrate possible results based upon a combination of variables (such as multiples of price and quantity to reflect gross sales). An earnings claim must include a *description of its factual basis* and the *material assumptions underlying its preparation* and presentation.

The catch-22 was created by the original strictness of these rules. Prospective franchisees *wanted* to know what they were likely to earn, and franchisors wanted to tell them, but many franchisors could not meet the strict standards contained in the federal and state regulations. Others feared that the earnings claim would be misused or misunderstood by the prospect and only come back to haunt them in subsequent litigation. As a result, the majority of franchisors did not provide prospective franchisees with earnings claims primarily because:

- The detailed substantiation requirements of federal and state law made compliance difficult and expensive, *especially for early-stage franchisors.*
- Many franchisors feared that the documents would "come back to haunt them" in subsequent disputes with disgruntled or disappointed franchisees.
- Differences between the geographic location, actual performance, and number of units in the system made it difficult to have a sufficient foundation from which to compile the earnings information.

Pressures from members of the franchise community resulted in certain changes to the rules affecting earnings claims in 1987, which were designed to provide greater flexibility in franchise sales and marketing practices. The primary reasons cited for the changes, aside from "political" pressures, included the following: (1) Efforts by start-up and early-stage franchisors to sell franchises had been severely restricted; and (2) Sophistication had grown (education, net worth, professional advisors, etc.) among prospective franchisees who *wanted* and *needed* to know what to expect financially when buying a franchise.

Amendments to the earnings claim disclosure rules under Item XIX of the Uniform Franchise Offering Circular (UFOC) were unanimously adopted by the North American Securities Administration Association (NASAA) on November 21, 1986. The changes liberalized the rules governing earnings claims provided by franchisors to prospective franchisees. On June 9, 1987, the Federal Trade Commission (FTC) approved for its disclosure format the amendments to Item XIX that were adopted by NASAA. The FTC permitted use of either the old version of Item XIX or the new version through December 31, 1988. As of January 1, 1989, the commission allows use of *only* the new version to comply with the Item XIX earnings claim disclosure requirements. The new Item XIX is entitled *Representations Regarding Earnings Capabilities*. It has been adopted by every state regulating disclosure and registration except the state of New York, which, for the most part, has retained the old Item XIX disclosure requirements with its own variations and legends.

Special Topics in Compliance: Material Changes

As the franchise system grows, the franchisor is likely to experience a wide variety of challenges that may result in significant changes to the corporate structure, franchise program, financial statements, or relationships with its franchisees.

Figure 6-2. Earnings claim requirements.

If an earnings claim is made, the basic disclosure made in Item 19 must include:

- A concise summary of the basis for the claim including a statement of whether the claim is based upon actual experience of franchised units and, if so, the percentage of franchised outlets in operation for the period covered by the earnings claim that have actually attained or surpassed the stated results
- A conspicuous "disclaimer" that a new franchisee's individual financial results are likely to differ from the results stated in the earnings claim
- A statement that substantiation of the data used in preparing the earnings claim will be made available to the prospective franchisee on reasonable request

---

When these significant structural or program changes occur, they must be disclosed to the prospective franchisee through an update to the FOC. The laws that dictate how and when these updates must be made are commonly referred to as the "material change" regulations.

The determination of what constitutes a "material change" can be difficult, and federal and state law provide for a significant degree of discretion. For example, the term *material change* is defined by the FTC as "any fact, circumstance, or set of conditions which has a substantial likelihood of influencing a reasonable franchisee or a reasonable prospective franchisee in the making of a significant decision relating to a named franchise business or which has any significant financial impact on a franchise or prospective franchisee."

With respect to the timing of offering circular amendments, it is important to keep in mind the danger of continuing to grant franchises with knowledge of a material event or change that may require disclosure. The longer an amendment is deferred, the greater the risk that sales made prior to the amendment will be challenged as illegal or be subject to rescission, which essentially grants the franchisee an "option" rather than a binding and enforceable franchise agreement. Amendments filed to the disclosure document in registration states will cause a short delay in the ability of the franchisor to offer and sell franchises in that (those) state(s). However, the cost of this delay should be viewed as minor compared to the benefits of a "legal" sale.

Examples of Material Changes

The following list provides examples of facts and circumstances that have been considered by federal and state franchise regulators to constitute a material change:

1. A change in any franchise or other fee charged, or significantly increased costs of developing or operating a franchised outlet
2. The termination, closing, failure to renew, or repurchase of a significant number of franchises. Whether the number is significant depends on the number of franchises in existence and whether the area in which the above occurred is the same area in which new franchises will be offered, except where specific state regulations define what constitutes a significant number (e.g., Hawaii and New York).
3. A significant *adverse* change in any of the following:

   - The obligations of the franchisee to purchase items from the franchisor or its designated sources
   - Limitations or restrictions on goods or services that the franchisee may offer to its customers
   - The obligations to be performed by the franchisor
   - The key terms of the franchise agreement
   - The franchisor's financial situation, resulting in a 5 percent or greater change in net profits or losses in any six-month period

- The services or products offered to consumers by the franchisees of the franchisor
- The identity of persons affiliated with the franchisor and any franchise brokers
- The current status of the franchisor's trade or service marks

4. Any change in control, corporate name, state of incorporation, or reorganization of the franchisor
5. A significant change in status of litigation or administrative matters that have been disclosed in the FOC. In addition, a franchisor should be alert to provide for the addition of any new claims or counterclaims that have been filed against the franchisor which may need to be disclosed.
6. Any recent developments in the market(s) for the products or services sold by the franchisees that could increase competition or create operating problems for franchisees
7. A change in the accuracy of earnings claims information (if applicable) disclosed

Compliance in the Nonregistration States

According to Section 436.2(n) of the Federal Trade Commission Trade Regulation Rule relating to disclosure requirements and prohibitions concerning franchising and business opportunity ventures, the terms *material, material fact,* and *material change* include any fact, circumstance, or set of conditions that has a substantial likelihood of influencing a reasonable franchisee or a reasonable prospective franchisee in the making of a significant decision relating to a named franchise business or that has any significant financial impact on a franchisee or prospective franchisee. According to the FTC's interpretative guide to this rule, the disclosure document must be promptly updated, on at least a quarterly basis, whenever a material change occurs in the information contained in the disclosure document. The material change disclosure may be attached to the FOC as an addendum.

Compliance in the Registration States

The following overview shows how each of the registration states handle the filing and registration of a "material change."

California: California is a registration state that requires a franchisor to promptly notify the Commissioner of Corporations, in writing, by an application to amend the registration, of any material change in the information contained in the application as originally submitted, amended, or renewed.

Hawaii: Hawaii is a registration state that defines *material event* or *material change* to include, but not be limited to, the following:

1. The termination, closing, or failure to renew during any three-month period of:

- The greater of one percent or five of all franchises of a franchisor or subfranchisor regardless of location
- The lesser of 15 percent or two of the franchises of a franchisor or subfranchisor located in Hawaii

2. Any change in control, corporate name or state of incorporation, or reorganization of the franchisor whether or not the franchisor or its parent, if the franchisor or subfranchisor is a subsidiary, is required to file reports under section 12 of the Securities Exchange Act of 1934

3. The purchase by the franchisor of in excess of 5 percent of its existing franchises during any three-month period on a continuous basis

4. The commencement of any new product, service, or model line involving, directly or indirectly, additional investment by any franchisee or the discontinuation or modification of the marketing plan or system of any product or service of

the franchisor where the total sales from such product or service exceeds 20 percent of the gross sales of the franchisor on an annual basis

Illinois: Illinois is a registration state that defines a "material change" as follows:

> A change in information contained in the disclosure statement is *material* within the meaning of the Act if there is a substantial likelihood that a reasonable prospective franchisee would consider it significant in making a decision to purchase or not purchase the franchise. Without limitation, examples of changes which could be material include:

1. Any increase or decrease in the initial or continuing fees charged by the franchisor
2. The termination, cancellation, failure to renew, or reacquisition of a significant number of franchises since the most recent effective date of the disclosure statement
3. A change in the franchisor's management
4. A change in the franchisor's or franchisee's obligations under the franchise or related agreements
5. A decrease in the franchisor's income or net worth
6. Limitations or significant prospective limitations regarding sources of supply that are known to or should reasonably be anticipated by the franchisor
7. Additional litigation or a significant change in the status of litigation including:

   - The filing of an amended complaint alleging or involving violations of any franchise law, fraud, embezzlement, fraudulent conversion, restraint of trade, unfair or deceptive practices, misappropriation of property, or breach of contract
   - The entry of any injunctive or restrictive order relat-

ing to the franchise; or the entry of any injunction under any federal, state, or Canadian franchise securities, antitrust trade regulation, or trade practice law

- The entry of a judgment that has or would have any significant financial impact on the franchisor. Such a judgment is considered to have significant financial impact if it equals 15 percent or more of the current assets of the franchisor and its subsidiaries on a consolidated basis.

Indiana: Indiana is a registration state that requires a franchisor to promptly notify the Indiana Securities Commissioner of any material change in the information contained in an effective registration by filing an application to amend the registration. Such an amendment to an effective registration is effective five days after the date the amendment is filed.

Maryland: Maryland is a registration state that defines a "material event" or "material change" to include but not be limited to the following:

- The termination, closing, or failure to renew during any three-month period of either the greater of one percent or five of all franchises of a franchisor regardless of location, or the lesser of 15 percent or two of the franchises of a franchisor located in the state

- Any change in control, corporate name or state of incorporation, or reorganization of the franchisor whether or not the franchisor or its parent, if the franchisor is a subsidiary, is required to file reports under section 12 of the Securities Exchange Act of 1934

- The purchase by the franchisor of more than 5 percent of its existing franchises during any three-month period on a running basis

- The commencement of any new product, service, or model line requiring, directly or indirectly, additional investment by any franchisee or the discontinuation or modification of the marketing plan or system of any product or service of the franchisor in which the total sales from this product or service exceeds 20 percent of the gross sales of the franchisor on an annual basis

Michigan: Michigan is a registration state that requires a franchisor to file with the Department of the Attorney General promptly in writing any change in the notice as originally submitted or amended.

Minnesota: Minnesota is a registration state that requires a franchisor with a registration in effect to notify the Commissioner of Commerce of any material change in the information on file with the commissioner. Such notification must take place by an application to amend the registration accompanied by a fee of $50. "Material event" or "material change" includes, but is not limited to the following:

1. The termination, closing, or failure to renew by the franchisor during any consecutive three-month period after registration of 10 percent of all franchises of the franchisor, regardless of location, or 10 percent of the franchises of the franchisor located in the state of Minnesota

2. Any change in control, corporate name, or state of incorporation, or reorganization of the franchisor

3. The purchase by the franchisor during any consecutive three-month period after registration of 10 percent of its existing franchises, regardless of location, or 10 percent of its existing franchises in the state of Minnesota

4. The commencement of any new product, service, or model line involving, directly or indirectly, an additional investment in excess of 20 percent of the current average investment made by all franchises or the discontinuation or modification of the marketing plan or marketing system of any product or service of the franchisor where the average total sales from such product or service exceed 20 percent of the average gross sales of the existing franchisees on an annual basis

5. Any change in the franchise fees charged by the franchisor

6. Any significant change in:

- The obligations of the franchisee to purchase items from the franchisor or its designated sources
- The limitations or restrictions on the goods or services the franchisee may offer to its customer
- The obligations to be performed by the franchisor
- The franchise contract or agreement, including all amendments thereto

New York: New York is a registration state that requires a franchisor to promptly notify the New York State Department of Law, by application to amend its offering, of any material changes in the information contained in the prospectus as originally submitted or amended. As used in New York, the term *material change* includes, but is not limited to:

1. The termination, closing, or failure to renew, during a three-month period, of the lesser of ten or 10 percent of the franchises of a franchisor, regardless of location
2. A purchase by the franchisor in excess of 5 percent of its existing franchises during six consecutive months
3. A change in the franchise fees charged by the franchisor
4. Any significant adverse change in the business condition of the franchisor or in any of the following:

- The obligations of the franchisee to purchase items from the franchisor or its designated sources
- Limitations or restrictions on the goods or services the franchisee may offer to its customers
- The obligations to be performed by the franchisor
- The franchise contract or agreements, including amendments thereto

- The franchisor's accounting system resulting [in] a 5 percent or greater change in its net profit or loss in any six-month period.
- The service, product, or model line

5. Audited financial statements of the preceding fiscal year

North Dakota: Although North Dakota is a registration state, the Commissioner of Securities has not defined what shall be considered a material change. Therefore, the definition used in nonregistration states should be consulted in preparing amendments to the offering circulars registered in North Dakota.

Oregon: While Oregon is a registration state, the Director of the Department of Insurance and Finance has not defined what shall constitute a material change and therefore the definition used in the nonregistration states should be consulted.

Rhode Island: Rhode Island is a registration state that requires a franchisor to promptly notify the Director of Business Regulation in writing, by an application to amend the registration, of any material change in the information contained in the application as originally submitted, amended, or renewed. The director has not defined what constitutes a material change and therefore the definition used in the nonregistration states should be consulted.

South Dakota: South Dakota is a registration state that requires franchisors with a registration in effect, within thirty days after the occurrence of any material change in the information on file with the Director of the Division of Securities, to notify the director in writing of the change, by an application to amend the registration accompanied by a fee of $50. The director has not defined the term *material change* and therefore the definition used in the nonregistration states should be consulted.

Virginia: Virginia is a registration state that requires the franchisor to amend its registration upon the occurrence of any material change. Virginia defines *material change* to include any fact, circumstance, or condition that would have a substantial likelihood of influencing a reasonable prospective franchisee in making a decision related to the purchase of a franchise.

Washington: Washington is a registration state that requires a supplemental report to be filed as soon as reasonably possible (and in any case before the further sale of any franchise) if a material adverse change occurs in the condition of the franchisor. Because the term *material adverse change* is not defined, the definition used in nonregistration states should be consulted.

Wisconsin: Wisconsin is a registration state that requires a franchisor to amend its registration within thirty days after any material event that affects a registered franchise. As defined in Wisconsin, the terms *material event* or *material change* include, but are not limited to, the following:

1. The termination, closing, or failure to renew during any three-month period of (1) the greater of one percent or five of all franchises of a franchisor regardless of location or (2) the lesser of 15 percent or two of the franchises of a franchisor located in the state of Wisconsin

2. Any change in control, corporate name or state of incorporation, or reorganization of the franchisor whether or not the franchisor or its parent, if the franchisor is a subsidiary, is required to file reports under section 12 of the Securities Exchange Act of 1934.

3. The purchase by the franchisor in excess of 5 percent of its existing franchises during any three-month period on a running basis

4. The commencement of any new product service or model line involving, directly or indirectly, additional investment by any franchisee or the discontinuation or modification of the marketing plan or system of any product or service of the franchisor where the total sales from such product or service exceeds 20 percent of the gross sales of the franchisor on an annual basis

5. An adverse financial development involving the franchisor or the franchisor's parent company, controlling persons, or guarantor of the franchisor's obligations. In this paragraph, *adverse financial development* includes, but is not limited to:

- The filing of a petition under federal or state bankruptcy or receivership laws
- A default in payment of principal, interest, or sinking fund installment on indebtedness that exceeds 5 percent of total assets that is not remedied within thirty days of the default

Special Topics in Compliance: Advertising Regulations

Certain states have enacted laws that regulate the use of advertising by a franchisor which is directed at prospective franchisees. Many of these states require the filing and approval of these advertising and marketing materials *prior to their use*. Below is a discussion of those states with special provisions that must be built into the overall compliance program.

California: No advertisement offering a franchise may be published in California unless a copy of the advertisement has been filed in the office of the California Commissioner of Corporations at least three (3) business days prior to the first publication. Additionally, all advertising must contain the following legend (in not less than ten-point type):

THESE FRANCHISES HAVE BEEN REGISTERED UNDER THE FRANCHISE INVESTMENT LAW OF THE STATE OF CALIFORNIA. SUCH REGISTRATION DOES NOT CONSTITUTE APPROVAL, RECOMMENDATION OR ENDORSEMENT BY THE COMMISSIONER OF CORPORATIONS NOR A FINDING BY THE COMMISSIONER THAT THE INFORMATION PROVIDED HEREIN IS TRUE, COMPLETE AND NOT MISLEADING.

Illinois: In order to publish, distribute, or use any offering to sell or to purchase a franchise in the state of Illinois, the franchisor must file two true copies of the proposed advertisement *at least* five days before the first publication, distribution, or use thereof. If the advertisement is not in compliance with the Illinois Franchise Disclosure Act, the Illinois Attorney General will notify the franchisor of any objections within five days of receipt of the advertisement. Failure of the administrator to respond within five days does not constitute approval of the advertisement but will preclude the administrator from objecting on grounds of the five-day filing requirement.

Indiana: A copy of any advertising the franchisor intends to use in Indiana must be filed in the office of the Indiana Securities Commissioner at least five days prior to the first publication of such advertising.

Maryland: A franchisor may not publish any advertisement offering a franchise unless the advertisement (in duplicate) has been filed with the Securities Commissioner in the Office of the Attorney General at least seven *business* days before the first publication of the advertisement. An advertisement may not be used unless and until it has been cleared for use by the Division of Securities.

Michigan: The Michigan Department of the Attorney General *may* by rule or order require an advertisement to be filed that is addressed or intended to be distributed to prospective franchisees, as well as any other sales literature or advertising communication having the same purpose.

Minnesota: The franchisor must file one true copy of any advertisement, proposed for use in Minnesota, with the Office of the Commissioner of Commerce at least three business days before the first publication thereof. If not disallowed by the commission within three business days from the date filed, the advertisement may be published.

New York: All sales literature must be submitted to the New York Department of Law at least seven days prior to its intended use. The franchisor must verify, in writing submitted with the sales literature, that it is not inconsistent with the filed prospectus. All sales literature must contain the following statement (in easily readable print) on the cover of all circulars, flyers, cards, letters, and other literature intended for use in New York:

> This advertisement is not an offering. An offering can only be made by a prospectus filed first with the Department of Law of the State of New York. Such filing does not constitute approval by the Department of Law.

In all classified-type advertisements, not more than 5 inches long and no more than one column of print wide, and in all broadcast advertising thirty seconds or less in duration, the following statement may be used in lieu of the statement provided above:

> This offering is made by prospectus only.

North Dakota: The franchisor must file a true copy of any advertisement proposed for use in the state with the Office of the Commissioner of Securities at least five *business* days before the first publication.

Oklahoma: All sales literature and advertising must be filed with the administrator and approved prior to use. A filing shall include the sales literature and advertising package, a review fee of $25, and a representation by the seller that reads substantially as follows:

> I,_____ , hereby attest and affirm that the enclosed sales literature or advertising package contains no false or misleading statements or misrepresentations of material facts and that all information contained therein is in conformity with the most recent disclosure document relating to the particular business opportunity offered thereby on file with the Administrator.

Rhode Island. No advertisements may be published in Rhode Island unless a true copy of the advertisement has been filed in the Office of the Director of Business Regulations at least three business days prior to the first publication.

Washington. The franchisor must file one true copy of any advertisement proposed for use in the state with the Office of the Director of Licensing at least seven days before publication.

Wisconsin. The franchisor must file two copies of all proposed advertisements in the Office of Securities at least five days before first publication, distribution, or use thereof.

7

Structuring Franchise Agreements, Area Development Agreements, and Related Documents

The principal document that sets forth the binding rights and obligations of each party to the franchise relationship is known as the franchise agreement. The franchise agreement contains the various provisions binding on the parties for the life of their relationship and therefore must maintain a delicate balance of power. On one hand, the franchisor must maintain enough control in the franchise agreement to enforce uniformity and consistency throughout the system, yet at the same time be flexible enough to anticipate changes in the marketplace and modifications to the franchise system and to meet the special considerations or demands resulting from the franchisee's local market conditions.

The franchise agreement can and should reflect the business philosophy of the franchisor and set the tenor of the relationship. A well-drafted franchise agreement will reflect the culmination of literally thousands of business decisions and hundreds of hours of market research and testing. The length, term, and complexity of the franchise agreement will (and should) vary from franchisor to franchisor and from industry to industry. Many start-up franchisors make the critical mistake of "borrowing" terms from a competitor's franchise agreement. Such a practice can be detrimental to the franchisor and the franchisee because the agreement will not accurately reflect the actual dynamics and economies of the relationship.

Early-stage franchisors should resist the temptation to copy from the franchise agreement of a competitor or to accept the "standard form and boilerplate" from an inexperienced attorney or consultant. The relationship between the franchisor and franchisee is far too complex to accept such compromise in the preparation of such a critical document. For example, suppose that the three principal competitors of Prof-Finders are charging a monthly royalty of 7 percent on gross sales. Not wanting to make waves, Theoryman decides to mimic this practice by also charging 7 percent. However, there may be fundamental differences between his costs and expenses and those of his competitors.

Suppose that his New England location afforded him a lower overhead than his New York- and California-based competitors had. Perhaps he ought to pass these cost savings along to his franchisees by charging only a 5 percent royalty. This could still preserve healthy profits for Prof-Finders and result in more franchises being sold over his competitors. Along the same lines, Theoryman's cash flow requirements may differ from those of his competitors, suggesting that a weekly royalty payment may be more beneficial than a monthly payment. Additionally, Prof-Finders may wish to reward high-performing franchisees by adopting a sliding scale of 4 percent if a certain sales level is reached and 3 percent if an even higher sales level is reached. As you can see, a provision as simple as the royalty rate raises a wide variety of issues that must be considered by the management team of the franchisor. Merely adopting the practices and provisions of a competitor is not sufficient for building a solid foundation for franchising.

There are a wide variety of drafting styles and practices among those attorneys who regularly practice in the area of franchise law. Some franchise lawyers prefer to "roll every-thing" into a single agreement (which can result in quite a behemoth), while others prefer to address the equipment leases, product purchasing requirements, personal guaranty, site development obligations, security interests, options for assignment of leases, and other key aspects of the relationship in "supplemental agreements " that are separate from the ac-tual franchise agreement. The advantage to this latter ap-proach, which I have come to appreciate over the years, is that the franchisee and its counsel are not overwhelmed (or intim-idated) by the complexity and depth of a single document. We will examine the key elements of a basic franchise agreement and then turn to some of the various supplemental agreements that further define the long-term rights and obligations of the franchisor and franchisee.

Key Elements of the Basic Franchise Agreement

Regardless of size, stage of growth, industry dynamics, or spe-cific trends in the marketplace, all basic franchise agreements should address the following key topics:

• *Recitals.* The recitals or preamble of the franchise agree-ment essentially sets the stage for the discussion of the con-tractual relationship. This section provides the background information regarding the development and ownership of the proprietary rights of the franchisor which are being licensed to the franchisee. The preamble should always contain at least one recital specifying the obligation of the franchisee to oper-ate the business format in strict conformity with the opera-tions manual and quality control standards provided by the franchisor.

• *Grant, term, and renewal.* The typical initial section of the franchise agreement is the grant of a franchise for a speci-fied term. The length of the term is influenced by a number of factors including market conditions, the franchisor's need to periodically change certain material terms of the agreement, cost of the franchise and franchisee's expectations in relation to start-up costs, length of related agreements necessary to the franchisee's operations such as leases and bank loans, and anticipated consumer demand for the franchised goods and services. The renewal rights granted to a franchisee, if included at all, will usually be conditioned upon the franchisee being in good standing (e.g., no material defaults by franchisee) under the agreement. Other issues that must be addressed in any provisions regarding renewal include renewal fees, obligations to execute the "then current" form of the franchise agreement, and any obligations of the franchisee to upgrade its facilities to the "latest" standards and design. The franchisor's right to relocate the franchisee, adjust the size of any exclusive territory granted, or change the fee structure should also be addressed.

• *Territory.* The size of the geographic area granted to the franchisee by the franchisor must be specifically discussed in conjunction with what exclusive rights, if any, will be granted to the franchisee with respect to this territory. These provisions address whether the size of the territory is a specific radius, city, or county and whether the franchisor will have a right to either operate company-owned locations and/or grant additional franchises within the territory. Some franchisors designate a specific territory within which market research indicates that a given number of locations could be successful without market oversaturation, and then sell that exact number of franchises, without regard to specific location selected within the geographic area. Any rights of first refusal for additional locations, advertising restrictions, performance quotas relating to territory, and policies of the franchisor with regard to territory are addressed in this part of the franchise agreement.

• *Site selection.* The responsibility for finding the specific site for the operation of the franchised business will rest either with the franchisor or franchisee. If the franchisee is free to choose its own site, then the franchise agreement will usually provide that the decision is subject to the approval of the franchisor. Some franchisors provide significant assistance in site selection in terms of marketing and demographic studies, lease negotiations, and securing local permits and licenses, especially if a "turnkey" franchise is offered. Site selection, however, can be the most difficult aspect of being a successful franchisee, and as a result most franchisors are reluctant to take on full responsibility for this task contractually. For additional protection and control, some franchisors insist on becoming the landlord to the franchisee through a mandatory sublease arrangement once an acceptable site has been selected. A somewhat less burdensome method of securing similar protection is to provide for an automatic assignment of the lease to the franchisor upon termination of the franchise.

▪ *Services to be provided by the franchisor.* The franchise agreement should clearly delineate which products and services will be provided to the franchisee by the franchisor or its affiliates, both in terms of the initial establishment of the franchised business ("preopening obligations") and any continuing assistance or support services provided throughout the term of the relationship ("postopening services"). The preopening obligations generally include a trade secret and copyright license for the use of the confidential operations manual, recruitment and training of personnel, standard accounting and bookkeeping systems, inventory and equipment specifications and volume discounts, standard construction, building and interior design plans, and grand opening promotion and advertising assistance. The quality and extent of the training program is clearly the most crucial preopening service provided by the franchisor and should include classroom as well as on-site instruction. Postopening services provided to the franchisee on a continuing basis generally include field support and troubleshooting, research and development for new products and services, development of national advertising and promotional campaigns, and the arrangement of group purchasing programs and volume discounts.

• *Franchise, royalty, and related fees payable to the franchisor and reporting.* The franchise agreement should clearly set forth the nature and amount of fees that will be payable to the franchisor by the franchisee, both initially and on a continuing basis. The initial franchise fee is usually a nonrefundable lump sum payment due upon execution of the franchise agreement. Essentially this fee is compensation for the grant of the franchise, the trademark and trade secret license, pre-opening training and assistance, and the initial opening supply of materials, if any, to be provided by the franchisor to the franchisee.

A second category of fees is the continuing fee, usually in the form of a specific royalty on gross sales. This percentage can be fixed or be based on a sliding scale for different ranges of sales achieved at a given location. Often minimum royalty payment will be required, regardless of the franchisee's actual performance. These fees should be payable weekly and submitted to the franchisor together with some standardized reporting form for internal control and monitoring purposes. A weekly payment schedule generally allows the franchisee to budget for this payment from a cash flow perspective and provides the franchisor with an early warning system if there is a problem, and also allows the franchisee to react before the past due royalties accrue to a virtually uncollectible sum.

The third category of recurring fees is usually in the form of a national cooperative advertising and promotion fund. The promotional fund may be managed by the franchisor, an independent advertising agency, or even a franchisee association. Either way, the franchisor must build a certain amount of control into the franchise agreement over the fund in order to protect the company's trademarks and ensure consistency in marketing efforts.

Other categories of fees payable to the franchisor may include the sale of proprietary goods and services to the franchisee, consulting fees, audit and inspection fees, lease management fees (where franchisor is to serve as sublessor), and renewal or transfer fees.

The obligations of the franchisee to provide periodic

weekly, monthly, quarterly, and annual financial and sales reports to the franchisor should also be addressed in the franchise agreement.

   ▪ *Quality control.* A well-drafted franchise agreement always includes a variety of provisions designed to ensure quality control and consistency throughout the franchise system.
Such provisions often take the form of restrictions on the
franchisee's sources of products, ingredients, supplies, and
materials, as well as strict guidelines and specifications for operating procedures. These operating procedures will usually
specify standards of service, trade dress and uniform requirements, condition and appearance of the facility, hours of business, minimum insurance requirements, guidelines for
trademark usage, advertising and promotional materials, accounting systems, and credit practices. Any restrictions on the
ability of the franchisee to buy goods and services or requirements to purchase from a specific source should be carefully
drafted within the perimeters of applicable antitrust laws. If
the franchisor is to serve as the sole supplier or manufacturer
of one or more products to be used by the franchisee in the
day-to-day operation of the business, then such exclusivity
must be justified by a product that is truly proprietary or
unique.

   ▪ *Insurance, record keeping, and other related obligations of the franchisee.* The franchise agreement should always address the minimum amounts and types of insurance
that must be carried by the franchisee in connection with its
operation of the franchised businesses. Typically the franchisor is named as an additional insured under these policies.
Other related obligations of the franchisee that must be set
forth in the franchise agreement include the keeping of proper
financial records (which must be made available for inspection by the franchisor upon request); the obligation to maintain and enforce quality control standards with its employees
and vendors; the obligation to comply with all applicable employment laws, health and safety standards, and related local
ordinances; the duty to upgrade and maintain the franchisee's

facilities and equipment; the obligation to continue to promote the products and services of the franchisor; the obligation to reasonably process requests by patrons for franchising information; the obligation not to produce goods and services that do not meet the franchisor's quality control specifications or that may be unapproved for offer at the franchisee's premises (such as video games at a fast-food restaurant or X-rated material at a bookstore); the obligation not to solicit customers outside its designated territory; the obligation of the franchisee personally to participate in the day-to-day operation of the franchised business (required by many but not all franchisors); and the general obligation of the franchisee to refrain from any activity that may reflect adversely on the reputation of the franchise system.

• *Protection of intellectual property and covenants against competition.* The franchise agreement should always contain a separate section on the obligations of the franchisee and its employees to protect against misuse or disclosure the trademarks and trade secrets being licensed. The franchisor should provide for a clause that clearly sets forth that the trademarks and trade names being licensed are the exclusive property of the franchisor and that any goodwill is established to the sole benefit of the franchisor. It should also be made clear that the confidential operations manual is "on loan" to the franchisee under a limited use license, and that the franchisee or its agents are prohibited from the unauthorized use of the trade secrets both during and after the term of the agreement. To the extent that such provisions are enforceable in local jurisdictions, the franchise agreement should contain covenants against competition by a franchisee, both during the term of the franchise agreement and following termination or cancellation.

• *Termination of the franchise agreement.* One of the most important sections of the franchise agreement is the section discussing how a franchisee may lose its rights to operate the franchised business. The various "events of default" should be carefully defined and tailored to meet the needs of the specific type of business being franchised. Grounds for termination can range anywhere from the bankruptcy of a franchisee to failure to meet specified performance quotas or strictly abide by quality control standards. Certain types of violations will be grounds for termination, while other types of default will provide the franchisee with an opportunity for cure. This section should address the procedures for notice and opportunity to cure, as well as the alternative actions that the franchisor may pursue to enforce its rights to terminate the franchise agreement. Such clauses must be drafted in light of certain state regulations that limit franchise terminations to "good cause" and have minimum procedural requirements. The obligations of the franchisee upon default and notice of termination must also be clearly spelled out, such as the duty to return all copies of the operations manuals, pay all past-due royalty fees, and immediately cease using the franchisor's trademarks.

- *Miscellaneous provisions.* As with any well-prepared business agreement, the franchise agreement should include a notice provision, a governing law clause, severability provisions, an integration clause, and a provision discussing the relationship of the parties. Some franchisors may want to add an arbitration clause, a "hold harmless" and indemnification provision, a reservation of the right to injunctions and other forms of equitable relief, specific representations and warranties of the franchisee, attorney's fees for the prevailing party in the event of dispute, and even a contractual provision acknowledging that the franchisee has reviewed the agreement with counsel and has conducted an independent investigation of the franchise and is not relying on any representations other than those expressly set forth in the agreement.

An Overview of Some Sample Supplemental Agreements Commonly Used in Franchising

In addition to the franchise agreement, there are a wide variety of other contracts that may be necessary to govern the rights and the obligations of the franchisor and franchisee. These include:

- *General release.* The general release should be executed by all franchisees at the time of renewal of their franchise agreement and/or at the time of a transfer of the franchise agreement or their interest in the franchised business. The document serves as a release by the franchisee of the franchisor from all existing and potential claims that the franchisee may have against the franchisor. In recent years, however, some courts have restricted the scope of the release if it is executed under duress or where its effect will run contrary to public policy.
- *Personal guaranty.* For a wide variety of tax and legal purposes, many franchisees want to execute the franchise agreement in the name of a closely held corporation that has been formed to operate the franchised business. Under the circumstances, it is highly recommended that each shareholder of the franchise corporation be personally responsible for the franchisee's obligation under the franchise agreement. A sample personal guaranty, specially designed for multiple shareholders, may be found in Figure 7-1.
- *Sign lease agreement.* There are a wide variety of reasons why a franchisor may want to separately lease the signage bearing its trademarks to the franchisee. Aside from the additional rental income, the sign lease should contain cross-default provisions that allow the franchisor to immediately remove the signs upon termination of the franchisee. The sign lease agreement sets forth the specific rental terms and conditions to which the franchisee is bound. A sample sign lease agreement may be found at Figure 7-2 of this chapter.
- *Site selection addendum to franchise agreement.* A site selection addendum to the franchise agreement should be executed at the time that a *specific site* within the geographic area established in the Franchise Agreement, has been secured for the center. The addendum will modify the initial designation of the territory initially agreed to at the time the franchise agreement is signed.

(Text continues on page 138.)

Figure 7-1. Sample personal guaranty for multiple shareholders.

In consideration of, and as an inducement to, the execution of the foregoing Franchise Agreement ("Agreement")
dated _____ by Franchisor, each of the undersigned Guarantors, as shareholders of XYZ corporation,
agree as follows:

1. The Guarantors do hereby jointly and severally uncon-
ditionally guarantee the full, prompt, and complete performance of the Franchisee under the Agreement of all the terms,
covenants, and conditions of the Agreement, including without
limitation the complete and prompt payment of all indebtedness to Franchisor under the Agreement and any revisions,
modifications, and amendments thereto (hereinafter collectively referred to as the "Agreement"). The word indebtedness
is used herein in its most comprehensive sense and includes
without limitation any and all advances, debts, obligations,
and liabilities of the Franchisee, now or hereafter incurred,
either voluntarily or involuntarily, and whether due or not due,
absolute or contingent, liquidated or unliquidated, determined
or undetermined, or whether recovery thereof may be now or
hereafter barred by any statute of limitation or is otherwise
unenforceable.

2. The obligations of the Guarantors are independent of
the obligations of Franchisee and a separate action or actions
may be brought and prosecuted against the Guarantors, or
any of them, whether or not actions are brought against the
Franchisee or whether the Franchisee is joined in any such action.

3. If the Franchisee is a corporation or partnership, Franchisor shall not be obligated to inquire into the power or authority of the Franchisee or its partners or the officers,
directors, or agents acting or purporting to act on the Franchisee's behalf and any obligation or indebtedness made or created in reliance upon the exercise of such power and authority
shall be guaranteed hereunder. Where the Guarantors are
corporations or partnerships, it shall be conclusively pre-
sumed the Guarantors and the partners, agents, officers, and
directors acting on their behalf have the express authority to

bind such corporations or partnerships and that such corporations or partnerships have the express power to act as the Guarantors pursuant to this Guaranty and that such action directly promotes the business and is in the interest of such corporations or partnerships.

4. Franchisor, its successors, and assigns, may from time to time, without notice to the undersigned (a) resort to the undersigned for payment of any of the liabilities, whether or not it or its successors have resorted to any property securing any of the liabilities or proceeded against any other of the undersigned or any party primarily or secondarily liable on any of the liabilities; (b) release or compromise any liability of any of the undersigned hereunder or any liability of any party or parties primarily or secondarily liable on any of the liabilities; and (c) extend, renew, or credit any of the liabilities for any period (whether or not longer than the original period); alter, amend, or exchange any of the liabilities; or give any other form of indulgence, whether under the Agreement or not.

5. The undersigned further waives presentment, demand, notice of dishonor, protest, nonpayment, and all other notices whatsoever, including without limitation: notice of acceptance hereof; notice of all contracts and commitments; notice of the existence or creation of any liabilities under the foregoing Agreement and of the amount and terms thereof; and notice of all defaults, disputes, or controversies between Franchisee and Franchisor resulting from such agreement or otherwise, and the settlement, compromise, or adjustment thereof.

6. In the event any dispute between the Franchisor and the Guarantors cannot be settled amicably, the parties agree said dispute shall be settled in accordance with the Commercial Rules of the American Arbitration Association. The Arbitration shall be held at the Franchisor's headquarters in [Franchisor's headquarters]. The undersigned agrees to pay all expenses paid or incurred by Franchisor in attempting to enforce the foregoing Agreement and this Guaranty against Franchisee and against the undersigned and in attempting to collect any amounts due thereunder and hereunder, including reasonable attorneys' fees if such enforcement or collection is by or through an attorney-at-law. Any waiver, extension of

Figure 7-1. continued

time, or other indulgence granted from time to time by Franchisor or its agents, successors, or assigns, with respect to the foregoing Agreement, shall in no way modify or amend this Guaranty, which shall be continuing, absolute, unconditional, and irrevocable.

7. This Guaranty shall be enforceable by and against the respective administrators, executors, successors, and assigns of the Guarantors and the death of a Guarantor shall not terminate the liability of such Guarantor or limit the liability of the other Guarantors hereunder.

8. If more than one person has executed this Guaranty, the term *the undersigned,* as used herein shall refer to each such person, and the liability of each of the undersigned hereunder shall be joint and several and primary as sureties.

IN WITNESS WHEREOF, each of the undersigned has executed this Guaranty under seal effective as of the date of the foregoing Agreement.

_____
Signature

_____
Printed Name

_____
Home Address

_____
Home Telephone

_____
Business Address

_____
Business Telephone

_____
Date

Figure 7-2. Sample sign lease agreement.

SIGN LEASE AGREEMENT

THIS AGREEMENT made this __day of _____, 19__, by and between FRANCHISOR, a corporation organized under the laws of the State of _____, with its principal offices at _____(address of headquarters)_____ (hereinafter referred to as "Franchisor"); and _____with its principal offices at _____ _____(hereinafter referred to as "Franchisee").

W I T N E S S E T H:

WHEREAS, on _____, 19_____, Franchisor and Franchisee entered into a written Franchise Agreement by the terms of which Franchisee has been licensed to operate a _____ ("Center") to be operated in accordance with Franchisor's System and Proprietary Marks at the premises located at_____ and has a valid lease for possession of, or has title to, said premises for that purpose; and

WHEREAS, the Franchisee is desirous of leasing certain building, window, and street signage (collectively "the Signage") for advertising and identifying the Center from the Franchisor for use at the Center.

NOW, THEREFORE, in consideration of the mutual covenants herein contained, it is mutually agreed as follows:

1. *Lease of Signs.* Franchisor hereby leases and rents to Franchisee the Signage (which is more particularly described in Appendix "A" attached hereto and incorporated herein by this reference). The Signage shall be erected and used only at the premises of and in the operation of the Center as described herein.

Figure 7-2. continued

2. *Title To Signs.* The parties acknowledge and agree that title to the Signage leased under this Agreement is in the Franchisor and the Signage shall always remain the property of Franchisor or its successors, assignees, or designees herein.

3. *Security Deposit and Rental.* Franchisee shall pay a security deposit of _____Dollars ($_____) to Franchisor, as collateral to secure the care and maintenance of the Signage, upon the execution of this Agreement. Franchisee shall thereafter pay to the Franchisor as and for rent for the use of the Signage_____ Dollars ($_____) per year, payable monthly in advance, the first payment of _____ Dollars ($_____) to be made upon delivery of the Signage and each subsequent payment shall be made not later than the tenth day of each month thereafter together with any and all payments due to Franchisor pursuant to said Franchise Agreement. Any default in the payment of rent for the Signage shall be treated in the same manner as a default in the payment of franchise or royalty fees, except that the remedy provided in Paragraph Six (6) or Nine (9) below shall be in addition to and not in lieu of any other remedy available to the Franchisor under any other document for such default in payment of fees or royalties.

4. *Term.* The term of this Agreement shall commence at the time that the Signage is installed and shall continue for such period of time as Franchisee shall maintain and operate a Center at the premises described herein.

5. *Installation and Maintenance.* All Signage shall be installed by Franchisee at its expense pursuant to the plans and specifications of Franchisor. Franchisee shall not remove the Signage without first receiving written permission from Franchisor. Franchisee shall secure the necessary public permits and private permission to install all Signage. Franchisee shall pay the cost, if any, of such permits and shall comply with all laws, orders, and regulations of federal, state, and local authorities. Franchisee shall be responsible for all repair and maintenance of the Signage as may be required from time to time and as may be specified by Franchisor. Franchisee shall pay all taxes and assessments of any

nature that may be assessed against or levied upon the Signage before the same become delinquent.

6. *Right of Entry and/or Repossession.* If, for any reason, Franchisee should be in default of its obligations hereunder, its obligations under the Franchise Agreement, its obligations under the lease of the premises described herein, or any stiuplation executed by Franchisee, Franchisor shall have the right to enter upon the premises of the Center at any hour to take possession of the Signage leased hereunder without liability therefor. Franchisee agrees that Franchisor shall not be required to obtain prior permission to enter upon the premises and remove the Signage. Franchisee hereby grants Franchisor the limited power of attorney to obtain an order and judgment in Franchisor's behalf in any court of competent jurisdiction that orders and authorizes the entry of Franchisor on the premises and the removal of the Signage. Franchisee further agrees that if Franchisor is forced to resort to this procedure by any interference with the Franchisor's rights hereunder or for any other reason, Franchisee shall pay all attorney's fees and other costs associated with Franchisor's obtaining such order and judgment on its behalf. Franchisee further agrees to reimburse Franchisor for any costs or expenses incurred in connection with any such removal or detachment. Franchisee shall be liable and hereby assumes responsibility for any damage done to the building, premises, or the Signage as a result of the removal thereof.

7. *Repairs.* The Franchisee shall keep the Signage in the same condition as when delivered and shall make all necessary repairs in order to maintain such condition. The Franchisee shall be responsible for any damage to the Signage and shall pay the Franchisor at Franchisor's option the current replacement cost of the Signage if destroyed or the cost of repairing the damage. If the Franchisee shall fail to make any necessary repairs, Franchisor shall have the right to repair the Signage on the premises, or off the premises if Franchisor resorts to its repossession under Paragraph Six (6) for the purpose of repairing the Signage. Franchisee shall pay to the Franchisor the cost of such repairs or the current replacement cost, to be paid in one lump sum along with the next royalty payment that becomes due under the Franchise Agreement. Franchisee agrees that his rental fee obligations under Par-

Figure 7-2. continued

agraph two (2) for the term hereof shall continue even though the Signage is damaged or destroyed. Franchisee shall not make any alterations or additions to the Signage without the prior written consent of Franchisor.

8. *Transfers or Encumbrances.* Franchisee shall not pledge, loan, mortgage, or part with possession of the Signage or attempt in any other manner to dispose of or remove the Signage from the present location or suffer any liens or legal process to be incurred or levied thereupon.

9. *Default.* The occurrence of any of the following shall constitute an event of default hereunder:

(a) Failure of Franchisee to pay when due any installment of rent hereunder or any other sum herein required to be paid by Franchisee; and
(b) Franchisee's failure to perform any other covenant or condition of this Agreement or the Franchise Agreement or any stipulations thereunder.

Any default hereunder shall constitute and be considered a default of the Franchise Agreement, wherefor Franchisor shall be entitled to the enforcement of any and all rights under said Franchise Agreement or this Agreement.

10. *Warranties and Insurance.* Franchisor, upon written request of Franchisee, shall assign and transfer to Franchisee without recourse all assignable or transferable manufacturer's warranties, if any, which Franchisor may have with respect to the Signage. Franchisee agrees and acknowledges that Franchiosr has made no representations or warranties, either express or implied, with respect to the Signage. Franchisee hereby assuumes any and all risk and liability for the Signage including but not limited to the possession, use, operation, and maintenance thereof; injuries or death to person; and damage to property however arising or damage or destruction of the Signage however arising therefrom. Franchisee, at its own expense, shall carry adequate liability insurance coverage on the Signage, naming the Franchisor and Franchisee as named insureds, affording protection from and against

damages, claims, and expenses however caused and shall provide Franchisor a copy of said insurance policy upon request.

11. *Return.* Upon termination of this Agreement, the Franchisee shall at its own expense return the Signage to the Franchisor at the Franchisor's place of business in the same condition as when received, less ordinary wear and tear. If Franchisee fails to return the Signage, the Franchisor may, by his agents, take possession of the Signage, with or without process of law, and for this purpose may enter upon any premises of the Franchisee without liability and remove all or any of the Signage in the manner provided in Paragraph Six (6) above. Franchisee shall pay to Franchisor and any third parties all costs and expenses incurred in connection with such removal.

12. *Joint Liability; Gender.* If there be more than one person comprising the party designated as Franchisee, then all reference in this Agreement shall be deemed to refer to each such person jointly and severally, and all such persons shall be jointly and severally liable hereunder. Words of any gender used in this Agreement shall be construed to mean corresponding words of any other gender, and words in the singular number shall be construed to mean corresponding words in the plural, when the context so requires.

13. *Successors.* All terms and conditions of this Agreement shall be binding upon the successors, assignees, and legal representatives of the respective parties hereto.

IN WITNESS WHEREOF, the parties, intending to be legally bound hereby, have signed this Agreement and affixed their seals on the day and year above written.

WITNESS: **FRANCHISOR:**

_____   _____

                                 FRANCHISEE:

_____   _____

- *Option for assignment of lease.* The option for assignment of lease agreement provides the franchisor with the option, exercisable upon the termination of the franchisee for any reason, to be substituted as the tenant under franchisee's lease with its landlord for the premises on which franchisee's center is located.

- *Employee noncompetition and nondisclosure agreement.* This agreement should be executed by all employees of the franchisees. This agreement will ensure that all information disclosed to said employees will be kept confidential and also imposes noncompetition restriction on employees of the franchisees.

- *Acknowledgment of receipt of FOC and FA.* This document should be executed at the time that the franchisor releases a franchise offering circular and franchise agreement to a prospective franchisee for his/her review and consideration. It serves as an acknowledgment of receipt and notifies prospective franchisees that the documents remain the property of the franchisor and contain trade secrets that are confidential and must be treated as such.

- *Special disclaimer.* This document should be initialed and signed by the franchisee at the time of closing. It serves as a written acknowledgment that no earnings claims, representations, or warranties not contained in the offering circular have been made by the franchisor or relied upon by franchisee. It also serves as an acknowledgment that the proper offering circular and related documents were provided to franchisee on a timely basis.

- *Inventory purchase agreement.* The inventory purchase agreement defines the rights and obligations between the franchisor and the franchisee with respect to the purchase of certain items of inventory, supplies, and other items available for purchase through the franchisor or its affiliates. A sample inventory purchase agreement may be found at Figure 7-3 of this chapter.

- *Assignment of franchise agreement or franchised business.* This agreement is executed at the time of an assignment

(Text continues on page 144.)

Figure 7-3. Sample inventory purchase agreement.

INVENTORY PURCHASE AGREEMENT

THIS AGREEMENT is made and entered into this ___day of _____, 19___, by and between FRANCHISOR, an ____ corporation, (the "Franchisor"), and _____ (the "Purchaser").

W I T N E S S E T H:

WHEREAS, Franchisor has attained prominence in the _____ industry and through its _____ techniques and methods has developed numerous products;

WHEREAS, Purchaser entered into a Franchise Agreement with Franchisor, on _____, 19___ by the terms of which Purchaser as Franchisee has been granted the right and license to operate a _____ (the "Center");

WHEREAS, Purchaser is obligated by the terms of the Franchise Agreement to purchase certain merchandise, products, and other supplies (the "Products") solely from Franchisor or its approved suppliers;

WHEREAS, Purchaser has agreed to maintain Franchisor's uniformly high standards of quality for its products and services, which Purchaser acknowledges to be critical to the Franchisor's positive image and the protection of Franchisor's good will, and which, if not maintained, would result in irreparable harm to the Franchisor and the Purchaser; and

WHEREAS, Purchaser desires to purchase from Franchisor and Franchisor desires to sell to Purchaser certain merchandise, products, and supplies to be used in connection with its operation of the Center.

Figure 7-3. continued

NOW, THEREFORE, in consideration of the mutual promises, covenants, and conditions contained herein and for other good and valuable consideration, the receipt and sufficiency of which is hereby acknowledged, the parties agree as follows:

1. *Orders.* Orders for Products placed by Purchaser with Franchisor shall be subject to acceptance by Franchisor and Franchisor reserves the right to wholly or partially accept or reject any order placed by Purchaser. Franchisor also reserves the right to limit the amount of credit it will extend to Purchaser, to suspend shipments, to make shipments only after all prior orders shipped to Purchaser have been paid in full, to make shipments on a cash in advance or C.O.D. basis or on any other terms that Franchisor in its discretion deems to be appropriate.

2. *Price.* Franchisor agrees to sell the Products to Purchaser at the prices set forth in the Price Schedule attached hereto as Exhibit A and incorporated herein by this reference. The Price Schedule may be changed by Franchisor from time to time in the normal course of business. Any lists of suggested retail prices that Franchisor may provide to Purchaser for the sale of the Products to its customers shall be nothing more than suggested prices. Purchaser shall be free to set its prices for resale as it sees fit. Purchaser shall be free to set itsprices for resale as it sees fit. Franchisor, in its sole discretion, shall make price adjustments in accordance with then current market conditions.

3. *Payments.* Purchaser shall submit full payment for its orders and all shipping and handling charges at the time that said order is submitted to the Franchisor in accordance with the Price Schedule attached as Exhibit A, which may be amended from time to time by the Franchisor. Purchaser agrees to pay Franchisor for all orders pursuant to Franchisor's then current payment terms and policies, which terms and policies may be changed by Franchisor from time to time in its sole discretion without incurring any liability to Purchaser.

4. *Security Interest.* In order to secure prompt payment of all amounts due to Franchisor hereunder, the Purchaser grants Franchisor a security interest in Purchaser's accounts receivable, contract rights, inventory, equipment, fixtures, personal property, and all other assets whether now owned or hereafter acquired. Purchaser agrees to execute a Security Agreement and such financing statements as may be required under the Uniform Commercial Code in order to secure Franchisor's interest in the aforementioned assets of Purchaser.

5. *Delivery.* Franchisor understands that time is of the essence in the fulfillment of orders submitted by Purchaser and will make a good faith effort to fill all orders in a timely manner. Franchisor shall not be responsible for delays or failures in manufacture or delivery, due to any cause beyond its control.

6. *Warranties.* Franchisor hereby assigns to Purchaser, when such assignment may be made, each and every warranty for Products manufactured or supplied by others which is provided to Franchisor. Franchisor makes no other warranty of any nature concerning the Products supplied to Purchaser. FRANCHISOR MAKES NO OTHER WARRANTY, EXPRSSED, STATUTORY, OR IMPLIED, INCLUDING ANY WARRANTY OF FITNESS FOR A PARTICULAR PURPOSE OR WARRANTY OF MERCHANTABILITY. FRANCHISOR SHALL HAVE NO OTHER LIABILITY NOR DOES IT AFFIRM ANY REPRESENTATION BEYOND THE DESCRIPTION SET FORTH HEREIN OR ON THE LABEL OF ANY PRODUCT. Franchisor may, at its option, issue a credit to the Purchaser for damaged or defective merchandise provided that the Purchaser returns said merchandise to Franchisor in accordance with its standards and procedures for the return of merchandise. Franchisor will issue said credit upon receipt of the damaged or defective merchandise from Purchaser. Franchisor shall not be liable for incidental, consequential, or other damages suffered by the Purchaser due to defective products.

7. *Term.* The term of this Agreement shall be the same as the term of the Franchise Agreement dated _____, 19__

Figure 7-3. continued

by and between Purchaser and Franchisor including all renewal terms. Upon termination or expiration of this Agreement, the Purchaser must return to Franchisor, within seven (7)
days, any Products in the Purchaser's possession that have
been provided on a consignment basis or that have been
shipped to Purchaser by Franchisor for which payment has not
been received.

8. *Waiver.* The failure of either party to enforce at any
time of the provisions hereof shall not be construed to be a
waiver of such provisions or of the right of any party thereafter
to enforce any such provisions.

9. *Assignment.* This Agreement and the rights hereunder
are not assignable by Purchaser and the obligations imposed
on Purchaser are not delegable without the prior written consent of Franchisor.

10. *Modification.* No renewal hereof, or modification or
waiver of any of the provisions herein contained, or any future
representation, promise, or condition in connection with the
subject matter hereof, shall be effective unless agreed upon
by the parties hereto in a signed writing.

11. *Independent Contractor.* This Agreement shall not be
construed so as to characterize Purchaser as an agent, legal
representative, joint venturer, partner, employee, or servant of
Franchisor for any purpose whatsover; and it is understood
between the parties hereto that the Purchaser shall be an independent contractor and in no way shall Purchaser, its officers, directors, agents, or employees be authorized to make
any contract, agreement, warranty, or representation on behalf of Franchisor or to create any obligation, express or implied, on behalf of Franchisor.

12. *Guaranty of Franchisee's Shareholders:* All shareholders of the Purchaser hereby undertake to guarantee the
performance by the Purchaser of any and all obligations imposed upon the Purchasers under this Agreement.

13. *Notices.* Any and all Notices required or permitted

under this Agreement shall be in writing and shall be personally delivered or mailed by certified or registered mail, return receipt requested, to the respective parties at the addresses set forth below, unless and until a different address has been designated by a written Notice to the other party. Notice by mail shall be deemed received five (5) days after deposit with the United States Postal Service.

14. *Entire Agreement.* This instrument contains the entire agreement between the parties. This Agreement supersedes and is in lieu of all existing agreements or arrangements between the parties relating to the Products heretofore sold or delivered to Purchaser, and with respect to any fair trade agreement that may be in existence as of the effective date hereof.

15. *Execution of Documents.* Purchaser agrees to execute any and all documents or agreements and to take all action as may be necessary or desirable to effectuate the terms, covenants, and conditions of this Agreement.

16. *Binding Effect.* This Agreement shall be binding upon the parties hereto, their heirs, executors, successors, assigns, and legal representatives.

17. *Severability.* If any provision of this Agreement or any part thereof is declared invalid by any court of competent jurisdiction, such act shall not affect the validity of this Agreement and the remainder of this Agreement shall remain in full force and effect according to the terms of the remaining provisions or part provisions hereof.

18. *Remedies.* The rights and remedies created herein shall be deemed cumulative and no one of such rights or remedies shall be exclusive at law or in equity of the rights and remedies that Franchisor may have under this Agreement or otherwise.

19. *Attorney's Fees.* If any action is instituted by any party to enforce any provision of this Agreement, the prevailing party shall be entitled to recover all reasonable attorney's fees and costs incurred in connection therewith.

Figure 7-3. continued

20. *Construction.* This agreement shall be governed by and construed in accordance with the laws of the State of ___.

IN WITNESS WHEREOF, the parties hereto have caused this Purchase Agreement to be executed on the day and year first above written.

ATTEST   **FRANCHISOR:**

_____   By: _____
Secretary

ATTEST   **PURCHASER**

_____   By: _____
Secretary

by a franchisee of its rights, title, and interest in the franchise agreement or the franchised business. It serves as the formal assignment agreement as well as a consent to the assignment by the franchisor and imposes certain obligations upon the franchisee (assignor) and the assignee.

• *Addendum to lease agreement regarding assignment.* This addendum is executed at the time of closing. It contains various provisions that must be contained in the franchisee's lease agreement for the premises on which the franchised business is located.

• *Special consulting agreement.* This agreement should be used in the event that the franchisor intends to provide special support services to a franchisee or assume interim control of a franchisee's facility in the event of death or disability of the franchisor.

Figure 7-4. Tips for the negotiation of franchise agreements.

There are two distinct philosphies among franchise sales-persons: "No negotiations" represents the disciplined camp who fear reprimand from the franchisor's sales director and outside legal counsel, and the "everything's negotiable" camp who fear the wrath of their spouses if there is no sales commission revenue to pay the monthly mortgage. Neither camp represents the proper approach in franchise sales and franchise agreement negotiation. The Franchise Agreement is not to be presented as a "contract of adhesion." It is within the human nature of the prospective franchisee (and its legal counsel) to request and expect some degree of negotiation of the Franchise Agreement. This must be balanced against both the need for uniformity and consistency throughout the franchise system as well as the material change rules (which trigger an amendment to the offering circular) as discussed in the previous chapter. Certain states, such as New York and California, have developed strict regulations that govern the negotiations of Franchise Agreements. Each request by the prospective franchisee to modify a key term of the Franchise Agreement should be carefully considered from an economic and quality control perspective, as well as be reviewed by franchise counsel in order to identify potential legal problems and disclosure obligations.

Area Development Agreements and Subfranchising

Most franchises are sold to individual owner/operators who will be responsible for managing a single site in accordance with the franchisor's business format and quality control standards. And it has been the context of the single-unit franchisee that this chapter has addressed thus far. A recent trend in franchising, however, has been the sale of "multiple-unit franchises" to more aggressive entrepreneurs who will be responsible for the development of an entire geographic region.

The two primary types of multiple-unit franchises are (1) *subfranchisors*, who act as independent selling organizations that are responsible for the recruitment and ongoing support of franchisees within their given region; and (2) *area developers*, who have no resale rights but rather are themselves directly responsible for meeting a mandatory development schedule for their given region. There are a wide variety of variations on these two principal types of multiple-unit franchises. For example, some franchise relationships that are initially single units wind up as multiple-unit owners through the use of option agreements or rights of first refusal. Other franchisors have experimented with co-development rights among adjacent franchisees of a nearby territory, franchises coupled with management agreements (under circumstances where the franchisee deserves to be more passive), equity participation by franchisors in franchisees (and vice-versa), employee ownership of franchisor-operated units, and co-development rights between the franchisor and franchisee.

As a general rule, the inclusion of multiple-unit franchises in a franchisor's development strategy allows for even more rapid market penetration and less administrative burdens. Often the franchisee demands the right to develop and operate multiple units. However, a wide range of legal and strategic issues must be addressed when multiple-unit franchises are included in the overall franchising program.

Structuring Area Development Agreements

The key issues in structuring an area development agreement usually revolve around the size of the territory, fees, the mandatory timetable for development, and ownership of the units. The franchisor usually wants to reserve certain rights and remedies in the event that the franchisee defaults on its development obligations. The area developer must usually pay an umbrella development fee for the region, over and above the individual initial fee that is to be due and payable as each unit becomes operational within the territory. The amount of the fee varies, depending on factors such as the strength of the

(Text continues on page 152.)

Figure 7-5. Selected key provisions from a typical area development agreement.

A. *Recitals*

WHEREAS, Franchisor, as the result of the expenditure of time, skill, effort, and money, has developed and owns a unique system (hereinafter, the "System") relating to the establishment, development, and operation of_____ (the "Franchised Business" or "Center");

WHEREAS, the distinguishing characteristics of the System include, without limitation, unique_____ techniques; technical assistance and training in the operation, management, and promotion of the Franchised Business; specialized bookkeeping and accounting methods; and advertising and promotional programs, all of which may be changed, improved, and further developed by Franchisor;

WHEREAS, Franchisor is the owner of certain rights, title, and interest in the trade name, trademark, and service mark and such other trade names, trademarks, and service marks as are now designated (and may hereafter be designated by Franchisor in writing) as part of the System (hereinafter referred to as the "Proprietary Marks");

WHEREAS, Franchisor continues to develop, expand, use, control, and add to its Proprietary Marks for the benefit and exclusive use of itself and its franchisees in order to identify for the public the source of products and services marketed thereunder and to represent the System's high standards of quality and service;

WHEREAS, Area Developer desires to obtain the exclusive right to develop, construct, manage, and operate a series of Centers within the marketing territory specified hereunder as the "Designated Marketing Territory" (a geographic map of which is attached hereto as Exhibit "A") under the System and Proprietary Marks, as well as to receive the training and other assistance provided by Franchisor in connection therewith; and

Figure 7-5. continued

WHEREAS, Area Developer understands and acknowledges the importance of Franchisor's uniformly high standards of quality and service and the necessity of operating the
Centers in strict conformity with Franchisor's quality control
standards and specifications.

B. *Grant*

1. Franchisor hereby grants to Area Developer the right
and license to develop, construct, operate, and manage _____
(_____) Centers in strict accordance with the System
and under the Proprietary Marks within the marketing territory
("Designated Marketing Territory") as described in Exhibit "A"
attached hereto. Each Center shall be operated according to
the terms of the individual Franchise Agreement with respect
thereto.

2. If the Area Developer complies with the terms of this
Agreement, the Development Schedule, and the individual
Franchise Agreement for each Center, then Franchisor will not
franchise or license others, nor will it itself directly or indirectly
develop, own, lease, construct, or operate in any manner, any
Centers in the Designated Marketing Territory during the term
hereof.

3. This Agreement is not a franchise agreement and Developer shall have no right to use in any manner the Proprietary Marks of Franchisor by virtue hereof.

C. *Development Fee*

Area Developer shall pay to Franchisor a nonrefundable
development fee of Five Thousand Dollars ($5,000) per Center
to be developed by Area Developer, which shall be paid upon
execution of this Agreement, which fee shall be fully earned
by Franchisor in consideration of its execution of the Agreement and its services and forbearance in offering franchises in
the Designated Marketing Territory that is the subject of this

Agreement. With respect to all Centers to be developed under this Agreement, Franchisor and Area Developer shall enter into an individual Franchise Agreement for each such Center within thirty (30) days prior to the grand opening thereof, which Agreement shall be in the form of the then current Franchise Agreement offered to new franchisees; provided, however, that the royalty fees shall remain the same as those royalty fees set forth in the individual Franchise Agreement being executed currently herewith.

D. *Development Schedule*

Area Developer shall open and continuously operate the Centers in accordance with the System and the development schedule set forth in Exhibit B (the "Development Schedule"). In the event that Area Developer opens and operates a greater number of Centers than is required to comply with the current period of the Development Schedule, the requirements of the succeeding period(s) shall be deemed to have been satisfied to the extent of such excess number of Centers. Except as otherwise provided herein, nothing herein shall require Area Developer to open Centers in excess of the number of Centers set forth in the Development Schedule, nor shall Area Developer be precluded from opening additional Franchised Businesses subject to the prior approval of Franchisor.

E. *Location of Centers*

The location of each Center shall be selected by Area Developer, within the Designated Marketing Territory, subject to Franchisor's prior approval, which approval shall take into account the marketing information and report provided by Area Developer. The acquisition of any proposed site by Area Developer prior to approval of Franchisor shall be the sole risk and responsibility of Area Developer and shall not obligate Franchisor in any way to approve the same. The approval of a proposed site by Franchisor does not in any way constitute a warranty or representation by Franchisor as to the suitability of such site for location of a Center.

Figure 7-5. continued

F. *Assignment and Ownership of the Centers*

1. *By Franchisor.* Franchisor shall have the absolute right to transfer or assign all or any part of its rights or obligations hereunder to any person or legal entity.

2. *By Area Developer.*

A. Area Developer understands and acknowledges that the rights and duties set forth in this Development Agreement are personal to Area Developer and are granted in reliance upon the personal qualifications of Area Developer. Area Developer has represented to Franchisor that Area Developer is entering into this Development Agreement with the intention of complying with its terms and conditions and not for the purpose of resale of the development and option rights hereunder.

B. Neither Area Developer nor any partner or shareholder thereof shall, without Franchisor's prior written consent, directly or indirectly sell, assign, transfer, convey, give away, pledge, mortgage, or otherwise encumber any interest in this Agreement or in Area Developer. Any such proposed assignment occurring by operation of law or otherwise, including any assignment by a trustee in bankruptcy, without Franchisor's prior written consent shall be a material default of this Agreement.

C. If Area Developer is in full compliance with this Agreement, Franchisor shall not unreasonably withhold its approval of an assignment or transfer to proposed assignees or transferrees who are of good moral character, have sufficient business experience, aptitude, and financial resources and otherwise meet the Franchisor's then applicable standards for area developers and are willing to assume all obligations of Area Developer hereunder and to execute and be bound by all provisions of the Franchisor's then current form of Area Development Agreement for a term equal to the remaining term hereof. As a condition to the granting of its approval of any such assignee or transferee, Franchisor may require Area Developer or the assignee or transferee to pay to the Franchisor its then current transfer fee as specified in Subsection F to defray expenses incurred by the Franchisor in connection with the assignment or transfer, legal and accounting fees, credit and other investigation charges and evaluation of the assignee or transferee, and the terms of the assignment or transfer. Franchisor shall have the right to require Area Developer and its owners to execute a general release of Franchisor in a form satisfactory to Franchisor as a condition to its approval of the assignment of this Agreement or ownership of Area Developer.

G. Change in Territory

The parties acknowledge that the development of the Designated Marketing Territory as anticipated hereunder has been determined according to the needs of the existing individuals who constitute Area Developer's targeted market in the Designated Marketing Territory, as determined by Franchisor, as of the date of execution of this Agreement. The parties agree that if there is an increased public demand for the products and services offered by Franchisor due to an increase in the number of individuals in the Designated Marketing Territory, as may be determined by a future demographic study, Franchisor shall have the right to demand that additional Centers be established within the Designated Marketing Territory. Area Developer shall have the right of first refusal to establish any such additional Centers deemed necessary and Franchisor agrees that such additional Centers shall be established only under the following terms and conditions:

(i) Any additional Centers shall be governed by the then current individual Franchise Agreement; and

(ii) Additional Centers will only be deemed necessary if the number of individuals in the Designated Marketing Territory increases by _____persons.

Figure 7-5. continued

H. *Acknowledgments*

1. Area Developer acknowledges and recognizes that different terms and conditions, including different fee structures, may pertain to different Development Agreements and Franchise Agreements offered in the past, contemporaneously herewith, or in the future, and that Franchisor does not represent that all Development Agreements or Franchise Agreement are or will be identical.

2. Area Developer acknowledges that it is not, nor is it intended to be, a third-party beneficiary of this Agreement or any other agreement to which Franchisor is a party.

AREA DEVELOPER REPRESENTS THAT IT HAS READ THIS AGREEMENT, THE OFFERING CIRCULAR, FRANCHISE AGREEMENT, AND ALL EXHIBITS THERETO IN THEIR ENTIRETY AND THAT IT HAS BEEN GIVEN THE OPPORTUNITY TO CLARIFY ANY PROVISIONS AND INFORMATION THAT IT DID NOT UNDERSTAND AND TO CONSULT WITH AN ATTORNEY OR OTHER PROFESSIONAL ADVISOR. AREA DEVELOPER UNDERSTANDS THE TERMS, CONDITIONS, AND OBLIGATIONS OF THIS AGREEMENT AND AGREES TO BE BOUND THEREBY.

---

franchisor's trademarks and market share, the size of the territory, and the term (and renewal) of the agreement. This development fee is essentially a payment to the franchisor that prevents the franchisor from offering any other franchises within that region (unless there is a default). Sample key provisions of the area development agreement may be found in Figure 7-5.

Structuring Subfranchising Agreements

Subfranchise agreements present a myriad of issues that are not raised in the sale of a single-unit franchise or an area development agreement, primarily because the rewards and responsibilities of the subfranchisor differ from those of the area developer or single-unit operator. In most subfranchising relationships, the franchisor will share a portion of the initial franchise fee and ongoing royalty with the subfranchisor, in exchange for the subfranchisor assuming responsibilities within the given region. The proportions in which fees are shared usually have a direct relationship to the exact responsibilities of the subfranchisor. In addition, the subfranchisor receives a comprehensive regional operations manual that covers sales and promotions, training, and field support over and above the information contained in the operations manuals provided to the individual franchisees. Some of the key issues that must be addressed in the subfranchise relationship include:

- How will the initial and ongoing franchise fees be divided among franchisor and subfranchisor? Who will be responsible for the collection and processing of franchise fees?
- Will the subfranchisor be a party of the individual franchise agreements? Or will direct privity be limited to franchisor and individual franchisee?
- What is the exact nature of the subfranchisor's recruitment, site selection, franchising, training, and ongoing support to the individual franchisees within its region?
- Who will be responsible for the preparation and filing of franchise offering documents in the states where the subfranchisor must file separately?
- What mandatory development schedules and related performance quotas will be imposed on the subfranchisor?
- Will the subfranchisor be granted the rights to operate individual units within the territory? If yes, how will these units be priced?
- What will the subfranchisor be obligated to pay the franchisor initially for the exclusive rights to develop the territory?

- What rights of approval will the franchisor retain with respect to the sale of individual franchises (e.g., background of the candidate, any negotiated changes in the agreement, decision to terminate, etc.)?
- What rights does the franchisor reserve to modify the size of the territory or repurchase it from the subfranchisor?

A subfranchisor enters into what is typically referred to as a regional development agreement with the franchisor, pursuant to which the subfranchisor is granted certain rights to develop a particular region. The regional development agreement is not in itself a franchise agreement to operate any individual franchise units; rather it grants the subfranchisor the right to sell franchises to individuals using the franchisor's system and proprietary marks solely for the purpose of recruitment, management, supervision, and support of individual franchisees. To the extent that the subfranchisor itself develops units, then an individual franchise agreement for each such unit must be executed. Some of the key terms, conditions, and obligations that make up the subfranchising relationship include:

- *Grant.* The franchisor grants the subfranchisor the right and exclusive license to develop or grant franchises for the establishment and operation of franchises in a stated geographic region for a stated term (generally ten years or more).
- *Fees.* The subfranchisor generally pays to the franchisor a development fee in exchange for the grant of the right and exclusive license to operate and sell franchises in the designated region. Typically, this development fee is paid upon execution of the regional development agreement, although it may be paid in installments.
- *Development of region.* The subfranchisor is obligated to develop and operate a franchise sales, marketing, and development program for its designated region which will include advertising and promotion of the franchisor's system,

the offer and sale of franchises in the designated region, and the provision of support and assistance to franchisees in the establishment and ongoing operation of their franchises.

Traditionally, a performance schedule is set in the regional development agreement for the development of the designated region. This schedule will set forth the number of franchises the subfranchisor will be required to develop and/or sell in the designated region over the term of the agreement. Generally, if the subfranchisor fails to meet the development schedule, the franchisor may do one or more of the following:

1. Accelerate the development schedule
2. Withdraw the territorial exclusivity granted to the subfranchisor
3. Redefine the designated region to encompass a smaller territory
4. Terminate the regional development agreement

• *Franchisor's obligations.* Most of the obligations of a franchisor under a franchise agreement with an individual franchisee in turn become obligations of the subfranchisor to the franchisee in a subfranchising relationship. The franchisor does typically, however, have several distinct obligations to the subfranchisor, including:

1. Provision of training
2. Provision of materials, layouts, promotional items, operations, and other manuals (sometimes including a regional development manual)
3. Overseeing subfranchisor's operations and techniques and suggesting improvements thereto
4. Promoting the business and goodwill of the franchisor's system and proprietary marks

• *Subfranchisor's obligations.* By far, the most extensive portion of the Regional Development Agreement is the recitation of the subfranchisor's obligations. These obligations flow to the franchisor and to the individual franchisees in the designated region. They include the obligation to:

1. Locate and maintain an office within the designated region
2. Submit for franchisor's prior approval all proposed advertising, promotional, and sales materials that relate to the recruitment of franchisees
3. Offer and sell franchises only to persons/entities who meet franchisor's qualifications for experience, competence, reputation, and financial responsibility
4. Submit to franchisor written applications for all qualified prospective franchisees for franchisor's approval
5. Ensure the proper execution of franchise and related agreements by the franchisee
6. Ensure that each franchise in its designated region is developed and operated in accordance with franchisor's standards and specifications
7. Comply with all federal and state laws and all regulations enacted by appropriate regulatory bodies with respect to the offer and sale of franchises
8. Provide ongoing support and assistance to franchisees in the designated region, including on-site supervision, inspection, training, and provision of marketing/advertising techniques and materials
9. Submit all periodic reports required by the franchisor

- *Renumeration of the franchisor and subfranchisor.*

1. Initial franchise fees paid by franchisees. Generally, the franchisor and subfranchisor split the initial franchise fee charged to and collected from individual franchisees in the designated region. Typically, at the outset (e.g., first twenty-five franchises) the franchisor is entitled to a higher percentage of the initial franchise fee. The percentages are gradually readjusted (as an incentive to stimulate sales in the region) as more franchises are sold by the subfranchisor.

2. *Royalty fees.* Additionally, the franchisor and sub-franchisor share the royalty fees collected from each franchisee in the designated region. Similarly, the franchisor collects a greater percentage of said royalties at the outset (e.g., first twenty-five or so franchises sold by subfranchisor), but as more franchises are sold the subfranchisor's percentage of royalties increases.

The relationship between franchisor and subfranchisor is unique and somewhat complicated. If the appropriate individual is chosen for this role, the relationship can be mutually beneficial. The advantages of such a relationship to the franchisor include rapid market penetration, the delegation of obligations it would otherwise be required to fulfill to each franchisee in its network, and the ability to collect a percentage of the initial franchise fee and royalty fees from each franchisee, generally without the same level of effort that would be required in a single-unit relationship.

8

Protecting Intellectual Property

At the foundation of every successful franchise system is the franchisor's intellectual property that has been developed, improved, and expanded over the years to create a unique concept, product, or service readily identifiable by consumers. The intellectual property of a franchise system consists primarily of (1) trademarks, (2) trade secrets, and (3) copyrights.

Trademarks and Service Marks

A trademark or service mark is a word, name, symbol, or device used to indicate the origin and ownership of a product or service. A trademark is used in the advertising and marketing of a product while a service mark typically identifies a service. A trademark or service mark identifies and distinguishes the products or services of one person from those of another person.

A trademark also provides a guarantee of quality and consistency of the product or service it identifies. It assures the consumer that the products and services purchased today at one location are of the same quality as those purchased at another location. Consumer recognition of and confidence in the product or service identified by the trademark is the lifeline of a successful franchise system.

In a franchise system the franchisor grants the franchisee a *nonexclusive* license to use the franchisor's trademarks in connection with the franchisee's sale of the products and services or the identification of the business that constitutes the franchise system.

Types of Marks

Not all words or phrases are entitled to trademark protection. The mark must, as a preliminary matter, identify the products or services as coming from a particular source. The goodwill and name recognition established by the franchisor is the most valuable component of the franchise for the franchisee. The mark may not, however, be generic in nature or be merely descriptive of the type of products or services it identifies. Marks that are generally protectable are coined, fanciful, arbitrary, or suggestive.

- *Coined, fanciful, or arbitrary.* This is the strongest category of mark that can be protected. The trademark is either a coined word, such as Xerox, or a word in common usage that has no meaning when applied to the goods and services in question, such as Dove for dish detergent or body soap. Such marks are inherently distinctive for legal and registration purposes; however, as a result of the obscurity of the mark, the burden is on the manufacturer to establish goodwill.
- *Suggestive.* A suggestive mark requires the consumer to use some degree of imagination in determining what product or service is represented and as such is the next strongest category of mark that may be protected. Owners of suggestive trademarks are usually not required to establish "secondary meaning" (see below). Examples of suggestive marks include Seven-Up or Orange Crush, which merely suggest that they identify refreshing beverages.
- *Descriptive.* Trademarks that are descriptive of the goods or services they identify *cannot* be protected unless the manufacturer can establish distinctiveness. This requires

demonstration that the public associates this particular mark with the goods of the specific producer (known as "secondary meaning"). This category would include names like Holiday Inn, for motels, which is descriptive but nevertheless registered because it is distinctive.

The host of marks that will be refused registration include those that:

- Are immoral, deceptive, or scandalous
- May disparage or falsely suggest a connection with persons, institutions, beliefs, or national symbols or bring them into contempt or disrepute
- Consist of or simulate the flag or coat of arms or other insignia of the United States, or of a state or municipality or any foreign nation
- Are the name, portrait, or signature of a particular living individual unless he or she has given written consent; or are the name, signature, or portrait of a deceased President of the United States during the life of his widow, unless she has given her consent
- So resemble a mark already registered in the U.S. Patent and Trademark Office (USPTO) as to be likely, when applied to the goods of the applicant, to cause confusion or to cause mistake or to deceive
- Are primarily geographically descriptive or deceptively misdescriptive of the goods or services of the applicant
- Are primarily a surname

A mark will not be refused registration on the grounds listed above if the applicant can show that, through use in commerce, the mark has become distinctive so that it now identifies to the public the applicant's products or services. Marks that are refused registration on the grounds listed above may be registered on the Supplemental Register, which contains terms or designs considered capable of distinguishing the owner's goods or services but have not yet been used.

Protections Afforded by Registration

Trademark rights arise from either (1) use of the mark or (2) a bona fide intention to use the mark along with the filing of an application to federally register the mark on the Principal Register. A federal trademark registration is not required to protect a trademark, and a mark may be used without securing registration. However, registration does provide a number of advantages, as listed in Figure 8-1.

A mark that is an actual use in commerce though it does not qualify for registration on the Principal Register for one or more reasons (i.e., it is merely descriptive or a surname) may be registered with the USPTO on the Supplemental Register. Registration on the Supplemental Register does not provide the mark the same level of protection afforded by registration on the Principal Register, but does give the registrant:

- The right to sue in federal court and obtain statutory remedies for infringement
- In foreign countries whose laws require prior registration in the home country, a possible right to foreign registration
- Protection against federal registration by another identical or confusingly similar mark
- The right to use the encircled R symbol on goods

Registration on the Supplemental Register allows the owner of the mark to put the world on notice of his use and rights to the mark. Further, registration of a descriptive mark on the Supplemental Register may be advantageous for a period of time while the mark's use is increased to the point where it becomes so substantial as to acquire "secondary meaning." It is at this time that the mark may qualify for registration on the Principal Register. It may be advantageous for a start-up franchisor to take advantage of registration on the Supplemental Register, if registration is denied on the Principal Register until a few franchises are sold and the mark,

Figure 8-1. Advantages of registration.

1. The filing date of the application, a constructive date of first use of the mark in commerce, which gives the registrant nationwide priority as of that date, except as to certain prior users or prior applicants
2. The right to bring legal action in federal court for trademark infringement
3. Recovery of profits, damages, and costs in a federal court infringement action and the possibility of triple damages and attorneys' fees
4. Constructive notice of a claim of ownership (which eliminates a good faith defense for a party adopting the trademark subsequent to the registrant's date of registration)
5. The right to deposit the registration with customs in order to stop the importation of goods bearing an infringing mark
6. Prima facie evidence of the validity of the registration, registrant's ownership of the mark, and registrant's exclusive right to use the mark in commerce in connection with the goods or services specified in the certificate
7. The possibility of incontestability, in which case the registration constitutes conclusive evidence of the registrant's exclusive right, with certain limited exceptions, to use the registered mark in commerce
8. Limited grounds for attacking a registration once it is five years old
9. Availability of criminal penalties and triple damages in an action for counterfeiting a registered trademark
10. A basis for filing trademark applications in foreign countries

through increased use, gains secondary meaning. This would bolster the marketability of the franchises much more than would an unregistered trademark licensed by the franchisor.

Overview of the Registration Process

Prior to the passage of the Trademark Law Revision Act of 1988, eligibility for federal registration of a trademark arose only if the mark has been *actually used* in interstate commerce. This requirement was different than that of most other countries, which generally allow a company to register a mark even if no actual use had been established. This generally meant that a substantial amount of time and expense might be invested in a proposed trade identity for a new product or service, with virtually no assurance that the mark could ever be properly registered and protected.

Under the new law, a franchisor may file an application to register a trademark based on actual use *or* upon a "bona fide intention" to use the mark in interstate commerce. This allows the franchisor to conduct some market research and further investigation without the need to actually put the mark into the stream of commerce as a prerequisite to obtaining federal protection.

The USPTO has developed guidelines for registration under the new "intent to use" provisions. The following procedures have been established:

1. Company files application for registration, which is subject to all of the current tests for registrability (e.g., likelihood of confusion, descriptiveness, etc.), *except for* proof of use in interstate commerce and the requirement for actual specimens of the mark. If the mark is used in interstate commerce prior to approval of the application by the examiner, an amendment to the application should be made to allege that use of the mark in interstate commerce has occurred.
2. When the application is approved by the examiner, a Notice of Allowance will be issued to the applicant.

3. If actual use does not occur until after the application
is approved, the applicant will then have six months
from the date of allowance to actually use the mark in
interstate commerce and file a Statement of Use, with
actual specimens attached. After review of the Statement of Use and specimens, the mark will be registered. An applicant may request extensions of time for
filing of the Statement of Use for up to four successive
six-month periods. Failure to file by this deadline will
result in an abandonment of the mark.

Regardless of whether a franchisor files under the "actual
use" or "intent to use" provisions, an application must be prepared and filed at the USPTO for the trademark in the classification that is appropriate for the goods and services offered.
A trademark examiner will then review the application to determine if it meets the statutory requirements and whether
similar trademarks have already been registered in the same
or similar lines of business. The examiner's concerns are usually enumerated in a formal office action. Legal counsel is then
required to respond to all of the concerns of the examiner.
This process continues until the application is either finally
refused or recommended by the examiner for publication in
the Official Gazette, which serves as notice to the general public. Anyone who believes that he or she would be injured by
registration may file a Notice of Opposition within thirty days
of the publication date. Failure of the parties to resolve any
differences will result in a hearing before the Trademark Trial
and Appeal Board (TTAB). The TTAB is also the appropriate
body to appeal the examiner's final refusal to register.

Registration is a complex and often lengthy process (anywhere from twelve to eighteen months even if there are only
minimal problems), but the commercial rewards may be substantial if the registered mark is properly used to provide the
franchisor with a competitive edge. A registration under the
Lanham Act is effective for ten years but may be renewed for
additional ten-year terms thereafter so long as it is still in
actual use in interstate commerce. The registration may,
however, be canceled after six years unless an affidavit of con-

tinued use is filed with the USPTO which demonstrates that the registrant has not abandoned the trademark.

Maintaining Rights in the Trademarks

Because a trademark provides consumers a guarantee of quality, the owner of a trademark is responsible for protecting and ensuring the quality of the products or services associated with the trademark. For a franchisor that has licensed its trademark to franchisees and may be located all over the coutry, maintaining a certain level of quality of the products and services identified by the mark is certainly a challenge.

Along with the rights conferred as the owner of a registered trademark there are responsibilities. The licensor/franchisor must actively police the mark to ensure that an established level of quality is maintained by its licensees/franchisees. A carefully drafted franchise/license agreement should set forth, in detail, the specific obligations of the franchisee with respect to the trademarks. The franchise/license agreement must provide the franchisor with supervisory control over the product or service that the mark represents. If such controls are not retained by the franchisor, the "naked" license of the trademarks could be found to be invalid. It is, therefore, imperative that a franchisor provide its franchisees with both guidelines for use of the trademarks and guidance on the level of quality and uniformity of the products and services which must be maintained.

Protecting the trademarks under the franchise agreement. Every franchise agreement should have a section devoted to the proper use and care of the franchisor's trademarks, which should stipulate the following:

- The identity of the trademarks that the franchisor licenses its franchisees to use
- That the franchisee use only the trademarks designated by the franchisor and use them only in the manner required or authorized and permitted by the franchisor

- That the franchisee use the marks only in connection with the right and license to operate the center granted to the franchisee

- That, during the term of the franchise agreement and any renewal thereof, the franchisee must identify itself as a licensee and not the owner of the trademarks and shall make any necessary filings under state law to reflect its status as a license. In addition, the franchisee is required to identify itself as a licensee of the trademarks on all invoices, order forms, receipts, business stationery, and contracts, as well as display a notice in such form and content and at such conspicuous locations as the franchisor designates in writing.

- That the franchisee's right to use the trademarks is limited to uses authorized under the franchise agreement, and any unauthorized use is an infringement of the franchisor's rights and grounds for termination of the franchise agreement

- That the franchisee must not use the trademarks to incur or secure any obligation or indebtedness

- That the franchisee must not use the trademarks as part of its corporate or other legal name

- That the franchisee must comply with the franchisor's instructions in filing and maintaining the requisite trade name or fictitious name registrations and must execute any documents the franchisor or its counsel deems necessary to obtain protection for the trademarks or to maintain their continued validity and enforceability

- That the franchisee will promptly notify the franchisor if litigation involving the marks is instituted or threatened against the franchisee and will cooperate fully in defending or settling such litigation

Additionally, the franchisee should be required to expressly acknowledge that:

- The franchisor is the owner of all right, title, and interest in the trademarks and the goodwill associated with the symbolized by them

- The trademarks are valid and serve to identify the franchisor's system and those who are licensed to operate a franchise in accordance with the system
- The franchisee will neither directly or indirectly contest this validity nor the franchisor's ownership of the trademarks
- The franchisee's use of the trademarks according to the franchise agreement does not give the franchisee any ownership interest or other interest in or to the trademarks, except a nonexclusive license.
- Any and all goodwill arising from the franchisee's use of the trademarks in accordance with the franchisor's system is solely and exclusively to franchisor's benefit, and upon expiration or termination of the franchise agreement, no monetary amount will be assigned as attributable to any goodwill associated with the franchisee's use of the system or the trademarks
- The license and rights to use the trademarks granted to the franchisee are nonexclusive, and the franchisor may therefore: (1) itself use the trademarks and grant franchises and licenses to others to use them; (2) establish, develop, and franchise other systems different from the one licensed to the franchisee, without offering or providing the franchisee any rights in, to, or under such other systems; and (3) modify or change, in whole or in part, any aspect of the trademarks so long as the franchisee's rights are in no way materially harmed.
- The franchisor reserves the right to substitute different names and trademarks for use in identifying the system, the franchise, and other franchised businesses operating under the franchisor's system
- The franchisor has no liability to the franchisee for any senior users that may claim rights to the franchisor's trademarks
- The franchisee will neither register nor attempt to register the trademarks in the franchisee's name or that of any other person, firm, entity, or corporation

Trademark protection and quality control program. Every franchisor should develop an active trademark protection program designed to educate the franchisor's field staff, key vendors, advisors, officers, employees, and all of its franchisees as to the proper usage and protection of the trademarks. Development of a franchise agreement that imposes all of the obligations described above is a vital component of this program, but alone is insufficient to prevent misuse of the trademarks and enforce quality control standards. A Trademark Use Compliance Manual, which contains more detailed guidelines for proper trademark usage, grammar, and quality, also plays an important role in a successive trademark protection program. The compliance manual may comprise a section of the franchisor's operations manual and specify the following:

- Proper display of the marks (use of ™, block *TM*, or *SM* symbol)
- Required state filings (fictitious name registrations) and instructions for said filings by franchisee to reflect its status as a licensee of the marks
- All documents, correspondence, and other materials on which franchisee must display the trademarks and identify itself as a licensee
- All authorized uses of the marks and prohibited uses (i.e., they may not be used as part of franchisee's corporate name)

In addition to a compliance manual, strategies should be developed to monitor franchisees, competitors, and other third parties in order to detect and prevent improper usage or potential infringement of the mark. A staff member of the franchisor should be designated to read trade publications; business press; marketing materials of competitors; and in-house production, labeling, and correspondence to ensure that the mark is properly used by franchisees and not stolen by competitors. If an infringing use is discovered by a clipping service, company field representative, franchisee, trade association, or supplier, then the franchisor must be vigilant in its protection of the marks. This will require working closely with trademark counsel to ensure that all potential infringers receive letters demanding that such practices be immediately discontinued and infringing materials destroyed. As much evidence as possible should be gathered on each potential infringer and accurate files kept in the event that trademark infringement litigation is necessary to settle the dispute. The registrant considering litigation should carefully weigh the costs and likely result of the suit against the potential loss of goodwill and market share. It may be wiser to allocate those funds toward advertising rather than toward legal fees, especially if the likelihood of infringement is remote.

Trademark Infringement and Dilution

The principal reason a trademark monitoring program must be maintained by every franchisor is to guard against trademark infringement or dilution. Under the Lanham Act, infringement is a demonstration by the owner of a registered mark that some third party is using a reproduction or imitation of the registered mark in connection with the offer or sale of goods and services in such a way as to be likely to cause confusion, mistake, or deception from the perspective of the ordinary purchaser.

The exact definition of the "likelihood of confusion" standard has been the source of much debate over the years. The focus has always been on whether the ordinary purchaser of the product in question is likely to be confused as to the source of origin or sponsorship. There are a wide variety of factors that the courts have listed as criteria for determining whether a likelihood of confusion exists, such as:

- The degree of similarity and resemblance of the infringer's marks to the registered marks (in terms of visual appearance, pronunciation, interpretation, etc.)
- The strength of the registered mark in the relevant industry or territory
- The actual or constructive intent of the infringer

- The similarity of the goods or services offered by the infringer and the owner of the registered mark
- The overlap (if any) in the distribution and marketing channels of the infringer and the owner of the registered mark
- The extent to which the owner of the registered mark can demonstrate that consumers were actually confused (usually demonstrated with consumer surveys and affidavits)

In addition to a federal cause of action for trademark infringement, many state trademark statutes provide owners of registered marks with an antidilution remedy. This remedy is available when a third party is using a mark in a manner that "dilutes" the distinctive quality of a mark registered under the state statute or used under common law. The owner of the registered mark and the diluting party need not be in actual competition, nor must a likelihood of confusion be demonstrated. However, in order to make a claim for dilution, the trademark must have a "distinctive quality," which means that it must enjoy very strong consumer loyalty, recognition, and goodwill.

Trademark rights are often the most valuable asset of a franchisor in today's competitive marketplace. The goodwill and consumer recognition that trademarks and service marks represent have tremendous economic value and are therefore usually worth the effort and expense to properly register and protect them. Management must also implement and support a strict trademark compliance program that includes usage guidelines for all franchisees, as well as suppliers, service providers, and distributors.

Trade Secrets

A franchisor's advantage over its competitors is gained and maintained in large part through its trade secrets and proprietary information. A franchisor's trade secrets will typically consist of its confidential formula, recipes, business format and plan, prospect lists, pricing methods, and marketing and distribution techniques.

Not all ideas and concepts are considered to be trade secrets. Courts have generally set forth three requirements for information to qualify for trade secret protection:

1. The information must have some commercial value.
2. The information must not be generally known or readily ascertainable by others.
3. The owner of the information must take all reasonable steps to maintain its confidentiality. In order to preserve legal protections for its trade secrets, a franchisor must follow a reasonable and consistent program for ensuring that the confidentiality of the information is maintained. This presents a difficult problem in the franchising context where the franchisor, as the owner of the trade secrets, licenses sometimes hundreds (and even thousands) of people and/or companies to use its trade secrets. It is, therefore, important to continuously strive to maintain the confidential nature of the trade secrets in the hands of franchisees and their employees.

There are many factors, however, in addition to those discussed above, that courts have considered in deciding the extent to which protection should be afforded for trade secrets. Among those factors most often cited are:

- The extent to which the information is known by others outside the company
- The measures employed within the company to protect its secrets
- The value of the information, including the resources expended to develop the information
- The amount of effort that would be required by others to duplicate the effort or "reverse engineer" the technology

- The nature of the relationship between the alleged infringer and the owner of the trade secret

Implementing a Trade Secret Protection Program

There are some fundamental, affordable, and practical measures franchisors can readily adopt to protect the trade secrets that constitute the heart of their competitive advantage.

Steps to be Taken by the Franchisor and Its Franchisees.
Even in an effort to protect trade secrets, there is such a thing as overkill. In fact, like the boy who cried wolf, if a franchisor tries to protect every aspect of its operation by classifying everything in sight as "trade secret," virtually nothing at all will likely be afforded protection when put to the test. Genuine trade secrets may be diluted if you try to protect too much.

The process of establishing a trade secret protection and compliance program should start with a "trade secret audit" to identify which information is *genuinely* confidential and proprietary. Although each franchisor has its own priorities, all types of franchised businesses should consider financial, technical, structural, marketing, engineering, distribution documents, recipes, business plans, operations manuals, and pricing techniques to be candidates for protection. A portion of the franchisor's operations manual should identify all information the franchisor considers to be trade secrets and discuss the use and protection of those trade secrets it licenses to franchisees.

Trade secret protection must be a part of the franchisee's training program, during which a full briefing should be given on their continuing duty and legal obligation to protect the secrets of the franchisor. Franchisees should be instructed that trade secrets should only be disclosed to employees who have a genuine need to know the information in order to perform their job. Those employees who have access to the franchisor's trade secrets should also be informed of their continuing duty and legal obligation to protect the trade secrets. For certain key employees it may be advisable to require that the franchisee obtain a signed Confidentiality and Noncompetition Agreement them.

The critical rules of the franchisor's compliance program to which franchisees must also adhere are as follows:

- Ensure that adequate security measures are taken, which may include restricting access to certain proprietary documents and information (recipes, manuals); implementing log-in procedures prior to gaining access to locked desks, files, and vaults for proprietary documents; and posting signs and notices in all appropriate places.

- Purchase stamps to be placed on documents that are trade secrets in order to give notice to users of their proprietary status, and restrict the photocopying of these documents to limited circumstances.

- Designate a Trade Secret Compliance Officer to be in charge of all aspects relating to the proper care and monitoring of trade secrets.

- Carefully review advertising and promotional materials and press releases to protect trade secrets. Restrict access by reporters and other members of the media.

- Ensure that *all* key employees, marketing representatives, service providers, franchisees, prospective investors or joint venturers, customers, suppliers, or anyone else who has access to the company's trade secrets has signed a carefully prepared Confidentiality and Nondisclosure Agreement. See Figure 8-2.

- Police the activities of former employees, suppliers, and franchisees. Include post-term obligations in agreements which impose a duty on the employee to keep his or her former employer aware of his or her whereabouts.

- If trade secrets are contained on computers, use passwords and data encryption to restrict access to terminals and telephone access through modems.

- Establish controlled routing procedures for the distribution and circulation of certain documents.

(Text continues on page 178.)

Figure 8–2. Noncompetition and nondisclosure agreement (for use by employees of franchisee).

This AGREEMENT is made and entered into this _____ day of _____, 19___, by and between _____, a corporation, (the "Franchisee"); Prof-Finders, a _____ corporation, (the "Franchisor"); and _____ ("Employee").

W I T N E S S E T H

WHEREAS, the Franchisor and Franchisee have entered into a franchise agreement dated _____, _____, (the "Franchise Agreement"), pursuant to which Franchisee shall receive access to Confidential Information [as that term is defined in Paragraph _____ of the Franchise Agreement] and trade secrets of the Franchisor which Franchisee may, in certain instances, need to convey to Employee, in order to operate its Prof-Finders academic referral centers (the "Center"); and

WHEREAS, Franchisor and Franchisee desire to protect said Confidential Information and trade secrets from disclosure and unauthorized use by the Employee.

NOW, THEREFORE, in consideration of the employment of Employee by Franchisee and the mutual promises and covenants herein contained, and other valuable consideration the receipt and sufficiency of which is hereby acknowledged, the parties hereto, intending to be legally bound, hereby agree as follows:

A. *Covenant Not to Compete.*

Employee specifically acknowledges that due to its employment by Franchisee, Employee will receive valuable, specialized training and Confidential Information [as that term is defined in Paragraph _____of the Franchise Agreement] and information regarding academic referrals, operational, sales and marketing methods and techniques of Franchisor and its System. Employee covenants that during the term of his employment and subject to the post-termination provisions contained herein, except as otherwise approved in writing by Franchisor, Employee shall not, either directly or indirectly, for himself or through, on behalf of, or in conjunction with any person, persons, partners, or corporation:

1. Divert or attempt to divert any business, customer, or employees of the Franchisor or Franchisee to any competitor, by direct or indirect inducement or otherwise, or do or perform, directly or indirectly, any other act injurious or prejudicial to the goodwill associated with Franchisor's Proprietary Marks and the System.

2. Employ or seek to employ any person who is at that time employed by Franchisor or Franchisee, by any other franchisee or developer of Franchisor, or otherwise directly or indirectly induce such person to leave his or her employment.

3. Own, maintain, engage in, be employed by, advise, assist, invest in, franchise, or have any interest in any business which is the same as or substantially similar to that of the Franchisor or Franchisee.

Employee covenants that, except as otherwise approved in writing by Franchisor, Employee shall not, for a continuous uninterrupted period commencing upon the expiration of termination of his employment with Franchisee, regardless of the cause for termination, and continuing for _____(__) years thereafter, either directly or indirectly, for himself or through, on behalf of, or in conjunction with any person, persons, partnership, or corporation, own, maintain, engage in, be employed by, advise, assist, invest in, franchise, make loans to, or have any interest in any business that is the same as or sub-

Figure 8-2. continued

stantially similar to that of the Franchisor or Franchisee and that is located within a radius of _____(__) miles of the Franchisee's Designated Territory, or the location of any Center operated under the System [as that term is defined in the Franchise Agreement] that is in existence on the date of termination of Employee's employment relationship with Franchisee. Employee acknowledges and agrees that these covenants will survive the termination of his employment. This Section shall not apply to ownership by Employee of less than a five percent (5%) beneficial interest in the outstanding equity securities of any publicly held corporation.

B. *Nondisclosure and Confidentiality.*

1. Franchisor and Franchisee may make available to Employee certain designated materials, operational techniques, and information pertinent to the franchise being operated by the Franchisee pursuant to the Franchisor's System and Proprietary Marks.

2. Employee acknowledges and agrees that all materials and information shall be used solely for the purposes of conducting his duties as an employee of the Franchisee's Center.

3. Employee agrees to hold in strict trust and confidence all such materials and information that the Franchisor or Franchisee furnishes or otherwise makes available to Employee.

4. Neither the Employee nor his/her relatives, agents, or representatives will use such material or information for any purpose other than stated herein and shall not copy, reproduce, sell, reveal, or otherwise disclose any such materials and information to any persons or parties.

5. Employee shall not be subject to the restrictions imposed herein with respect to any information or data obtained by it from the Franchisor or Franchisee during his employment with Franchisee if the information or data:

(a) was known to the Employee or has been independently developed by the Employee at the time of the receipt of the proprietary materials and information thereof from the Franchisor or Franchisee; or

(b) was or hereafter is obtained by Employee from another source; however, the burden of proof shall rest on the Employee to demonstrate that such information or materials were not provided by the Franchisor or Franchisee.

C. Not an Employment Agreement.

Employee is being employed by Franchisee under separate arrangements that form no part of this Agreement. Franchisee is not obligated by this Agreement to continue to employ Employee for any particular time period, or under any specific terms or conditions. This Agreement does not create an employment relationship between Franchisor and Employee.

D. Severability.

The parties agree that each of the foregoing covenants shall be construed as independent of any other covenant or provision of this Agreement. If any or all portions of the covenants in this Section are held unreasonable or unenforceable by a court or agency having valid jurisdiction in an unappealed final decision to which Franchisor and Franchisee are parties, Employee expressly agrees to be bound by any lesser covenant subsumed within the terms of such covenant that imposes the maximum duty permitted by law, as if the resulting covenant were separately stated in and made a part of this Agreement.

E. Governing Law

This Agreement shall be construed in accordance with the laws of the State of _____, which law shall govern in the event of a conflict of laws.

Figure 8-2. continued

IN WITNESS WHEREOF, the parties have signed this Agreement and affixed their seals on the day and year above written.

Employee

_____

Prof-Finders

By:_____

Franchisee

_____

• Purchase a paper shredder and use it where appropriate.

• Restrict photocopying of documents and *prohibit* photocopying of confidential operations manuals. Use legends and maintain logbooks on the whereabouts of the original.

• Monitor the trade press and business journals for any news indicating a possible compromise and/or exploitation of your trade secrets by others.

• Conduct exit interviews with all employees who have had access to the franchisor's trade secrets. Remind them of their obligations not to use or disclose confidential and proprietary data owned by the franchisor, and of the costs and penalties for doing so. Notify the future employer in writing of these obligations, especially if it is directly or indirectly competitive. Conversely, in order to avoid litigation as a defendant, remind new employees of the franchisor's trade secret policies and that they are being hired for their skills and expertise, not for their knowledge of a former employer's trade secrets.

Confidentiality Provisions in the Franchise Agreement. An important component of the trade secret protection program is the franchise agreement. A properly drafted agreement should contain confidentiality provisions, covenants against competition (both in-term and post-termination), and obligations with respect to the use and care of the franchisor's proprietary operations manuals.

Provisions regarding the franchisor's proprietary operations manuals should contain the following:

- The franchisee will conduct its business in strict compliance with the operational systems, procedures, policies, methods, and requirements prescribed in the franchisor's manual(s) and any supplemental bulletins, notices, revisions, modifications, or amendments thereto.

- Franchisee acknowledges receipts of a copy of the franchisor's manual that has been provided *on loan* for the term of the franchise agreement. The franchisor should have an identifying number on each manual it distributes to franchisees, and franchisees should be required to sign a receipt acknowledging receipt of the manual(s).

- Franchisee acknowledges that the franchisor is the owner of all proprietary rights in and to the system and manual(s) and any changes or supplements to the manual(s).

- Franchisee acknowledges that all of the information contained in the manual(s) is proprietary and confidential and franchisee shall use all reasonable efforts to maintain such information as confidential.

- Franchisee acknowledges, knows, and agrees that designated portions of the manuals are trade secrets known and treated as such by the franchisor.

- The trade secrets must be accorded maximum security consistent with franchisee's need to make frequent reference thereto. Franchisees shall strictly limit access to the manuals to employees who have a demonstrable and valid "need to know" the information contained therein in order to perform their position and strictly follow any provisions in the manuals regarding the care, storage, and use of the manuals and all related proprietary information. The franchisor should reserve the right to designate which employees of the franchisee shall execute confidentiality agreements, in a form provided by the franchisor.

- Franchisee shall not at any time, without franchisor's prior written consent, copy, duplicate, record, or otherwise reproduce in any manner any part of the manuals, updates, supplements, or related materials, in whole or in part, or otherwise make the same available to any unauthorized person.

- The manuals at all times remain the sole property of franchisor. Upon the expiration or termination, for any reason, of the franchise agreement, franchisee shall return to franchisor the manuals and all supplements thereto.

- Franchisor retains the right to prescribe additions to, deletions from, or revisions of the manuals which shall become binding upon franchisee upon being mailed or otherwise delivered to franchisee, as if originally set forth therein. The manuals and any such additions, deletions, or revisions thereto, shall not alter franchisee's rights and obligations under the franchise agreement.

- Franchisee shall at all times ensure that its copies of the manuals are kept current and up-to-date, and in the event of any dispute as to the contents of the manuals, the terms contained in the Master Set (#0001) of the manuals maintained by franchisor at franchisor's headquarters shall be controlling.

- If one or more of the volumes comprising the manuals is lost, stolen, or destroyed, franchisee shall pay franchisor a nonrefundable replacement fee for replacement manuals.

Covenants of Confidentiality and Noncompetition. Every franchise agreement should contain covenants of confidentiality and noncompetition. Likewise, every key employee of the franchisee should be required to execute similar covenants of confidentiality and noncompetition. To ensure that franchisee's employees execute these agreements, franchisee should be obligated, by the terms of the franchise agreement, to obtain such an agreement from certain defined employees (i.e., managers). Those employees required to execute such agreements should be identified in the franchisor's manual. The employee Confidentiality and Noncompetition Agreement should name the franchisor as a third-party beneficiary of the agreement between franchisee and employee.

Misappropriation of Trade Secrets

The first step in protecting trade secret rights is to establish a duty of those who come in contact with the information not to disclose or use it in any way not in the best interest of the franchisor. There must generally be some duty established, which must be breached before a cause of action will arise. The only exception to this rule is wrongful misappropriation by improper means such as theft or bribery, ascertained according to applicable state criminal statutes.

The simplest way to create such a duty is by agreement. A franchisor should have a written employment agreement with each employee who may have access to the employer's trade secrets. The employment agreement should contain provisions regarding the nondisclosure of proprietary information as well as covenants of nonexploitation and noncompetition applicable to both during and after the term of employment. These covenants will be upheld and enforced by a court if they are reasonable, consistent with industry norms, and not overly restrictive. See Chapter 2 for a more detailed discussion of the covenants to be included in a typical employment agreement.

Agreements like these, as well as similar provisions in the franchise agreement, will go a long way toward proving to a court that the franchisor intended to and in fact took reasonable steps to protect the trade secrets in the event of any subsequent litigation. These agreements should only be the beginning, however, of an ongoing program to make the franchisee and franchisor employees mindful of their continuing duty to protect the trade secrets of the franchisor.

Proving an Act of Misappropriation

The key elements of a cause of action for misappropriation of trade secrets are:

1. Existence of a trade secret
2. *Communication* of it to the defendant
3. Misappropriation while defendant was in a *position of trust or confidence* (some duty not to disclose)
4. Information constituting the trade secrets *used* by the defendant to the *injury of the plaintiff*

In analyzing whether these essential elements are present, the court considers the following factors:

1. Was there any *relationship of trust and confidence,* either by express agreement or implied, that was breached?
2. How much time, value, money, and labor has been expended in developing the trade secret?
3. Had the trade secret reached the public domain? Through what channels?
4. Has the franchisor maintained a conscious and continuing effort to maintain secrecy (agreements of nondisclosure, security measures, etc.)?
5. What were the mitigating circumstances surrounding the alleged breach or misappropriation?
6. What is the value of the secret to the franchisor?

Remedies for Misappropriation

The most important and most immediate remedy available in any trade secret misappropriation case is the temporary restraining order and preliminary injunction. This remedy immediately restrains the unauthorized user from continuing to use or practice the trade secret, pending a hearing on the owner's charge of misappropriation. Prompt action is necessary to protect the trade secret from further unauthorized disclosure. If the case ever makes it to trial, the court's decision will address the terms of the injunction and may award damages and profits resulting from the wrongful appropriation of the trade secret.

Franchisors, however,should be aware that there are certain risks to evaluate before instituting a trade secret suit. The franchisors may face the risk that the trade secret at issue, or collateral trade secrets, may be disclosed during the course of the litigation. Certain federal and state rules of civil procedure and laws of evidence will protect against this risk to a limited extent. The franchisor should also consider that trade secret law is very unsettled and often turns on the facts of each case. Establishing the "paper trail" needed to prove all of the elements of misappropriation may be virtually impossible in some cases. Such lengthy litigation is likely to be prohibitively expensive for the average early-stage franchisor. This is all the more reason why preventive and protective measures are a far more attractive alternative than litigation.

Copyrights

The legal basis for copyright protection is found in the United States Constitution, which empowers Congress to enact legislation to promote the progress of science and the useful arts by securing for limited times to authors and inventors the exclusive right to their respective writings and discoveries.

Congress, pursuant to the power granted by the Constitution, has enacted the Copyright Revision Act (the "Act") which provides protection to all "original works of authorship fixed in any tangible medium of expression." This definition includes not only literary materials but also pictorial, graphic, and sculptural works. Operations manuals, promotional and advertising materials, training films and videos, forms, architectural plans, and computer programs typically developed and used by franchisors are copyrightable work within the definition of the Act.

Protections Afforded to Owner of Copyright

The Act provides protection from the following to the owner of a copyright in an original work:

1. Unauthorized reproduction
2. Preparation of derivative works
3. Distribution of entire or partial copies of the work
4. Infringement

A copyright protects only the *expression of an idea,* not the idea itself. A copyright protects only the original labor of the author that gave substance to the idea, not the underlying abstract idea or concept of the author. Once copyright ownership is established, it may be transferred or licensed to others.

How to Obtain Copyright Protection

According to the Act, copyright protection arises *as soon as the work is created and fixed in a tangible medium* of expression. The work need not be registered prior to its publication; however, registration is necessary so that the author may commence legal proceedings against infringers. The right to sue for infringement includes the ability to obtain injunctive relief and damages. Therefore, materials are protected, *without registration,* provided they contain the required statutory notice of copyright (as described below). Prior to registration, it is advisable to examine whether registration would compromise the confidentiality of the trade secrets contained in the work. For example, the contents of a new marketing brochure are a natural candidate for copyright registration; however, the contents of a confidential operations manual should not be registered due to its proprietary nature.

The author of a work protectable by copyright must use a notice of copyright, which puts the world on notice that the author claims the work as a copyright. The prescribed notice consists of (1) © or the word *copyright* or the abbreviation *copr.*, (2) the year of first publication of the work, and (3) the name of the copyright owner.

Work Made for Hire

Typically the author of the work is the owner of the copyright. Under the doctrine of "work made for hire," works developed by an employee are considered to be works owned by the employer. Whether copyright materials prepared by an employee or outsider are the property of the employer depends on whether the work is considered "work made for hire." The Act defines "works made for hire" as follows:

1. A work prepared by an employee within the scope of his or her employment
2. A work specially ordered or commissioned for use as a contribution to a collective work, as a part of a motion picture or other audiovisual work, as a translation, as a supplementary work, as a compilation, as an instructional text, as a test, as answer material for a test, ". . . if the parties expressly agree in a written instrument signed by them that the work shall be considered a work made for hire. . . ."

A "work made for hire," therefore, must either be prepared by an "employee" or fit within one of the nine narrow categories enumerated in subsection 2 above.

All materials used by the franchisor that constitute "original works" may be protected by the Act. Registration is advisable for all major nonproprietary works that are an integral part of a franchise system, and the appropriate notice must appear on all such products.

9

Managing Disputes

Conflict in a franchise system between the franchisor and franchisee is inevitable. Resolving conflicts with franchisees, however, is an expensive and time-consuming process that can significantly impede the growth of a franchisor as well as distract the franchisor from the attainment of its business objectives. In my experience, protracted litigation yields no winners, only successful or unsuccessful litigants.

As a result, most franchisors prefer to engage in battle in the marketplace or in the boardroom rather than in the courtroom. Nevertheless, there are instances when an amicable resolution or settlement of a conflict seems unattainable. If a dispute with a franchisee or prospective franchisee matures into a courtroom battle, franchisors must understand the fundamental rules of litigation as well as alernate means of resolving disputes.

Problems Leading to Litigation

Inherent in the franchisor-franchisee relationship is a certain level of tension: The franchisor has invested a great deal of time, effort, and money in establishing a business format franchise. This involves quality control guidelines that must be followed. The franchisee, on the other hand, often desires to be his own boss and resists any such restrictions. The tension can often create an exciting and dynamic atmosphere that enables both parties to achieve their goals: growth for the franchisor and independence and satisfaction for the franchisee.

In many instances, however, the tension that is part and parcel of every franchise relationship leads to conflict and strife that distract the parties from their common objectives.

Ten Common Areas of Conflict

It is critical for franchisors to recognize and understand the problems that typically give rise to litigation and attempt, and if at all possible, to resolve these in an effort to avoid legal action. Following are ten areas in which conflict commonly arises:

Franchisee Recruiting. A franchised operation is only as strong as the franchisee operating it. The franchisor must carefully evaluate and screen prospective franchisees to ensure that only qualified individuals are accepted. Because the initial franchisees in a system set the tone for and establish the criteria for later applicants, it is essential that the first franchisees be carefully scrutinized to ensure they have the financial background and experience to successfully operate a franchise. The applicant should possess the requisite financial strength to meet the demands that can reasonably be expected to arise in a franchised business, including sufficient working capital for payroll, rent, unexpected complications, product purchases, taxes, and so on. Ideally, the candidate should have a background in some business similar to or compatible with the franchised business or other sufficient experience as a business owner or manager. The intangible factors that contribute to a franchisee's success such as motivation, loyalty, and commitment are, of course, almost impossible to evaluate from a written application and the franchisor should at a minimum speak with the applicant's references and his or her current employer, if there are any. A franchisee's level of motivation can also be evaluated by analyzing the franchisee's ownership interest or risk in the enterprise. A franchisee who is gambling with someone else's money will be far less committed to the business than the franchisee who has invested his or her own hard-earned dollars and personal savings. A franchisor can also learn a great deal about an individual simply through the initial screening process. An applicant who is hostile, contentious, and untruthful in the interview and negotiation process will in all likelihood be hostile, contentious, and untruthful as a franchisee. It is almost inevitable that such a franchisee will cause discord and dissension that may lead to litigation.

Many franchisors have discovered that claims of fraud, misrepresentation, and mistake commonly grow out of misunderstandings in the recruiting and sales process. Franchisors or their sales staff unintentionally make comments about other franchisees who have earned certain sums of money, and the prospective franchisee views this as a guarantee of a certain dollar amount. The sales staff may promise assistance and support that the franchisor does not commonly offer. These misunderstandings typically lead to litigation. In fact, a recent Indiana district court decision (which was later reversed) held that General Foods, the parent of Burger Chef, had made actionable misrepresentations to its franchisees that it planned to actively develop and promote its restaurant system when in fact General Foods planned to sell Burger Chef to Hardee's. Such comments in the sales process may go beyond mere puffery or inflated sales talk into the realm of fraud.

Although it is understandable that emerging franchisors are anxious to make sales, this eagerness should not be allowed to displace the franchisor's need for careful scrutiny of applicants and prudent communications with those prospective franchisees. In this regard, franchisors should take heed of the adage "If you want it badly, that's exactly how you'll get it."

Site Selection and Territorial Rights. Even the best franchise in the world cannot take root and flourish in a humble location. The franchise agreement typically imposes a duty on the franchisee to select a site for the location of the business. Often the franchisor lends some amount of assistance in this site selection process and invariably has the right to reject a site located by the franchisee. A franchisor should develop criteria to assist in the determination whether a site selected by the franchisee is acceptable. Some of the factors considered by franchisors in such a determination include size of the site, suitability of the location and surrounding area for the type of business being franchised, adequate parking, costs of development, zoning and traffic patterns, proximity and access to major thoroughfares, compatibility with other businesses in the area, and proximity to competing businesses.

Franchisees often expect a great deal of assistance in site selection and are quick to demand compliance with the terms of agreements that bind the franchisors to offer that support. For example, Avis Service, Inc., a subsidiary of the rental car company, has been besieged by recent lawsuits that allege that Avis has failed to help franchisees find sites for quick-lube businesses and rejects sites found by the franchisees as being too expensive or unsuitable. In many instances the franchisees have demanded refunds and have alleged fraud and misrepresentation. Franchisors must ensure that site selection staff fulfill their obligations to find and develop suitable locations and guard against oversaturation of the market.

Typically, a franchisee will be granted an exclusive area or territory within which to operate the business. So long as the franchisee performs its obligations under the franchise agreement, the franchisor will not establish any other franchises in this territory. The territory is often defined by population or some geographical criteria such as zip code or a certain radius area around the franchised business. While franchisors may be tempted to offer existing franchisees a right of first refusal to expand into adjacent or surrounding territories, such a right places burdensome restrictions on the franchisor, who is then precluded from selling in certain areas unless time-consuming and complicated notice procedures are followed. A franchisor's failure to strictly follow a right of first refusal and provide the appropriate notice to an existing franchisee who has been granted such a right will surely lead to litigation, and courts zealously and quite rightly protect these rights.

Another area of conflict is the operation of company-owned stores or businesses that will invariably compete with those owned and operated by franchisees. A Kentucky Fried Chicken franchisee has sued its franchisor for allegedly opening a company-owned restaurant too close to the franchisee's store in violation of a provision in the franchise agreement that guarantees that each franchisee will have a protected radius of one-fourth mile. Unless expressly allowed by the franchise agreement, the establishment of a company-owned store in a franchisee's territory will lead to the argument by a franchisee that the franchisor has breached its duty of good faith and fair dealing and has deprived the franchisee of the benefit of its bargain with the franchisor.

Similarly, direct or indirect competition within the territory by a franchisor is subject to scrutiny. Franchisees at Haagen-Dazs ice cream stores recently sued Pillsbury Co., alleging that Pillsbury aggressively sold its Haagen-Dazs brand in grocery stores, competing with the franchised shops. However, the language in the franchise agreement allowed the company to distribute the ice cream products not only through the franchised shops but through other distribution methods. Because this language unequivocally gave the franchisor the right to market the products in the grocery stores, the court held that the franchisees had no reason to expect that distribution through the ice cream shops would be exclusively protected. Therefore, the language in the franchise agreement should be carefully drafted to allow a franchiser to open company-owned stores or sell the products through other market channels if it so desires.

Accounting Practices and Procedures. The franchise agreement will impose various requirements on the franchisee to provide records, reports, and accounting information to the franchisor. Such records are needed to enable the franchisor to determine whether royalties are being calculated correctly, whether contributions to funds for advertising are being paid on time, whether gross sales are accurately reported, and so forth.

A clearly written franchise agreement sets forth the manner and time of such reporting, for which the franchisor must act swiftly and efficiently to enforce the deadlines. As soon as a royalty or advertising payment is overdue or an accounting report is tardy, the franchisor should notify the franchisee and demand compliance with the appropriate provision of the franchise agreement. Repeated failures by the franchisee to pay or report and account may justify termination of the franchise agreement.

Franchisors should be vigilant in observing and documenting these defaults because they may be warning signs of a failing franchisee in need of extra supervision and monitoring. Failure to properly and timely notify a franchisee may result in an assertion by the franchisee that the franchisor has given up or waived its right to insist on timely compliance with payment and record-keeping deadlines.

Misuse of Advertising Funds. Many franchisors require an advertising fee to be paid by all franchisees that is to be used for regional and/or national promotions and advertising programs. Fees paid into the advertising fund should be kept separate from the funds used by franchisors for their operating expenses and kept separate from the funds allocated toward advertising by the franchisor to attract new franchisees. Franchisors who experience temporary financial difficulties are often inclined to "borrow" from the advertising fund until their financial condition improves. Such "borrowing" will give rise to litigation based on the failure of the franchisor to use the funds for the specified purposes.

A recent California case focuses on this very issue. Thirty-six franchisees have sued Pioneer Take Out, the fast-food restaurant franchise, alleging, among other claims, that various rebates and allowances received by the franchisor when it purchased supplies and food products were not deposited into the advertising fund as required. The franchisees have further alleged that Pioneer, without informing the franchisees, has used their advertising contributions to pay advertising bills incurred by Pioneer prior to the date the franchisees purchased their franchises. The litigation is expected to be protracted and expensive. The temptation to use the advertising fund as a ready source of capital can be eliminated by establishing separate accounts and an advertising committee composed of franchisees as well as key members of the franchisor's management team.

Supervision and Support. While franchisees are usually independent individuals who desire to operate a business for themselves, they are also attracted to franchising because of the guidance and support offered by a franchisor who offers an established and proven business concept. A successful franchisor not only meets the contractual commitments established by the franchise agreement but typically goes beyond the agreement to offer additional support and supervision to the franchisees. This increased support results in two bonuses to the franchisor: The supervision alerts the franchisor to difficulties a franchisee may be having and demonstrates the franchisor's commitment to the system (which never hurts when prospective franchisees are talking to existing franchisees). While overzealous supervision by a franchisor is usually not needed and in fact may interfere with a franchisee's ability to run the business, maintaining routine phone contact and making occasional visits to the franchisee's place of business shows a willingness to assist with problems and an assurance that the franchisor is committed to the franchisee's goals.

A lack of such support often leads to conflict in the system and ultimately to litigations, as seen in the Pioneer case previously discussed and in which the franchisees have also alleged that the franchisor has diverted the chains' operating capital to other ventures and has failed to develop new products or support the franchisees. This contention is increasingly being leveled against franchisors. Franchisees are likewise alert to spinoffs, mergers, and other restructuring attempts by franchisors and view them as an abdication of the franchisor's duty to offer assistance and support. Burger King franchisees successfully blocked an attempt in 1988 by Pillsbury to spin off the Burger King franchise system as a defense against a takeover bid. Franchisees of the Diet Center system have sued the weight loss company following its leveraged buyout, which allegedly resulted in a 41 percent increase in royalty fees. When Marriott tried to sell its Straw Hat Pizza chain to Pizza Hut, many of the franchisees broke away and became their own franchisor by forming a cooperative. These disputes all arose out of a perceived lack of support and guidance by the franchisor and a fear that the franchisees would be burdened with a debt-ridden and undercapitalized new franchisor.

Support by the franchisor can be made available through regular meetings and seminars, newsletters, conventions, retraining programs, and the dissemination of published materials related to the franchised business.

Franchisors should respond promptly and in writing to specific questions and concerns of franchisees. Failure to respond to and manage the franchisees will not make the problem go away but will only compound it by creating an adversarial relationship between the parties. In this regard, franchisors should not attempt to interfere with or impede franchisees' efforts to form a franchisee association and, in fact, many states specifically declare any such interference to be unlawful.

Franchisors can also support franchisees by offering to provide management consulting services for special projects or general assistance at specified fees.

Communication between the parties and support and assistance offered by the franchisor serve not only to promote harmonious relations between the franchisor and franchisee but negate any argument that the franchisor was interested only in the initial franchisee fee and not in a long-term and mutually satisfactory relationship.

Quality Control. The essence of a successful franchisor is the protection of its business format, image, trademarks, the quality and nature of the goods and services sold, and the uniformity of its business operations. The franchisor must strictly protect and defend these interests; failure to do so will result in a weakened system with no identifiable image. Franchisors with a need for increased revenues are often tempted to force a franchisee to purchase goods, services, supplies, fixtures, equipment, and inventory from the franchisor on the basis that such items are integral to the franchisor's system and cannot be obtained elsewhere. Because courts strictly scrutinize such franchisor requirements, many franchisors no longer sell supplies but rather regulate the items franchisees purchase by requiring that franchisees utilize suppliers approved by the franchisor or purchase in accordance with specifications designated by the franchisor. Many franchisors pass through to the franchisees any discounts or rebates received by the franchisor from its suppliers. This practice greatly allays any misgivings the franchisee may have that the franchisor is profiting on items that can be easily obtained from other suppliers at a lower cost. One of the issues in the Pioneer Take Out litigation was an allegation by the franchisees that the franchisor was charging an excessively high price for one of its special product mixes. Likewise, a change in the product mix of Steve's Home-Made Ice Cream has resulted in litigation by a franchisee that alleged fraud and breach of contract.

Franchisors need to be watchful to ensure that franchisees do not substitute unapproved goods or items in place of those that meet the franchisor's quality control standards. Such action by franchisees erodes the goodwill and regional or national recognition that distinguish the franchised business from other business, and if not stopped by the franchisor will signal to other franchisees that the franchisor is not interested in protecting their investment in the system.

Unequal Treatment. While some circumstances may justify a decision by a franchisor to offer a benefit to one franchisee only, such as a grace period for the payment of royalties in the event of financial trouble, such advantages should be offered sparingly and only after a thorough analysis of the situation. Franchisees expect the system to operate uniformly and any perceived arbitrariness or inequality in treatment will lead to resentment and hostility, especially when the favorable treatment is afforded to company-owned stores. In addition to creating an atmosphere of tension, any deviation by the franchisor from established operating procedures will also raise the issue whether the franchisor has waived or foregone the right to demand compliance with the franchise agreement.

Just as some franchisees should not be singled out for more favorable treatment than others, those franchisees who are difficult and demanding should not be subjected to any form of treatment that could be viewed as retaliation or discriminatory. Any defaults or breaches of the franchise agreement by troublesome franchisees should be carefully documented and should be handled strictly in accordance with the franchise agreement. Franchisees who have made valid complaints against the franchisor or the system may not be subjected to any practice that a court would interpret as a reprisal for exercising their contractual rights. Such retaliatory treatment by franchisors leads only to litigation and further disruption of the system.

Transfers by Franchisees. A franchisee who wants to sell the franchised business should be assisted by the franchisor because an unhappy or unmotivated franchisee is unproductive and weakens the system. The franchisor may be able to steer potential buyers to the franchisee or might even consider purchasing the location and operating it as a company-owned store until a suitable purchaser can be found. The decision to purchase a franchisee's business, however, should be carefully evaluated by the franchisor because word of the repurchase will invariably spread to other franchisees, who may believe that such a practice is the established policy of the franchisor and an absolute right of a disgruntled or noncomplying franchisee. In the event a franchisee presents a prospective purchaser to the franchisor for approval, the franchisor must ensure that the purchaser satisfies the selection criteria established for all applicants. In a recent case involving the transfer of a Baskin-Robbins franchise, the court held that a "reasonableness" requirement should be read into the franchise agreement and the franchisor should not be allowed to arbitrarily reject a transfer without reference to some reasonable and objective standards. If the purchaser fails to meet such objective standards and fails to qualify, a written notification should be provided to the franchisee which explains the rejection and its basis.

Training for Franchisor's Management and Sales Team. Many of the problems that lead to litigation are caused by improperly trained members of the franchisor's staff. Salespeople are so eager to make a sale that the FTC regulations relating to the provision of the offering documents to the prospective franchisee at least ten days before the signing of the franchise agreement are sometimes ignored. On other occasions the salespeople make claims to prospective franchisees regarding anticipated earnings or bind the franchisor to a new contract term such as a lower initial franchise fee or payment of the fee in installments. While such acts might not be directed or authorized by the franchisor, the principles of agency law may result in the franchisor being bound by such acts performed by these agents. Therefore, it is critical that the franchisor have in place a training and compliance program to instruct the management and sales team with regard to the FTC requirements and the franchisor's philosophy and goals. Often legal counsel for the franchisor will participate in training and instructing the franchisor's staff. Form letters and checklists should be developed for routine transactions. Managers or salespeople who are "loose cannons" should be dealt with firmly to ensure that they do not "give away the store" in an effort to make a sale or retain a franchisee.

Documentation. While the goal of every successful franchisor is to manage the business rather than to manage disputes, when disputes arise the franchisor should be well-prepared to discuss and resolve the conflict. This cannot be accomplished unless the franchisor has kept adequate records, including notes of all conversations, telephone message slips, memos reflecting understandings reached at meetings, correspondence between the franchisor and franchisee, copies of all documents provided to or received from the franchisee, and copies of all inspection reports and notices to the franchisee. The franchisor should develop procedures for such record

keeping and file management and designate a reliable individual to assume responsibility for it. Meetings with a troubled
franchisee should be attended by at least two of the franchisor's employees to verify the nature of the meeting and what
was said.

Dealing With the Danger Signs

The problems described above are all areas of conflict that typically lead to litigation. It should be apparent that the common
thread running through all of these problems is lack of or poor
communication with the franchisee and inadequate documentation to support the franchisor's position. There are, however,
several warning signs such as those listed below in Figure 9-1
which are often seen in troubled franchisees and which
should be noted and managed by the franchisor before they
erupt into a need for legal intervention.

Litigation Planning and Strategy

If and when a franchisor determines that litigation is the most
sensible and efficient way to resolve a business dispute or
when a franchisee brings suit, the franchisor must develop
plans and strategies in light of the following principles:

- The franchisor must develop goals and objectives and
communicate them to legal counsel. A broad strategy such as
"kick the franchisee out" is not sufficient. Rather, counsel
must be made aware of any specific business objectives, bud-
getary limitations, or time constraints that affect the franchisor
well before the litigation is initiated.

- The franchisor must gather all documents relevant to
the dispute and organize them in advance of the time that the
opponent serves the first discovery request.

- The franchisor should explore alternative methods of
dispute resolution, clearly define parameters for settlement,
and communicate them to legal counsel.

Figure 9-1. Warning signs of troubled franchisees.

Danger Signal	Franchisor's Action
1. Late payment or non-payment of royalties	Notice of default to be followed by termination, if default is not remedied
2. Cancellation of franchisee's insurance by insurance company	Notice of default and if not remedied, procurement of policy by franchisor who assesses franchisee for said payment
3. Steadily declining royalties	Meet with franchisee to discuss problem, increase advertising, perform an audit to ensure reporting of sales is accurate
4. Complaints by franchisee's customers	Meet with franchisee, retrain franchisee and/or franchisee's staff, send "test" customers to franchisee's place of business to monitor and ensure compliance
5. Inability to contact or communicate with franchisee	Increase supervision of franchisee and make frequent unannounced visits to franchisee's business
6. Use of unauthorized products or unapproved advertising	Notice of default, retraining, and termination of franchise if default is not remedied
7. Standards of cleanliness and hygiene not followed	Notice of default and increased supervision of franchisee, including sending "test" customers to franchisee
8. Misuse of franchisor's proprietary marks	Notice of default and termination of franchise if default is not remedied after notice

9. Understaffing of fran- chisee's business	Increase supervision and in- spections and retrain fran- chisee and franchisee's staff
10. Unhappy or troubled franchisee	Increase communication with franchisee and offer to meet to resolve conflict

- The franchisor should discuss with legal counsel the risks, costs, and benefits of entering into litigation.
- The franchisor should review with counsel the terms of payment of legal fees (as well as those of any experts needed).
- The franchisor should review the terms of its insurance policies with its risk management team to determine whether there is insurance coverage for its defense costs or any judgment rendered against the franchisor.
- The franchisor should develop a litigation management system for monitoring and controlling costs.
- The franchisor should maintain clear lines of communication with legal counsel throughout all phases of the litigation and should appoint a responsible individual to serve as a liaison with counsel.

While litigation of franchise disputes does not significantly differ from litigation of other matters, the decision to resolve a dispute through litigation must be based on a genuine understanding of the legal rights, remedies, and defenses available. For example, suppose that a franchisee has stopped paying royalties with the argument that payment of royalties is excused by the franchisor's failure to provide adequate field support and supervision. Before filing a complaint to terminate the agreement, the franchisor should carefully review:

- Alternative methods for resolving the dispute
- The elements of proving a breach of the franchise agreement in the jurisdiction that governs the agreement

- The defenses that will be raised by the franchisee, such as lack of field support and supervision
- The perceptions and opinions of the other franchisees regarding this litigation
- The direct and indirect costs of litigation
- The damages that may accrue if a breach is successfully established
- The probability that the location can be easily sold to a new franchisee if the franchise agreement is terminated

Only after the franchisor is satisfied that the answers to these issues indicate that litigation is a viable alternative should formal action be pursued. Similarly, if the franchisor is sued by a franchisee, it should attempt to resolve the dispute before responding with a formal answer.

The Mechanics of Litigation

Suppose that Prof-Finders institutes legal action against Ziggy Freud for nonpayment of royalties. Prof-Finder's first step is to prepare and file a complaint. In the complaint, each allegation is stated in a separate paragraph and written in a clear and concise manner, with any necessary exhibits attached. Allegations should relate to a claim on which Prof-Finders is entitled to relief, and the complaint must make a demand for judgment.

If the complaint meets all statutory and procedural requirements, the clerk of the court then prepares a summons, which is served with the complaint on Mr. Freud. Usually a licensed or registered process server will serve the necessary papers on Ziggy and will file an affidavit with the court indicating the date, time, and place of service. The summons directs Ziggy to file an answer to Prof-Finder's complaint, usually within twenty days after service of process is made.

As an alternative to filing an answer, Ziggy may file certain preliminary motions. These motions, specific requests for the court to act, include motions to dismiss the complaint due to the lack of jurisdiction, improper service of process, etc.;

motions to dismiss due to failure to state a claim on which relief can be granted; motions to strike all or part of Prof-Finder's complaint; or motions for a more definite statement of Prof-Finder's claims. Once an answer is filed, the right to make these motions is usually waived.

An answer must contain three principal components:

1. Admission of any allegations in the complaint that are true
2. Denial of any allegations that Ziggy believes to be untrue
3. Allegation of any affirmative defenses to the claims brought by Prof-Finders

Ziggy must also file any counterclaims he may have against Prof-Finders arising out of the same transaction. Failure to raise such claims will result in a waiver by Ziggy.

If Ziggy does not file a response in the time allotted, Prof-Finders may obtain a default judgment for the amount requested.

The complaint, answer, and any counterclaims and answers to counterclaims are collectively referred to as the "pleadings."

Once all the pleadings and preliminary motions are filed, the parties begin the process of discovery. Discovery is a pre-trial procedure for obtaining information that serves a number of important functions, including the following:

- To narrow the issues that are actually in dispute
- To prevent surprises by allowing each party to find out the testimony, witnesses, and other evidence available for each issue in dispute
- To preserve information that may not be available at the trial, such as the statement of an ill witness
- To encourage resolution of the dispute prior to trial

Most information is discoverable, provided it is relevant and not subject to any category of evidentiary privilege.

(These privileges are usually limited to information exchanged between doctor and patient, attorney and client, priest and penitent, or husband and wife.)

Despite the benefits, discovery tends to increase significantly the legal fees and related expenses of the litigation.

The five principal discovery devices that are available to litigants are depositions, written interrogatories, requests for production of documents, physical and mental examinations, and requests for admissions (see Figure 9-2).

Once the discovery process is completed, litigation proceeds to the pretrial conference, the actual trial, the appeal, and any posttrial proceedings. Although a comprehensive discussion of the mechanics of a trial is beyond the scope of this book, it is safe to say that this process consumes two of a franchisor's most important resources: time and money. Therefore, when disputes with franchisees arise, franchisors should consider the various less expensive and less time-consuming alternatives to litigation.

Alternatives to Litigation

Franchise dispute litigation is invariably time-consuming and expensive and a franchisor might be portrayed by adverse counsel in a number of unflattering ways designed to engender the jury's support and emotion: as a huge impersonal corporate entity with no feeling for the small and defenseless franchisee; as a greedy corporate conglomerate interested in increasing its coffers at the expense of its loyal and diligent franchisees; as a vindictive and retaliatory entity motivated to get even with a franchisee that has merely exercised its contractual rights; or as a poorly managed business that has mishandled its affairs to the ruin of its franchisees. Because litigation involves these drawbacks and uncertainties, many franchisors seek to resolve their disputes with franchisees through alternative methods.

The many alternatives to litigation are broadly referred to as "alternative dispute resolution" (ADR) methods. Each method offers certain advantages and disadvantages that may make one process far more appropriate for resolving a partic-

Figure 9-2. Five commonly used discovery devices.

1. *Depositions.* A deposition is the pretrial examination and cross-examination by counsel of a witness under oath. The witness may be any person who has information relevant to the case, whether or not the witness is a party to the action. The written record of the deposition may be admitted at trial as evidence and may be used to impeach a witness whose testimony at trial is inconsistent with the prior deposition testimony. Depositions are usually the most productive discovery devices and are the most frequently used despite their cost, which may run as high as $1,000 per day of deposition testimony.

2. *Written Interrogatories.* An interrogatory is a written question that must be answered in writing, under oath, usually within thirty days of its receipt. Unlike depositions, interrogatories may be served only on parties to the litigation.

Most courts limit the number of interrogatories and the scope of the questions so that they are not overly burdensome and to prevent parties from engaging in mere "fishing expeditions" (i.e., asking questions without a specific reason, hoping to find useful information by chance). If a party objects to a specific interrogatory, it must state its grounds for refusing to answer. In such cases, the burden shifts to the proponent of the question to convince the court that the answer should be compelled.

An answer to an interrogatory may include a reference to a particular business document or set of records, provided that the other party is given an opportunity to inspect the documents. While interrogatories are less expensive than depositions, often the answers are provided or edited by the attorneys rather than the litigants and thus may not be as helpful as despositions.

3. *Requests to Inspect Documents or Land.* A party may request that another party produce and allow the inspection, copying, testing, or photocopying of business documents, tangible assets, financial books and records, or anything else that may be relevant to the litigation. Similarly, a party may request entry to the business premises of another party for the purpose

Figure 9-2. continued

of inspecting, photographing, surveying, or anything else that is relevant and not subject to an evidentiary privilege. These requests are limited to parties to the litigation, with the exception of a subpoena duces tecum, which is the demand to produce certain documents and records in connection with the deposition of a nonparty.

4. *Physical and Mental Examinations.* A party may request that another party submit to a physical and/or mental examination by a physician or psychiatrist. The mental or physical condition of the party, however, must be relevant to the dispute. The court will only grant such a request if good cause is shown, and it will usually limit the scope of the examination to the issues in controversy. This is the only discovery device that involves court intervention and is generally used in personal injury and paternity cases.

5. *Requests for Admissions.* A party may serve a request for admission on another party to authenticate specific documents, obtain the admission or denial of a specific matter, or confirm the application of a certain law to a given set of facts. Failure to respond to a request is deemed an admission. Therefore, the party upon which a request has been served must either deny the request, explain why it is unable to admit or deny, or file an objection to the request as improper within the specified period (usually thirty days).

If a party refuses to comply with discovery requests, the court may impose monetary sanctions, and in cases of willful or repeated refusals, the court may dismiss a plaintiff's complaint or enter judgment against a defendant.

ular dispute than another. Legal counsel can suggest the best ADR for each particular dispute.

Arbitration. Because franchise disputes often involve complex issues that are not readily disposed of and the issues arise in a business context that lacks jury appeal, many franchisors prefer to arbitrate rather than litigate and their agreements contain provisions requiring the submission of disputes to arbitration. These provisions are generally enforced by courts (assuming the party who seeks to arbitrate the dispute has not waived this right by an express statement or conduct that implies the party intends not to enforce the right to arbitrate).

There are many forms of arbitration. However, each is a process for parties in dispute to submit arguments and evidence in an informal and nonpublic fashion to a neutral person or persons who adjudicate their differences. The evidentiary and procedural rules are not nearly as formal as in litigation, and there tends to be greater flexibility in the timing of the proceedings and the selection of the actual decision makers.

Arbitration may be a voluntary proceeding that the parties have selected prior to any dispute. To help avoid litigation, ensure that arbitration clauses appear in all agreements with franchisees, especially the franchise agreement and any guaranty executed by a franchisee. These clauses should specify:

- The place of arbitration
- The method of selecting arbitrators
- Any limitations on the award that may be rendered by the arbitrator
- Which party will be responsible for the costs of the proceedings
- The enforceability of the arbitration award in court
- Any special procedural rules that will govern the arbitration

A key factor in arbitration is the question whether the arbitrator's decision will be binding or nonbinding. If both parties agree that the award will be binding, they must accept the results. Binding arbitration awards are usually enforceable by the local court, unless there has been a defect in the arbitration procedures.

The opinion rendered in a nonbinding arbitration is advisory only. The parties may either accept the result or reject the award and proceed with litigation. In this event, the parties have forgone any benefits of arbitration; it serves only as a dress rehearsal for a trial.

Another drawback of nonbinding arbitration is that after the award is made the losing party often threatens litigation (a trial de novo, or new trial) unless the monetary award is adjusted. Thus, the party that wins the arbitration is often coerced into paying or accepting less than awarded simply to avoid a trial after arbitration.

Unless the plaintiff, the defendant, and their legal counsel have specific rules and procedures in mind that will govern the arbitration, it is often best to follow the Commercial Arbitration Rules of the American Arbitration Association. To obtain copies of AAA rules and fees, write to the AAA at its national office, 140 W. 51st St., New York, NY 10020-1203, or call (212) 484-4000.

The services of the AAA are being utilized in disputes between franchisors and franchisees in ever-increasing numbers. In 1989 there was a 550 percent increase, representing 401 cases, over the mere 73 franchise disputes arbitrated during 1981. New York City had the largest number of arbitrated disputes in 1989 with 98 cases. This was followed by Los Angeles with 45 and nearby Orange County, California, with 30. The AAA has reported that this increase in caseload is expected to continue to rise with the growth of franchising. The franchisor-franchisee disputes arbitrated in the 35 AAA offices throughout the United States typically involve issues such as failure to pay fees or make reports, termination, territorial disputes, and failure to comply with contract provisions. Franchisors who wish to arbitrate disputes with franchisees may use the following clause recommended by the AAA:

> Any controversy or claim arising out of or relating to this contract, or the breach thereof, shall be settled by arbitration in accordance with the Commercial Arbitration Rules of the American Arbitration Association, and judgment rendered upon the award rendered by the arbitrator(s) may be entered in any court having jurisdiction thereof.

When AAA services are used, the plaintiff and the defendant are presented with a list of several AAA-approved arbitrators. Résumés of arbitrators are provided so the parties may select an individual experienced in the area of the dispute rather than rely on jurors who may not have the requisite business background to evaluate the various documents and testimony that will be introduced. The parties then will eliminate the arbitrators they prefer not to use until they select one who is mutually acceptable. A date for the arbitration is selected in a similar fashion. Arbitration under AAA rules is somewhat more formal than court-annexed arbitration but is still less rigid than a trial.

Court-annexed arbitration is court-ordered, nonbinding arbitration. The plaintiff and the defendant jointly agree on and select an arbitrator from a list of arbitrators on file with the court. The parties, therefore, can select an arbitrator who is an attorney with expertise in the area of the dispute. There usually is no fee or only a moderate fee.

In a jurisdiction in which the parties and attorneys know each other, conflicts of interest can often arise, particularly when the attorney who will arbitrate has or has had a social or business relationship with one of the other attorneys. The arbitrator selected should then withdraw from hearing the matter unless both parties consent to his/her arbitration despite this relationship. In a smaller community, it may be extremely difficult to locate an experienced arbitrator who is unknown to both parties.

Because the arbitrator selected is usually an attorney whose expertise may be negotiating rather than adjudicating, arbitration often results in "splitting the baby down the middle," not providing a clear award for one party or the other. Additionally, because no jury is involved, there is a low likelihood of recovering punitive or exemplary damages from an attorney or experienced arbitrator who will take a dim view of appeals to emotion rather than reason. As a result, some franchisors prefer to specify in the franchise agreement that only certain kinds of disputes will be submitted to arbitration (e.g., disputes over nonpayment of monies owed to the franchisor), while other types of disputes (those that might result in punitive or exemplary damages or that require injunctive relief or have jury appeal) will be litigated.

Private Judging. In many communities, retired judges are available at an hourly fee (often as high as $250 per hour) to hear and resolve disputes. Parties may agree in advance whether the decision will be legally binding.

The disadvantages of nonbinding arbitration also apply to nonbinding private judging. While private judging costs are substantially higher than court-annexed arbitration costs, private judging is considerably more flexible. A private judge may be retained without court intervention and without litigation first being instituted. The parties are free to select a judge and a mutually convenient date for the hearing. The hearing itself tends to be informal, and the rules of evidence are not strictly applied. The private judge often uses a settlement conference approach as opposed to a trial approach to achieve a resolution of the dispute.

Moderated Settlement Conferences. After litigation begins, a court may insist the parties participate in settlement discussions before a judge. If the court does not schedule a settlement conference, the parties can usually request one, often with a particular judge.

The attorneys are often required to prepare settlement briefs to inform the judge of each party's contentions, theories, and claimed damages. Parties, as well as attorneys, attend so the judge may explain his/her view of the case and obtain their consent to any proposed settlement. If a resolution is reached in the judge's chambers, the litigants often proceed to the courtroom so that the settlement (and the parties' consent to it) can be entered in the record to eliminate any further disputes.

Because moderated settlement conferences produce no out-of-pocket costs (other than attorney's fees), and information obtained or revealed is for settlement purposes only, they provide an excellent "last ditch effort" for resolving a dispute prior to trial.

Mediation. Mediation differs substantially from arbitration: An arbitrator renders a decision that is often binding; a mediator only makes suggestions or recommendations to resolve a dispute. Mediation costs are minimal and generally include only payment on an hourly basis to the mediator for his/her services. However, because the mediator has no authority to render a binding decision, the mediation process will only be effective if both parties are committed to achieving a voluntary resolution. The participants always have the ultimate authority in the mediation process, and they are free to reject any suggestion by the mediator.

Small Claims Matters. Matters that involve a small monetary amount (usually no greater than $2,500) are often best resolved in small claims court. Generally, litigants represent themselves and describe the dispute in an informal manner to a judge, who renders a decision at the time of the hearing. Court filing fees are moderate, and a trial date usually is set for within two or three months. Often a bookkeeper or credit manager may represent the franchisor as long as he/she is knowledgeable about the dispute and has supporting documentation.

Unfortunately, it is often difficult for a successful plaintiff to actually collect the judgment. Because of this, many courts have small claims advisers who can assist litigants in collecting the money awarded.

Part Three
Sales and Marketing Strategies

10

Developing Sales and Marketing Plans

At first blush, it would seem to be obvious that the heart of a successful franchise program is in the viability of the company's sales and marketing strategies. In fact, most early-stage franchisors are quick to recruit aggressive franchise salespeople well before they hire other key management positions, such as in the areas of operations, administration, and finance. Despite this commitment to marketing overall, if you were to ask most franchisors in this country to show you a recent copy of their formal franchise sales and marketing plan, you would see a dumbfounded expression on their faces. When asked how they go about selling franchises, they would respond, "Trade shows and advertisements in the Thursday edition of the *Wall Street Journal*."

These traditional approaches are simply not good enough in today's competitive and complex marketplace. Today's franchise sales and marketing plans require a genuine understanding of the needs and wants of the modern franchisee, a keen sense of target marketing, access to sophisticated databases, a detailed and well-designed strategic marketing plan, a well-educated sales team, and an ability to truly understand your competition. *The days of the fast-talking, leisure-suited, blue suede shoe franchise salesman are long gone.*

For the early-stage franchisor, the process of attracting

qualified leads and closing the sale is becoming increasingly more difficult. Some smaller franchisors have had such a tough time attracting qualified candidates that they have abandoned franchising altogether. Among the hurdles that young franchisors must overcome in the sales and marketing process are:

- A shrinking pool of qualified candidates who have the business acumen or financial resources to acquire some of today's "high ticket" retail and food franchises
- A growing competition to attract the qualified franchisee candidates as an increasing number of companies launch franchise programs each year
- A difficult time competing against larger and well-financed franchisors who can afford sophisticated media campaigns and marketing resources
- A fierce competition for quality retail sites, which is often won by the larger franchisors
- A reluctance by commercial lenders to extend financing to the franchisees of start-up franchisors
- A growing sense of prudence, skepticism, and cautiousness in the pool of qualified franchisees, as more and more reports of failing and failed franchisors (especially early-stage franchisors) find their way into the press
- A growing pressure to recoup the often significant sums spent for franchise development costs through franchise sales

The pressure to quickly achieve rapid franchise sales can result in lowering of the standards initially set to qualify a lead. Such a compromise will significantly lower the franchisee's likelihood of success, resulting in damage to the franchisor's goodwill and probably in litigation. Proper franchise sales and marketing requires *patience* and *planning*, two characteristics not often initially found among the entrepreneurs who are the pioneers of franchise systems.

Before examining the details of each component of a franchise sales and marketing plan, let's take a look at the critical factors in understanding the discipline of marketing.

What Is Marketing?

Marketing is the ongoing process of (1) determining the level of consumer demand for the company's products and services, (2) matching the company's strengths and weaknesses with the established demand, (3) delivering the products and services more effectively and more efficiently than do competitors, and (4) monitoring changes in consumer demand; industry trends; political, social, environmental, and legal issues; technology; and competition in order to ensure that the company's products and services remain competitive and consistent with consumer demand. In the context of franchising, this must always be done on two levels: (1) marketing to the prospective franchisee and (2) marketing to the prospective consumers of the franchisor's proprietary products and services.

Academics and consultants often identify the well-known "marketing mix" as the foundation of a marketing program. This mix is comprised of product, price, place, and promotion. All marketing plans and decisions stem from one or more of these components of the marketing mix. Some of the typical issues raised by each element of the marketing mix, as applied to franchising, are as follows:

Product
- What products and services will the franchisor offer to the consumer through its franchisees and company-owned centers?
- What are the various features, options, and styles that each product or service will include as being unique, of better quality, or proprietary?
- How will these products and services be packaged and offered to the consuming public?

- How will franchises be packaged to attract prospective franchisees?

Place
- In what manner will the franchisor's products and services be distributed to the marketplace? Dual distribution or exclusively through franchisees? Why has this strategy been selected?
- What are the various advantages and disadvantages of the distribution channels that are alternatives to franchising?
- In what geographic markets should the franchisor's products and services be offered? (determined through, e.g., demographics and population analysis, primary vs. secondary market studies, local competitor analysis, analysis of local and regional consumer habits) Will the franchisor be able to attract franchisees in these targeted markets?

Price
- What will consumers be willing to pay for the franchisor's products and services? How are prices determined? To what extent can price ranges be suggested to franchisees?
- What pricing policies will be developed with respect to discounts, credit terms, allowances, and introductory or special pricing schedules when products are sold directly by the franchisor to the franchisee? By the franchisees to the consumers? If the franchisor (or its franchisees) does engage in introductory or promotional pricing, have such policies been reviewed by legal counsel in connection with (1) Robinson-Patman Act considerations, (2) deceptive pricing regulations established by the Federal Trade Commission, or (3) prohibited predatory pricing practices?

Promotion
- What strategies will be implemented to ensure that targeted franchisees are aware of the franchisor's business format?

- What strategies will be implemented to ensure that the consuming public is *aware* of the company's products and services?
- What sales, advertising, and public relations plans, programs, and strategies will be adopted?
- How will human and financial resources best be allocated to these various advertising and promotional programs?

Key Components of the Marketing Program

The key components of a well-developed marketing program fall into three distinct stages: (1) marketing planning and strategy formulation, (2) implementation, and (3) monitoring and feedback. The balance of this chapter will be divided into these three stages.

Stage 1: Marketing Planning and Strategy Formulation

Effective marketing planning and strategy formulation typically fall into three distinct stages: marketing research, market analysis, and the development of a marketing plan. The activities of the management team during each stage are described below.

Marketing Research. Effective marketing planning begins with the development of a database of information regarding the history of the franchisor; its products, services, and personnel; trends in its industry; the size of its total marketplace; the characteristics of its typical customers and targeted franchisees; the strengths and weaknesses of its current competitors; and the various barriers to entry for prospective competitors. This information is typically the end result of *market research* that must be conducted prior to the development of a formal marketing plan. Market research need not be an expensive and time-consuming process for companies with minimal resources to devote to collecting data about the marketplace. There are essentially two types of data needed for conducting market research: external and internal. There are many sources of external data that are available virtually free of charge from state and local economic development agencies, chambers of commerce, trade associations such as the International Franchise Association, public libraries, local colleges and universities, and even federal agencies such as the Small Business Administration or the U.S. Department of Commerce. Internal sources of information include surveys; meetings with suppliers, customers, and the staff of the company in order to collect additional information regarding industry trends; consumer preferences; and the strengths and weaknesses of current marketing efforts.

Market Analysis and Segmentation. The information collected during the franchisor's market research must then be properly organized in order to be effective in the planning process. Unorganized data collected in a haphazard manner will have minimal benefit to the development of marketing plans and strategies. The end result of the marketing research should be a *market analysis,* which should include information on segmentation of the franchisor's targeted markets, trends within its industry, and an assessment of the franchisor's direct and indirect competitors. One of the key objectives of the market research is *segmentation* and *targeting* of the franchisor's market, which will serve as a starting point for market planning. Market segmentation is the process of dividing the total market into distinct groups of buyers based upon either demographic variables (e.g., age, income levels, gender, or race), geographic location of consumers, or even social-political trends and preferences. Market targeting is the evaluation and selection of one or more of these market segments toward which marketing efforts and resources will be directed. Once specific markets have been targeted, the franchisor must develop plans and strategies to *position* its franchise offering as well as its products and services in such a way as to attract these desired market segments. Market positioning involves manipulation of the elements of the marketing mix in order to effectively and efficiently reach the targeted consumer/franchisee.

Development of the Marketing Plan. A well-written marketing plan becomes the blueprint for the franchisor to follow in positioning its franchise offering as well as its products and services in the marketplace in order to meet its long-term growth objectives. The marketing plan becomes an integral part of the franchisor's overall strategic plan. And like strategic planning, marketing planning must be an ongoing process that will allow the franchisor to respond to changes in the marketplace, law, or technology so that its marketing strategies do not remain static or risk becoming quickly obsolete. Even more importantly, marketing planning must be *consistent* with the franchisor's overall strategies and objectives. Therefore, managers of *all* departments and at *varying levels* of the company must be involved in the marketing planning process and kept informed of marketing strategies as they are developed on an ongoing basis. For example, an aggressive marketing plan that is likely to triple the company's franchise sales should not be adopted without consulting the training and field support departments of the organization. Otherwise, neglected and improperly trained franchisees are likely to cripple the company.

Key Elements of the Marketing Plan. Naturally, the contents of a marketing plan vary for each franchisor in terms of topics to be addressed, relevant trends, extent of the market research, and resources that can be committed to the implementation of the plan. The elements of the plan vary from franchisor to franchisor depending on the specific industry in which the franchisor operates, the total cost of the franchise, and the desired profile of the targeted franchisee. Nevertheless, the following key components can and should be included in the marketing plan of franchisors of all types and sizes:

- *Executive summary.* This section should provide an overview of the principal goals and strategies that the market-

ing department of the franchisor plans to adopt. This summary should be distributed to all members of the franchisor's
management team for review and comment *prior* to time and
resources being devoted to the completion of the plan.

   ▪ *Assessment of the current state of affairs.* This section
must answer the classic planning question "Where are we and
how did we get here?" but this time from a marketing perspective. Although this section is primarily *historical* in nature, it
is also *analytical* because it must do more than simply tell a
story; it must also *explain* why the franchisor's marketing
strategies have evolved. This will often require a *marketing
audit*, which seeks to identify and assess current marketing
programs and strategies. This section should describe the franchisor's current products and services, the size and growth of
its marketplace, a profile of its current and targeted franchisees, and an assessment of its competitors. The importance of
competitive analysis should not be overlooked. Many entrepreneurs often make the statement "Our product/service is so
unique that we have no competition." Such a statement is very
dangerous and naive because it often reveals both a misunderstanding of the market as well as the likelihood of poorly
conducted market research. For example, suppose that a franchisor has developed a new form of recreational activity. To
the best of the franchisor's knowledge, no other company is
offering this activity to consumers, or this type of business
format to prospective franchisees. However, this could mean
that the franchisor has not conducted sufficient market research and/or that the company has not recognized that *all*
forms of recreation indirectly compete for the prospective
franchisee's investment income and/or the consumer's disposable income that will be allocated for leisure activities or investment in these types of businesses. Therefore, direct and
indirect competitors must be discovered through detailed
market research and then described in the marketing plan in
terms of size; financial strength; market share; sales and profits; product/service quality; and differentiation from the company's products and services, marketing strategies, and any

other characteristics that may be relevant to the development of a comprehensive marketing plan.

• *Discussion of current issues and opportunities.* This section should summarize the principal opportunities and threats, strengths and weaknesses, and issues and concerns that affect the franchisor's products and services as well as the market conditions affecting its ability to sell franchises. The principal question to be answered is "What market trends and factors should be exploited and what are the external/internal barriers that must be overcome before marketing strategies can be successfully implemented?" The "opportunities and threats" subsection should address the key *external* factors in the macroenvironment affecting the company's marketing strategies, such as legal, political, economic, or social trends. The exact impact of these trends will vary depending on the company's products and services. For example, a forthcoming recession could be a threat to automobile dealers because consumers will hold onto their cars longer, yet be an opportunity to a franchisor of miniature golf courses because market research has proved that consumers tend to spend even more money on low-cost entertainment during troubled economic periods.

The "strengths and weaknesses" subsection should address the key *internal* factors in the microenvironment affecting the franchisor's marketing strategies, such as resource limitations, research and development, organization structure and politics, protection of intellectual property, distribution channels, service and warranty policies, pricing strategies, and promotional programs. Once all of the strengths, weaknesses, opportunities, and threats have been identified, the last subsection, "issues and concerns," should discuss strategies and tactics for exploiting the franchisor's marketing strengths and compensating for its marketing weaknesses.

• *Marketing objectives and strategies.* This section should define the goals and objectives identified by the managers of the marketing department with respect to market share, advertising/promotion expenditures, franchise sales, and promotional methods. Strategies should then be discussed, outlining the specific steps and timetables involved to achieve marketing goals and objectives. Marketing strategy is essentially the "game plan" that must be adopted to achieve with respect to targeted markets, positioning of products and services, budgets for advertising, sales and public relations, and delegation of responsibility within the organization for specific projects. Because this section also involves dealing with sales and profitability projections, the franchisor's marketing staff must work closely with the finance department to ensure accuracy and consistency. As is true for all forms of planning, the statement of marketing objectives and strategies should be clear and succinct and not leave the reader (or user) hanging as to methodology. For example, a marketing objective of increasing franchise sales revenue by 10 percent could be achieved by increasing the franchise fee, increasing the total number of franchise units with the franchise fee structure remaining at current levels, or increasing fees and unit sales volume. Marketing managers must identify which course of action will be taken, based upon information ascertained from the market research as well as data and input received from other departments within the organization.

- *Execution of marketing program.* This section of the plan should set forth timetables for achieving specific goals and objectives, identify the persons who will be responsible for implementation, and project the anticipated resources that will be required to meet the goals developed.

- *Monitoring of marketing plans and strategies.* This section should discuss the establishment and operation of management systems and controls designed to monitor the franchise marketing plans and strategies implemented by the company. The relative success or failure of these programs should be measurable, so that performance can be properly assessed. Periodic reports should be prepared by the marketing department for distribution to other key members of the franchisor's management team.

- *Alternative marketing strategies and contingency plans.* This final section should address the alternative strategies available to the franchisor in the event of changes in the marketplace that have been identified in the plan. The ability to predict these positive or negative changes that may occur in the marketing plan and adopt alternative strategies in the event that they occur is at the heart of effective strategic marketing planning.

Remember that the marketing plan will continue to evolve and may be changed as often as monthly or be revised for specific targeted markets. The ability to quickly respond to consumer demands and prospective franchisee investment preferences is critical.

Stage 2: Implementation of the Marketing Program

Once market research has been conducted and a marketing plan prepared, the next step in the development of a marketing program is the actual *implementation* of the franchisor's objectives and strategies. At most growing franchisors, a separate marketing department is responsible for the implementation of the marketing plan.

The franchise marketing director and his staff must constantly interact with other departments, such as operations, finance, and administration as well as outside legal counsel in order to coordinate marketing efforts and to keep the marketing program consistent with the overall strategic plans and objectives of the franchisor. This will require the marketing department to establish certain procedures and controls to monitor marketing performance and to take corrective action where necessary to keep the franchisor on its course of growth and development. These periodic performance audits should also aim to make the franchisor more efficient by reducing unnecessary promotional expenditures and managing advertising costs.

Early-stage and growing franchisors typically experience

four distinct stages in the evolution of the department responsible for development and implementation of sales and marketing functions within the organization. At the inception of
the company, all founders are responsible for sales and marketing efforts. During this initial stage, marketing plans are
virtually nonexistent, marketing strategies are developed with
a "whatever works" approach and sales are to "anybody who
will buy" the franchise offered. Eventually, the founders of the
company are too busy with other demands to continue the
sales function, and as a result a professional franchise sales
staff is developed. As the franchisor reaches the third stage of
its growth, all sales and marketing efforts must be centralized
into a formal department. It is typically at this phase that formal marketing plans start being prepared by top marketing executives with guidance and input from managers of other
departments. As the franchisor experiences changes in its external and internal operating environment, the marketing
department experiences the fourth and final phase of reorganization, during which modifications in organizational structure are made in order to adapt and respond to these
environmental changes.

Developing the Franchise Sales Plan. As discussed in
Chapter 2, the responsibility for managing the franchise sales
program is typically vested with the vice-president of sales or
the director of franchise development. This individual is responsible for development of the *franchise sales plan,* which
is a critical step in the implementation of the overall marketing plan. The sales plan identifies the specific steps and resources required to attract prospective franchisees. Different
sales plans will need to be developed for each type of franchise offered by the company. For example, designing a program to attract a qualified prospect to serve as a subfranchisor
for the state of New York is quite different from attracting a
candidate for a single-unit franchise for the suburbs of Des
Moines.

The key to developing a successful franchise sales plan is
to ascertain a genuine understanding of the targeted franchi-

see. This requires the development of a detailed profile of the prospect, which includes an analysis of targeted age, gender, education, business sophistication, income levels, net worth, family size, health, communication skills, personality traits, hobbies, habits, and career objectives. Much of this information will be obtained through the use of a confidential franchise application and personal interviews. See Figure 10-1 for a sample franchise application. Many sophisticated franchisors have turned to detailed psychological testing methods as part of the qualification process for prospective franchisees. If the tests reflect a personality that resists following rules and procedures or lacks a certain attention to detail, then many franchisors will reject the candidate regardless of business acumen or financial net worth. There are a wide range of qualities and characteristics that franchisors look for in developing criteria for the appropriate type of franchisee. Naturally, the criteria vary from franchisor to franchisor and from industry to industry. Neither the know-it-all nor the naive are likely to make very good franchisees. Those who understand the importance of rules and procedures and display a willingness to follow them are likely to make the best franchisees. The franchisor is looking to attract those individuals whose personalities and experience are more suited to serve as sergeants, and not generals.

Once an accurate and objective set of criteria is developed for identifying the "model" franchisee, a sales plan must be developed to attract this prospect. Shots should always be fired with a rifle, not a canon. If experience has demonstrated that a model franchisee for your franchise system is an executive female, college-educated between the ages of 34 and 45, then an advertisement in *Working Woman* may be a better allocation of resources than an advertisement in *Inc.* magazine. The key elements of a franchise sales plan are as follows:

A. Introduction

    1. Description of the model franchisee
    2. Overview of the techniques and procedures to be imple-

(Text continues on page 230.)

Figure 10-1. Sample franchise application.

CONFIDENTIAL APPLICANT QUESTIONNAIRE

INTENTIONS AND EXPECTATIONS AS A
FRANCHISE OWNER

Why do you feel you are suited for the franchised business?

_____

_____

_____

What is your philosophy regarding the franchised business?

_____

_____

_____

What experience do you have?

_____

_____

_____

Do you feel that you possess the qualities necessary to:

1. Train and supervise staff members?
   [ ] Yes   [ ] No
2. Handle the everyday ongoing problems that arise in
   dealing with customers and staff?
   [ ] Yes   [ ] No

3. Handle the staff scheduling in both regular and flex-time modes?　　[ ] Yes　　[ ] No

Briefly explain why:

_____

_____

Who will operate the facility?

[ ] Self　　[ ] Spouse　　[ ] Other

Will one of you continue to work at your current place of employment after the franchise is awarded?　　[ ] Yes　　[ ] No

If yes, who?
[ ] Self　　[ ] Spouse　　[ ] Co-Applicant
[ ] Other

In what city, county, and state would you like to own a franchised business? Indicate first, second, and third choice.

City _____

County _____

State _____

How soon would you be available to operate the franchised business?

[ ] Immediately　　[ ] Within __ months

Do you now own any other franchises or business?

[ ] Yes　　[ ] No

If yes, please describe:

_____

Figure 10-1. continued

APPLICANT'S FINANCIAL INFORMATION

How do you plan to finance the acquisition of the franchise?

_____

_____

Do you anticipate the use of outside investors or commercial lenders?

_____

_____

_____

PLEASE ATTACH A COPY OF A RECENT PERSONAL FINAN-CIAL STATEMENT.

APPLICANT'S EDUCATION HISTORY

Dates of Attendance   School/College   Major/Degree

_____

_____

_____

CO-APPLICANT'S EDUCATION HISTORY

Dates of Attendance   School/College   Major/Degree

_____

_____

_____

APPLICANT'S EMPLOYMENT HISTORY

Dates From–To	Company	Position	Annual Income

CO-APPLICANT'S EMPLOYMENT HISTORY

Dates From–To	Company	Position	Annual Income

Other business affiliations (officer, director, owner, partner, etc.)

_____

_____

Have you ever failed in business or filed voluntary or involuntary bankruptcy?   [ ] Yes   [ ] No
(If yes, please list when, where, circumstances, including any remaining liabilities.)

_____

Are there any lawsuits pending against you?
[ ] Yes   [ ] No
If yes, please describe: _____

Figure 10-1. continued

Have you ever been charged with or convicted of a crime or act of moral turpitude?   [ ] Yes   [ ] No

If yes, please describe:_____

Are you a U.S. citizen?   [ ] Yes   [ ] No

If no, in which country do you hold a citizenship?_____

I certify that the information I have provided on this application, as well as the PERSONAL FINANCIAL STATEMENT attached hereto, is complete and correct. I hereby authorize the FRANCHISOR or its authorized agent to obtain verification of any of the above information and to conduct any necessary credit checks, and I authorize the release of such information to the FRANCHISOR or its authorized agent.

Signature of Applicant_____ Date_____
Signature of Applicant_____ Date_____

---

  mented to generate the maximum number of leads and prospects whose characteristics match those of the model franchisee

 3. Procedures for meeting, disclosing, and closing the sale
 4. Postclosing procedures

B. State of the Nation

 1. Why people buy franchises

  Job satisfaction in this nation has reached an all-time low. A wide variety of well-educated and financially secure executives and professionals lack the dreams and excitement they so sorely need to continue the daily grind. *Franchising offers these individuals an opportunity to be in business for themselves, but not by themselves.* It is an opportunity to be an entrepreneur, but without the risk and difficulty inherent in starting a nonfranchised business. For many of these individuals, franchising offers a happy compromise between being a middle-level executive paper pusher and a total maverick.

Once you understand *why* people buy franchises, you need to figure out why they will buy *your* franchise. A common misconception is that people currently operating within their industry are the best candidates for their franchise offering. Remember that considerably more frustrated accountants have purchased quick-lube and tune-up centers than have trained mechanics. With the notable exception of conversion franchising (e.g., Century 21), those with years of training and experience in a given industry are not likely to perceive the benefits of franchising in the same light as does a novice.

2. Why people buy your franchise

As a general rule, people will want to buy *your* franchise because of one or more of the following reasons:

a. They have an interest in your industry but lack the training skills to pursue this interest without assistance
b. They have a friend, relative, or business associate who is already a franchisee within your system
c. They have been consumers or employees of a franchise (or company-owned store) within your system and were impressed by the quality and consistency of your products and services
d. They were impressed by the quality and professionalism of your advertising matters, the integrity of your sales staff, and the excitement of your sales presentation

C. Lead Generation and Qualification

1. Selection of effective media and methods

a. *National/regional/local newspapers and magazines.* Direct advertising in specific publications with focuses such as business, income opportunity, general interest, topic-specific. Which are the most likely to attract the model franchisee? Which publications have rates within our budgets? How do we get the "biggest" bang for the buck? What should our advertisements say about the company? What image do we want to project?

b. *Direct mail.* Which mailing lists are readily available and most likely to contain a large number of our "model franchisees"? At what cost? Design of the marketing piece: What should the text say? What should the prospect's next step be? How often do we mail? Procedures for follow-up?

c. *Trade shows.* What is the quality of the trade show organizer and promoter? (I would strongly recommend the tradeshows sponsored by the International Franchise Association.) Of the facility? Of the average attendee? How elaborate should we make our booth? What type of promotional displays should be developed? How many people should we send? What literature should be available? How often should we participate? In what regions?

d. *Public relations.* What story do we tell to the media? What makes our franchise system and company different from the competition? How often do we send press releases? To whom? Saying what? When should we hold press conferences? For what events?

e. *Internal marketing.* Developing lead generation and incentive programs from the existing network of franchisees. Signs and brochures within the franchisee's facilities. Rewards to franchises and employees for generating qualified leads and actual franchise sales.

    f. *Miscellaneous sources of lead generation.* Leads for prospective franchisees can come from a variety of nontraditional sources such as military bases, college placement offices, local business organizations, outplacement offices of large corporations that have been "downsized," charitable organizations, personnel agencies, and investment clubs.

2. Procedures for qualifying a lead and making a presentation

    a. *Where and how should franchises be sold?* Avoid the motel bar; get the prospect to the franchisor's headquarters, if at all possible. Make prospects feel special once they arrive. Give them the red-carpet treatment and full-blown tour. Doors should be open, not closed. People should be smiling, not frowning.

    b. *Qualities of an effective franchise salesperson and presentation.* The sales staff should be there to *assist, not pressure,* the prospect. Remember that many prospects will base their decision more on personality traits of the salesperson than on the cold hard facts contained in the offering circular. The sales staff should *listen* to the *needs* and *questions* of the prospect; let the prospect make the decision to buy the franchise. The sales staff should be *confident, not pushy.* Franchises are *awarded, not sold.*

    c. *Data gathering on the prospect.* All relevant historical and financial data must be collected and verified. No detail should be overlooked. Employment and credit references should be checked carefully. Aptitude and psychological tests are commonplace and recommended. Carefully study the prospect, looking for any early warning signs of subsequent failure. A premium should be placed on the sales representative's "gut feel" assessment of the candidate's likelihood of success.

    d. *Materials and tools for the sales team.* Beyond the personal presentation, brochures, flip charts, and inspection of the franchisor's facilities, audiovisual materials are strongly recommended. Many franchisors have produced fifteen-minute videotapes designed to educate the prospect and help close the sale. *Legal compliance* (timing of disclosures, avoidance of unauthorized or improper earnings claims and misrepresentations concerning support and assistance, etc.) is *critical.* See Chapters 5 and 6.

D. Closing the Sale

    1. Stay in touch during the ten-day waiting period in order to offset the inevitable negative input, sweaty palms, and cold feet that the average prospect will be experiencing.
    2. Get all mystery and confusion regarding the rights and obligations of each party resolved *before signing the franchise agreement.*
    3. Consider the franchise closing *an event, not a mere procedure.* This is likely to be the biggest financial transaction of the prospect's life. Make it special.
    4. Stay in touch with the franchisee after execution of the franchise documents until formal training begins.

E. Managing the Sales Team

    1. Establishment of group and individual sales goals and objectives
    2. Timing and timetable for franchise sales
    3. Travel and promotional budgets to support sales efforts
    4. Personal, ethical, and professional expectations from

your sales team (no leisure suits, no gold chains, no lies, and no unauthorized earnings claims)

5. Reporting and record-keeping requirements (communications with prospects should be carefully documented; see Chapter 6)

6. Respect for prospect review and qualification procedures (data gathering and verification, committee approval, profile testing, etc.)

7. Ongoing sales and compliance training for the team (sales and closing methods and techniques, legal documents, etc.)

8. Coordination of efforts with other departments (operations, training, finance, legal, etc.)

9. Costs and benefits of the use of outside sales organization

Stage 3: Marketing Program Monitoring and Feedback

Once marketing and sales plans are developed and implemented, systems must be put into place that monitor the performance of the efforts of the sales and marketing department, as well as gather market and competitor intelligence. The market research division is usually responsible for acquiring data and intelligence, which are sometimes used as the first step in the development of the marketing plan and other times used in tracking the performance of marketing efforts in order to modify and refine marketing plans. Either way, systems must be developed to *gather and analyze the effectiveness of franchise sales and marketing efforts* as well as to study relevant market characteristics and trends affecting the franchisor's industry-competitive analysis and to monitor general business and economic, legal, political, and technological conditions. These intelligence-gathering systems are indispensable tools of a well-managed franchise marketing department and overall franchise organization.

A comprehensive monitoring and review system helps the franchise sales department to identify strengths and weaknesses of the plans and strategies initially adopted and implemented to attract prospective franchisees, measure the performance of those efforts, refine plans to adapt to changes in the marketing macroenvironment, and totally eliminate marketing strategies and sales techniques that have been a complete failure.

The key components of an effective monitoring and intelligence-gathering system include (1) acquiring and maintaining sufficient computer equipment capability to manage and organize market data; (2) tracking the development and problems of competitors; (3) remaining active in industry groups and trade associations; (4) regularly reading trade journals and industry publications; (5) meeting with key suppliers and customers to understand industry trends and preferences; (6) buying the products of competitors to observe pricing, packaging, labeling, and features; (7) keeping track of the information that may be readily available from federal, state, and local governments; and (8) staying abreast of political, economic, social, and legal trends and developments affecting marketing plans and strategies.

Franchisors should continue to monitor their sales and marketing efforts by interviewing those prospects who chose not to acquire the franchise (to find out why they did not buy) as well as collect data from recent franchisees (to find out why they did). If the lost prospect bought a franchise from another franchisor, then it is critical to find out why. Ask the lost prospect as well as the recent franchisee what they like and didn't like about the sales presentation and offering process. The franchise director should hold weekly meetings with his or her staff to analyze and deal with the common concerns and objections raised by the typical prospect. Tools and data should then be developed to overcome these concerns.

11

Taking Your Franchise Program Overseas

Just as the overwhelming popularity of franchising has captured the attention of the United States economy over the past ten years, it has also begun to attract attention among overseas markets. United States-based franchisors are currently operating in more than 160 countries worldwide. The reasons for this foreign expansion are strikingly similar to the reasons for domestic growth, including a greater demand for personal services, higher levels of disposable income, and an increased desire for individual business ownership. Foreign franchisees are responding eagerly to the greater levels of profitability and lower levels of risk inherent in the marketing of an established franchise system.

Domestic franchisors taking their products abroad face an already receptive consumer market. The fascination with our products and life-styles can often pave the way for successful business operations overseas. Beyond the fundamental interest in our products, many countries, particularly the less developed ones, view franchising as a readily acceptable source of technological development and system support that introduces know-how to a fledgling business community in a cost-effective manner.

There are many examples of successful worldwide franchise businesses such as McDonald's and Kentucky Fried Chicken. It is not unusual to see McDonald's doing a booming trade on the Champs-Elysées or the Via Venito, or even in Red

Square. However, it is vital to remember as a franchisor that no matter how popular your product or service is domestically, you are still entering a foreign country with all of its idiosyncrasies and its differences in culture, style, law, and politics. Domestic franchisors should not enter into foreign markets simply to feed their egos or because their competitors are doing it. There must be a set of valid business reasons, a comfort level within the company, and a commitment to fully understanding and developing the targeted overseas market(s).

When you embark on any franchise expansion program, but particularly an international expansion program, there is no substitute for a thorough investigation of the chosen market. Among the issues that should be reviewed in detail are the following key "barriers to entry" in foreign markets:

- *Language barriers.* Although it may seem simple enough at the outset to translate the operations manual into the local language, marketing the system and the product may present unforeseen difficulties if the concept itself does not "translate" well.

- *Taste barriers.* Franchisors marketing food products have frequently found that foreign tastes differ greatly from the American palate. The Japanese, for example, typically prefer foods with a lower sugar content and demand smaller portions than would be sold in the average United States fast-food establishments. These factors should be carefully reviewed with the assistance of local marketing personnel and product development specialists before you undertake any negotiations with suppliers and distributors.

- *Marketing barriers.* These barriers most frequently go to the deepest cultural levels. For example, whereas many overseas markets have developed a taste for "fast-food" burgers and hot dogs, differences in culture may dictate that the speed aspect is less important. Many cultures demand the leisure to be able to relax on the premises after eating a meal rather than taking a meal to go. These cultural norms can, in turn, be affected by factors such as the cost and availability of retail space. "Takeout" remains popular in Tokyo where space is at a premium and consumers are less inclined to expect the space and surroundings to be conducive to lingering after a meal. The opposite tends to be true in southern European and Middle Eastern markets where the pace is slower and the demand for retail space is not as great.

- *Legal barriers.* Domestic legislation may not be conducive to the establishment of franchise and distributorship arrangements. Tax laws, customs laws, import restrictions, and corporate organization and agency/liability laws may all prove to be significant stumbling blocks.

- *Access to raw materials and human resources.* Not all countries offer the open access to critical raw materials and skilled labor that can be found in the United States. A chain of steakhouse franchises would be very difficult and expensive to operate in a country experiencing severe meat shortages. Similarly, a tune-up franchisor will run into certain operational problems if there is a serious lack of skilled auto technicians.

- *Government barriers.* The foreign government may or may not be receptive to foreign investment in general or to franchising in particular. A given country's past history of expropriation, government restrictions, and limitations on currency repatriation may all prove to be decisive factors in determining whether the cost of market penetration is worth the potential benefits to be derived.

These potential stumbling blocks do not mean that overseas expansion is ill-advised. On the contrary, many times a review of the relevant market will indicate that such expansion holds great potential.

Specific Legal and Strategic Issues Relevant to Overseas Expansion

The first item necessary for a successful expansion abroad should be a strong domestic franchising program. Once the decision has been made to expand, a franchisor should spend considerable time reviewing the factors listed below with legal, accounting, and marketing representatives along with other individuals familiar with the franchise program and the targeted overseas markets. Careful consideration of the following points will provide a strong foundation upon which to build a successful international operation.

Selection of Specific Overseas Markets

The selection of an appropriate and accessible foreign market is the first step in embarking on an overseas franchise development program. As soon as a preliminary territory has been selected, whether an individual city or country or even broader geographic region, local market research will need to be conducted to determine whether the franchised product or service will appeal to the local consumers. As an example, many foreigners like the taste of U.S. fast foods, but do not like to eat "on the run." As such, the franchisor's product may be well-liked but sales may diminish rapidly once the initial novelty has passed, *if* you do not provide space for customers to sit and relax while they eat. Although the general enthusiasm for U.S. products may carry some products to the forefront of a foreign market, this enthusiasm may not be sufficient to sustain others. On the basis of the initial marketing research of existing consumption patterns and trends, a prudent franchisor will decide to either seek an alternate market or to adapt the present product and system to the local palate.

In addition to issues of product acceptance, some potential markets may raise more fundamental questions of accessibility. Franchisors should carefully review the availability of central transportation modes, such as air, sea, and internal road networks for moving goods vital to the franchisor's system. The availability of responsive communications systems such as fax, phone, and express mail services, though taken for granted domestically, may be surprisingly limited even in jurisdictions that are economically and politically advanced. The availability of financial resources as well as the applicable domestic taxation of commercial activities, labor resources, and the local real estate market will all dictate the selection of which foreign markets a franchisor will develop.

The threat of currency repatriation is also a primary concern in choosing appropriate foreign markets. This is particularly true in the newly developing Eastern European markets where hard currency is difficult to come by and removal of profits is often restricted by statute. Removal of hard currency is often further complicated by extensive paperwork and lengthy delays. These limitations may necessitate changes in the structure of the franchise system. Domestic suppliers of raw materials may have to be utilized to facilitate payment in local currencies. Royalties and ongoing fees may have to be taken in the form of soft currency or actual goods similar to a countertrade arrangement. For instance, a market with restrictive repatriation statutes may be able to cheaply and efficiently provide a raw material for export which is needed throughout the franchisor's system. This sort of raw material for technology exchange has proved viable in many developing economies.

The availability of domestic sources of financing both for the franchisor and for prospective franchisees will also have some bearing on the choice of venue. Once the choice of territory is made, the form of operation must be carefully considered.

Structuring Overseas Operations

Choosing the appropriate franchisee (or area developer) will undoubtedly be the single most important step in structuring an effective overseas franchise program. There is no substitute for face-to-face negotiations between parties, regardless of whether this individual is interested in a master development agreement or a single-unit franchise. The most promising candidates are often those with proven financial resources who have already established a successful business in the host country. Due diligence should be conducted on each prospective candidate. Beyond a certain point, however, only careful negotiating and contract preparation provides any degree of protection for a franchisor risking entry into a new market.

In structuring the actual franchise agreement, the franchisor should carefully consider the structure of the relationship, the term of the agreement, and the scope and length of nondisclosure and noncompete clauses. These provisions and their enforceability will take on increased importance when complicated by distance and differences in legal systems. Franchisors should also give careful thought to the structuring of the financial provisions of the franchise agreement. It is tempting to try to mitigate potential downstream losses by seeking a higher initial fee. This alternative, however, often results in uneasiness on the part of the prospective franchisees with respect to the franchisor's long-term commitment to the host country as a whole. In light of these considerations, a more balanced approach to fees and ongoing royalties should be considered.

Protecting the Franchisor's Intellectual Property Overseas.

The primary difficulty for franchisors in protecting their trademarks overseas is that in many countries a trademark belongs to the first person to register it, not the first person to conceive it or use it in commerce. Many franchisors have been unpleasantly surprised to find that local companies have already registered the franchisor's proprietary marks in the local jurisdiction. Therefore, the franchisor must then either buy back its own mark or attempt to operate unprotected in the market. According to the United States government, the eight worst violators are Brazil, China, India, Mexico, Saudi Arabia, South Korea, Taiwan, and Thailand; with Canada, Italy, and Japan close behind. The federal government is continuing to place pressure on these trading partners to promote more equitable treatment both through bilateral government-to-government negotiations, and the multilateral trade negotiations ongoing through the General Agreement on Tariffs and Trade (GATT). This renewed focus has in part provided a more favorable climate for international franchising. Still, as a precautionary measure, a franchisor considering expanding abroad should seriously consider applying for trademark/patent protection prior to commencing negotiations with any prospective franchisees. This process can be costly and time-consuming, but the protection is vital to successful operations.

Franchisors may also wish to consider test marketing their tradename before designing the overseas program. Many U.S. businesses have discovered the hard way that a foreign translation of a U.S. tradename may be unmarketable for a wide variety of reasons. Businesses in the past have had to face tradenames that translated into obscenities or meaningless words and phrases. Local sales and marketing people should be consulted at an early stage to prevent costly mistakes.

Foreign Laws Affecting the Structure of Franchise Agreements

Foreign law should always be carefully reviewed before you establish overseas franchise operations or negotiate franchise agreements in foreign countries. Distributorship, agency, and antitrust laws will all affect the viability of any given operation. Agency laws, for example, may place greater liability on a franchisor than it would be exposed to in this country. Distribution laws may restrict the way in which (1) termination clauses are enforced, (b) territories are divided, and (c) cooperative advertising programs are developed.

Foreign tax laws will also play a role in the structuring of the transaction. The presence or absence of a tax treaty with the United States generally dictates whether a foreign tax credit will be available to the franchisor. Foreign tax laws can work for and against a franchisor depending in large part upon the individual country's desire to encourage foreign investment. Tax credits and/or "tax holidays" may prove invaluable to a franchisor establishing a new enterprise in a higher-risk environment. In addition, countries seeking investment dollars and technology grants from developed nations may be willing to work out deals on an individual basis. Tax treatment of the franchisor's U.S. employees working abroad should also be considered.

Export Controls and Import Restrictions

Franchisors may face difficulties with respect to certain federal export control laws as well as foreign import controls. The U.S. limits, to a certain degree, the export of potentially sensitive technology for national security reasons. These restrictions can be imposed regardless of the proposed end use of the product. These export restrictions, however, have been easing in the past year as political tensions ease on a global scale. Franchisors should seek experienced legal counsel to ensure that all of the necessary export licenses and permits are applied for and received in a timely manner.

Having managed to export the necessary items, a franchisor may be presented with import restrictions at the receiving end. Local content legislation and other domestic production concerns may result in the imposition of domestic quotas and tariffs on U.S. products being brought into a foreign jurisdiction. These import restrictions should be reviewed with foreign counsel prior to the drafting of the price terms of the franchise offering documents. In some instances, a country's desire to benefit from foreign technology and know-how may result in duty-free importations and may provide a franchisor with the leverage to bargain for reductions on other import and re-export tariffs and fees.

Overview of Certain Foreign Laws Affecting International Franchising

The following is a random sampling of some of the international laws affecting the offers and sales of franchises in various parts of the world. These laws are changing rapidly, and it is imperative that legal counsel is consulted *before* entering into any of these foreign markets.

European Economic Community

The European Economic Community (EEC) was established by the Treaty of Rome in 1957 and now consists of twelve European Member States. The six original members, France, West Germany, Italy, and the three Benelux countries, were joined by the United Kingdom, Denmark, and Ireland in 1973, by Greece in 1981, and by Spain and Portugal in 1986. The goal of the EEC is to provide a unified internal and external market in goods and services for the member states.

The rules of play governing the EEC's legal system are contained in the Treaty of Rome itself. Article 85(1) of the treaty sets out certain restraints on trade that are automatically impermissible and as such *void ab initio*. Among these activities are agreements or concerted practices that directly fix prices or any other trading condition that affects interstate trade. In addition, agreements or concerted practices that limit or control supplies or are designed to share markets are also considered unacceptable. These activities are deemed to be harmful to the free flow of trade between the member states and as such are prohibited *unless* specifically exempted.

Quite clearly, the standard franchise arrangement has numerous provisions that would violate these statutory prohibitions. As such, large franchising concerns that operate across member states' borders in the EEC were obligated to seek a formal exemption from the commission on a case-by-case basis. These exemptions were granted with greater frequency following the European Court of Justice's decision in the *Pronuptia* case, indicating that franchise arrangements were not per se violative of Article 85(1). Since that time the European Commission has seen fit to establish by regulation a formal "block exemption" setting forth permissible franchising criteria that will automatically render a franchisor outside the scope of Article 85(1) competition rules. The regulation sets out in general terms the restrictions on competition and trade that may and may not be incorporated into a franchise agreement. Among the provisions specifically *permitted* are (1) clauses requiring the franchisee to refrain from attempting to solicit customers outside the franchised territory, (2) clauses requiring that operations be conducted solely from the franchised premises, and (3) anticompetition clauses restricting a franchisee's ability to manufacture or sell products that compete with the franchisor's products.

In addition, numerous provisions are deemed permissible but *only* insofar as they are necessary to protect the franchisor's intellectual property rights or to maintain the reputation and common identity of the franchise system. These provisions include clauses:

- Granting the franchisor exclusive rights to the know-how developed by the franchisee in the course of operating the franchised business
- Requiring the franchisee to refrain from engaging in a competing business for up to one year after the franchise agreement terminates
- Demanding that franchisees not enter into business arrangements with competitors of the franchisor, which would give the franchisee the power to influence the operations of the competitor
- Restricting a franchisee's ability to sell or use goods not made by the franchisor or a designated third party where establishing objective purchasing criteria is not practical
- Requiring nondisclosure of franchisor's know-how and restricting use of that know-how apart from the franchise system
- Prohibiting the transfer of the franchise location or any interests therein without the franchisor's consent

Franchisors are *not* permitted to prevent franchisees from supplying one another or from obtaining products from other authorized dealers, and franchisors may not restrict the franchisee's determination of prices for goods or services or prevent former franchisees from utilizing franchise know-how that has become part of the "public domain." These provisions are far more detailed than those in most foreign jurisdictions, and the laws of the individual member states will have to conform to these provisions. Specific provisions have also been established that address "block exemptions" for know-how licensing agreements.

Franchisors entering the EEC should notify the commission of their intent to do so, referring to the block exemption and providing details of the contemplated arrangements. If no opposition is lodged by the commission within six months of notification, an official exemption will issue.

North America

For many years Canada and Mexico have provided logical areas for initial international expansion by domestic franchisors. Proximity alone makes these markets attractive in terms of supervision of franchisees and a greater likelihood of common product interest. The following is a brief overview of the legal climates in these jurisdictions:

Mexico. New regulations have been put forward in Mexico, effective early in 1990, that radically liberalize the current market for franchise development. Until recently the Mexican government's position was that foreign investment in general should be severely restricted, and that franchising other than of high-tech products and services was not encouraged in light of the country's present state of cultural and economic development. Increasing pressure to liberalize what had been a very arbitrary system of foreign investment regulation has resulted in new policies designed to encourage an inflow of hard currency and technology into the nation's beleaguered economy.

The key provisions of the new regulation that will effect franchisors in particular are detailed below:

- A new registration system has been established that specifically defines a "franchise" as a relationship permitting a franchisee/licensee the right to use or exploit trademarks and commercial names while transmitting technical knowledge and providing technical assistance for producing/selling goods or performing services in line with the franchisor/licensor's standard commercial practices.

- Franchisors must file a model agreement with the appropriate agency every six months, whereupon a registration number is provided that may be cited by the franchisor in distributing the offering during the six-month interim period.
- Franchisors are now permitted to impose limits on research and technological developments by franchisees and may limit a franchisee's exports.
- Industrial secrets may now be protected for up to ten years, and contractual provisions may establish broader protections for these secrets.
- Payments of royalties have been liberalized and franchise/license parties may freely renegotiate provisions of their contracts with respect to royalty fees.
- Generalized strengthening of trademark and patent protection is being undertaken based upon pressure from other industrialized trading partners.
- A greater degree of freedom of contracting is permitted, provided that one of several demonstrable benefits will accrue to the country as a whole, including in part the creation of permanent jobs, manufacture of new products within the country (particularly if they take the place of imports), improvement of the balance of payments, and initiation or deepening of technological research and development activities in production units or in related domestic research centers.

Canada. In Canada only the province of Alberta has enacted legislation expressly regulating franchising. The Alberta laws specifically require disclosure and registration by any company that is "trading in franchises." The Alberta Franchises Act is very detailed and requires extensive disclosure into the background not only of the franchisor, but also of any individual who will be selling the franchise within the province. Detailed audited financial statements are also required for the prior two to three years of operations. There are limited exemptions from the Alberta Franchises Act, but these only encompass (1) franchisors with a minimum net worth of $5 million (Canadian dollars) and with at least twenty-five franchisees conducting business at all times during the five years immediately preceding commencement of operations in Alberta or (2) franchisors that have conducted this same business for five years prior to doing business in Alberta. Any franchisor considering selling franchises in Alberta should seek the advice of counsel familiar with the Alberta laws and recognize that the entire registration process will be expensive and time-consuming.

The regulation of franchising in provinces other than Alberta is generally governed by Canadian common law (with the exception of the province of Quebec, which continues to be governed under civil law principles). Most provinces have specific legislation governing motor vehicle dealers which requires registration of dealers and their associated salespersons. In addition, the province of Ontario enacted the Prepaid Services Act, which affects service businesses dealing in health, fitness, sports, dance, talent development, diet, and other similar matters. This statute restricts maximum initiation fees and maximum advance payments and limits the length of service contracts to one year. Customers are also granted certain recision rights with respect to these contracts.

Franchisors will be subject to a wide variety of antitrust provisions, securities regulations, and antifraud provisions. By and large, however, these statutes will be very similar in nature to their U.S. counterparts. Local counsel will be best equipped to provide guidance in this area. Trademark and other intellectual property protections are, generally speaking, more than adequate in most respects. A domestic trademark registration may be based upon intent to use as well as actual use, and as such, early stage registration is advisable.

Franchisors operating in Quebec will additionally be responsible for complying with French language translation requirements, which dictate that business in the province must also be conducted in French. This will generally affect franchisees more than it does the franchisor. There is, however, some question as to whether the original franchise agreement must be presented in French *and* in English or whether a mere statement in French recognizing that an agreement has been reached to provide an English translation is sufficient. The safest course is to present a French translation at the time that the franchise agreement is executed.

Pacific Rim. There are numerous potential franchise markets in the Pacific Basin with varying degrees of domestic regulation affecting franchisors. This subsection will provide a brief overview of the relevant domestic policies for each of the primary markets.

Hong Kong has virtually no restrictions on foreign investment and as such has been a mecca for foreign capital and products down the years. Although market access is relatively uncomplicated, political changes resulting from the relinquishment of the territory by the British in July 1997 may make certain investors reluctant to embark on substantial projects until after the transition is completed and stabilized.

Singapore, Taiwan, and New Zealand all fall into the category of jurisdictions not specifically regulating franchise activity per se. Singapore and New Zealand generally view foreign franchising as an acceptable and encouraged source of foreign investment. Taiwan, on the other hand, until recently encouraged foreign investment primarily in targeted high tech fields, most of which were not businesses susceptible to successful franchising. This attitude has changed recently as government policies are liberalizing. Foreign food franchises have already made inroads into the Taiwanese market. In all three jurisdictions, franchise relations will be governed by the standard laws of contract as well as local labor laws and health, safety, and antitrust provisions. A detailed discussion of these legal provisions in any detail is beyond the scope of this book, and therefore local counsel should be consulted prior to drafting the relevant franchise agreements. One area of the law worth mentioning briefly is the subject of intellectual property protection. The government of New Zealand has been relatively responsive to claims of infringement, and local policies provide adequate protection from infringement. Singapore and Taiwan, on the other hand, have a thriving market in pirated goods. Videotapes and computer software in particular have been hard hit. Pressure from the developed nations is slowly resulting in an increased awareness of the problems and certain concessions are being made. However, foreign businesspeople still complain that enforcement proceedings are slow and are generally given a low priority. Given the vital relationship of trademarks and service marks to a successful franchise system, you should carefully consider the ability to protect these marks before embarking on a franchise program in one of these jurisdictions.

Australia, Japan, Korea, and the Philippines all regulate, to some degree, franchising in their jurisdictions. The following segment will provide a brief overview of regulation in each of these jurisdictions.

Australia. Legislation is promulgated at the federal level and through each of the six state governments. The only federal legislation effecting franchising is the Petroleum Retail Marketing Franchise Act of 1980 which, as its name suggests, regulates petroleum retail sales. The various states have enacted other legislation that may well encompass franchise operations in general. New South Wales, Victoria, and South Australia all have Fair Trading Acts that prohibit false or misleading claims and the undertaking of unconscionable conduct with respect to the profitability or risk associated with a particular business. The various states also have provisions permitting the amendment of contract terms to prevent unjust consequences. A careful review of the relevant state and federal legislation should be undertaken prior to drafting the franchise documents.

Japan. The Law Concerning Development of Middle and Small Scale Retailers (the "Retailers Law") is part of a network of domestic legislation designed to support and encourage the development of small-scale retailers over department stores and supermarkets. The benefits provided by this legislation will frequently assist domestic franchisees of foreign franchisors. The following is a summary of laws effecting franchise establishment. However, the wide range of antimonopoly, price fixing, and fair trade provisions that will affect ongoing operations should be reviewed in detail.

The Retailers Law encompasses franchises through the definitions of *chain business* and *specific chain business*. A chain business is one that (1) involves middle- and small-scale retailers, (2) is based on a standard form agreement, and (3) is engaged in the continuous sale of goods and management assistance. Specific chain business is (1) the granting of trademarks, trade names, or other marks to an applicant for the business and (2) the payment by the applicant of a certain amount of money. Businesses that fit this definition, that are small or middle-scale retailers (with not more than 10 million yen in capital and continuously employing no more than fifty people) may seek designation of their small business plan. Designation will permit the enterprise to participate in investment incentives such as preferential loans and accelerated depreciation on certain depreciable assets.

Prospective franchisees in general must be provided with the following information in writing:

- Initial amount of money to be deposited or transferred by the applicant
- Method of sale of goods or provision of services
- Extent of management assistance to be rendered
- Trademarks or any other marks the applicant will be permitted to use
- Term, renewal, termination, and cancellation of the agreement
- Name, address, and representatives of the person or corporation operating the specific chain business
- Date of commencement of the specific chain business
- Money to be paid periodically by the applicant
- Obligation of the applicant with regard to structure, design, or layout of the franchised premises

Franchisors may also register voluntarily with the Japanese Franchise Association, providing additional information to be kept on file for reference by the prospective franchisee.

Intellectual property protection in Japan is notoriously weak. Furthermore, trademark registration is a slow process taking up to four years to complete. This is complicated by the fact that there is no penalty for infringement during the actual processing period. "Well-known" trade and service marks are protected in Japan; however, satisfactorily establishing that a mark is well-known can be extremely difficult.

Korea. Until recently, under the Foreign Capital Inducement Law, the Korean government provided a limited list of activities open to foreign investment. Recent amendments now provide for a smaller list of prohibited investment areas, with all others being presumably permissible.

Technology licensing arrangements of whatever kind must be approved at the federal level. Prior to mid-1986, a mere trademark license could not be accepted as a royalty-bearing "technology inducement agreement." Now a royalty-bearing trademark license agreement may be accepted even without the transfer of technology, if the trademark licensor waives any possible tax exemption. After submission of a technology inducement agreement, the relevant ministry must rule within twenty days or the report is deemed to be accepted as presented. Monopoly Regulation, Fair Trade Laws, and Foreign Exchange Control provisions also effect a franchisor's attempt to operate in Korea.

The United States government is closely monitoring Korean advances in the area of intellectual property protection. Recent threats of economic retribution have led to a preliminary overhaul of the notoriously lax protection system.

Philippines. As a general rule, franchising agreements that will promote exports are acceptable; however, franchise systems that do not transfer technology and have no economic benefits to the country are not accepted. This applies to foreign investment in general, encouraged only to the extent that capital-intensive projects are promoted that will utilize local labor and substantial amounts of domestic raw materials.

Protection of intellectual property rights is also relatively primitive. Domestic franchisors have had difficulties with local companies preregistering their trademarks and seeking payment from the foreign company in order to repurchase their own marks. In addition, a mark must be used continuously to avoid being dropped from the register. The situation is further complicated because enforcement of intellectual property rights is ineffective and enforcement resources are inadequate.

Eastern Bloc Expansion. The recent unprecedented changes in the Eastern Bloc nations have opened a potentially expansive new market to franchisors. To date, only the largest and most economically stable franchisors have undertaken expansion into these markets, given the lack of hard currency and the difficulties in repatriating profits. As the domestic economies build and develop, however, this should prove to be an increasingly attractive market and certainly one for early-stage and growing franchisors to seriously consider.

Franchisors actively seeking to expand into these markets will find that the federal government has developed technical assistance and financing programs to support and encourage this type of investment. Most franchising projects in the Eastern Bloc at present are being undertaken through joint venture arrangements. And even then only the more progressive countries such as Poland and Hungary are being targeted. The larger franchisors that have entered the market own their franchised sites in conjunction with their local joint venture partners. McDonald's, for example, has opened its Russian "franchise" in conjunction with the Moscow city authorities. The principal difficulties that arise with respect to proposed franchise-owned operations include:

- Short supplies of hard currency
- Difficulties in repatriation because of the nonconvertibility of currency and general currency controls

- Lack of necessary infrastructure, i.e., ineffective telephone networks and poor shipping and internal transport links
- Lack of satisfactory raw material supplies
- Difficulties finding prospective individual franchises with sufficient entrepreneurial/business background and sufficient cash reserves to cover franchise fees and general start-up costs

These factors indicate that at least initially the Eastern Bloc markets will be most viable for larger franchisors with greater flexibility that are able to take a long-term view of profitability. Some larger franchisors are already training prospective franchisees in Yugoslavia and Hungary. These individuals will make up a new class of business owners in Eastern Europe. Franchising in particular is a viable introduction to the for-profit world for a fledgling free-market economy. Bringing in a viable working system and providing support, know-how, and training in exchange for a monthly royalty is a positive step for both individuals and the economic infrastructure. The next five years will no doubt show incredible growth in this market. Local enthusiasm combined with U.S. government support both financially and ideologically will open a huge potential market even for small and growing franchisors.

Part Four
Financial Strategies

12

Raising Growth Capital

One of the most difficult tasks faced by the management team of a growing franchisor is the development and maintenance of an optimal capital structure for the organization. Access to affordable debt and equity capital continues to be a problem for the growing franchisor even though franchising has matured as a viable method of business growth.

Only recently have the investment banking and commercial lending communities given franchising the recognition it deserves. There are finally enough franchisors whose balance sheets have become more respectable, who have participated in successful public offerings, who have played (and won) in the merger and acquisition game, and who have demonstrated consistent financial appreciation and profitability. These developments have played a role in providing young franchisors access to affordable capital in recent years. Nevertheless, a growing franchisor must be prepared to *educate the source of capital* as to the unique aspects of financing a franchise company. And there *are* differences. Franchisors have different balance sheets (heavily laden with intangible assets), different allocations of capital (directed as expenditures for "soft costs"), different management teams, different sources of revenues, and different strategies for growth.

The amount of capital potentially available, as well as the sources willing to consider financing a given transaction, depends largely on the franchisor's current and projected financial strength, as well as the experience of its management team and a host of other factors, such as trademarks and franchise sales history, discussed in more detail in this chapter.

The Initial and Ongoing Costs of Franchising

Before examining the key elements of business planning and capital formation strategies, you should understand the specific nature of the capital requirements of the early-stage and emerging franchisor. Although franchising is less capital-intensive than is internal expansion, *franchisors still require a solid capital structure.* Grossly undercapitalized franchisors are on a path to disaster because they will be unable to develop effective marketing programs, attract qualified staff, or provide the high-quality ongoing support and assistance that franchisees need to grow and prosper.

Bootstrap franchising has been tried by many companies, but very few have been successful. In a bootstrap franchising program, the franchisor uses the initial franchise fees paid by the franchisee as its capital for growth and expansion. There is a bit of a catch-22, however, if the franchisor has not properly developed its operations, training program, and materials prior to the offer and sale of a franchise. Such a strategy could subject the franchisor to claims of fraud and misrepresentation, because the franchisee has good reason to expect that the business format franchise is complete and not still "under construction." A second legal problem with undercapitalization is that many examiners in the registration states will either completely bar a franchisor from offer and sales in their jurisdiction until the financial condition improves, or impose restrictive bonding and escrow provisions in order to protect the fees paid by the franchisee. A third possible legal problem is that if the franchisor is using the franchise offering circular to raise growth capital, then the entire scheme could be viewed as a securities offering, which triggers compliance with federal and state securities laws, as discussed in this chapter.

The start-up franchisor must initially put together a budget for the developmental costs of building the franchise system. This budget should be incorporated into the business plan, the key elements of which are discussed below. The start-up costs include the development of operations manuals, training programs, sales and marketing materials, personnel recruitment, accounting and legal fees, research and development, testing and operation of the prototype unit, outside consulting fees, and travel costs for trade shows and sales presentations. Naturally, there are a number of variables influencing the amount that must be budgeted for development costs, including:

- The extent to which outside consultants are required to develop operations and training materials
- The franchisor's location and geographic proximity to targeted franchisees
- The complexity of the franchise program and trends within the franchisor's industry
- The quality, experience, and fee structure of the legal and accounting firms selected to prepare the offering documents and agreements
- The extent to which products or equipment will be sold directly to franchisees, which may require warehousing and shipping capabilities
- The extent to which personnel placement firms will be used to recruit the franchisor's management team
- The use of a celebrity or industry expert to "endorse" the franchisor's products, services, and franchise program
- The difficulty encountered at the United States Patent and Trademark Office in registering the franchisor's trademarks
- The extent to which direct financing will be offered to the franchisees for initial opening and/or expansion
- The compensation structure for the franchisor's sales staff

- The difficulty encountered by franchise counsel in the registration states
- The extent to which the franchisor gets embroiled in legal disputes with the franchisees at an early stage
- The quality of the franchisor's marketing materials
- The type of media and marketing strategy selected to reach targeted franchisees
- The number of company-owned units the franchisor plans to develop
- The length and complexity of the franchisor's training program
- The rate at which the franchisor will be in a position to repay the capital (or provide a return on investment), which will influence the cost of the capital

Preparing a Business Plan for the Growing Franchisor

Owners and managers of growing franchisors have come to understand that meaningful and effective business planning is critical to the long-term success and viability of any business and to its ability to raise capital. Before you read about the various methods of financing available to the growing franchisor, you must understand the key elements of a business plan. Regardless of the financing method or the type of capital to be raised, virtually any lender, underwriter, venture capitalist, or private investor will expect to be presented with a meaningful business plan. A well-prepared business plan demonstrates management's ability to focus on long-term achievable goals, provides a guide to effectively implement the articulated goals once the capital has been committed, and constitutes a yardstick by which actual performance can be evaluated.

Business plans should be used by newly formed franchisors as well as established franchisors. The following is a broad outline of the fundamental topics to be included in a typical franchisor's business plan.

Executive Summary

This introductory section of the plan should explain the nature of the business and highlight the important features and opportunities offered by an investment in the company. The executive summary should be no longer than one to three pages and include (1) the company's origins and performance, (2) distinguishing and unique features of the products and services offered to *both* consumers and franchisees, (3) an overview of the market, and (4) the amount of money sought and for what specific purposes.

History and Operations of the Franchisor

In this first full section, the history of the franchisor should be discussed in greater detail: its management team (with résumés included as an exhibit); the specific program, opportunity, or project being funded by the proceeds; the prototype; an overview of the franchisor's industry, with a specific emphasis on recent trends affecting the market demand for the franchises; as well as the products and services offered by the franchisee. Figure 12-1 provides a list of questions to be addressed in this section.

Many of these issues will be described in greater detail in later sections of the plan. Therefore, each topic should be covered summarily in two or three paragraphs.

Marketing Research and Analysis

This section must present to the reader all relevant and current information regarding the size of the market for both franchisees and consumers, trends in the industry, marketing and sales strategies and techniques, assessments of the competition, (direct and indirect), estimated market share and projected sales, pricing policies, advertising and public relations, strategies, and a description of sales personnel. The following questions should also be addressed:

Figure 12-1. Questions to address in Section 1.

1. When and how was the prototype facility first developed?
2. Why has the company decided to expand its market share through franchising?
3. What are the company's greatest strengths and proprietary advantages with respect to its franchisees? Consumers? Employees? Shareholders? Competitors?
4. What are the nature, current status, and future prospects in the franchisor's industry?

- Describe the typical consumer. How and why is the consumer attracted to patronize the franchisee's facility? What relevant market trends affect the consumer's decision to purchase products and services from the franchisee's facility?
- Describe the typical franchisee. How and why is the prospective franchisee attracted to the franchisor's business format? What factors have influenced the prospect's decision to purchase the franchise?
- What is the approximate size of the total market for the services offered by the franchisee? The approximate market for franchisees?
- What marketing strategies and techniques have been adopted to attract franchisees and consumers? Where do referrals for prospective franchisees come from? Do existing franchisees make referrals? Why or why not? (Include sample promotional materials as an exhibit.)
- Describe the performance of the typical franchisee. Are the stores profitable? Why or why not?

Rationale for Franchising

This section should explain the underlying rationale for selecting franchising in lieu of the other growth and distribution strategies that may be available. Discuss whether a dual distribution strategy will be pursued. Under what circumstances will company-owned units be established? Explain to the reader which method(s) of franchising will be selected. Single units only? Sales representatives? Area developers? Subfranchisees? Special risks and legal issues, which are triggered by the decision to franchise, should also be discussed.

The Franchising Program

This section should provide an overview of the franchising program with respect to key aspects of the franchise agreement, a description of the typical site, an overview of the proprietary business format and trade identity, the training program, operations manual, support services to franchisees, targeted markets and registration strategies, the offering of regional and area development agreements, and arrangements with vendors. A detailed analysis of sales and earnings estimates and personnel needed for a typical facility should be included. Discuss marketing strategies relevant to franchising such as trade shows, industry publications, and sales techniques. Explain the typical length of time between the first meeting with a prospect through grand opening and beyond. What are the various steps and costs during this time period (from the perspective of both the franchisor and the franchisee)? Discuss strategies for the growth and development of the franchising program over the next five to ten years.

Corporate and Financial Matters

This section should briefly describe the current officers, directors, and shareholders of the corporation. An overview of the capital contributed to the company thus far should be provided, along with an explanation of how these funds have been allocated. Discuss the anticipated monthly operating costs to be incurred by the corporation, both current and projected, not only for operating and managing the prototype facility but also for the administrative expenses incurred in setting up a franchise sales and services office. Discuss the pricing of the franchise fee, royalties, and promotional fund contributions. Discuss the payment histories of the franchisees thus far. Are they complying with their obligations under the franchise agreement? Why or why not?

What portion of these fees collected from the franchisee will be net profit? Discuss the amount of capital that will be required for the corporation to meet its short-term goals and objectives. How much, if any, additional capital will be required to meet long-term objectives? What alternative structures and methods are available for raising these funds? How will these funds be allocated? Provide a breakdown of expenses for personnel, advertising and marketing, acquisition of equipment or real estate, administration, professional fees, and travel. To what extent are these expenses fixed and to what extent will they vary depending on the actual growth of the company?

Operations and Management

Provide the current and projected organizational and management structure. Identify each position by title with a description of duties and responsibilities and compensation. Describe the current management team and anticipated hiring requirements over the next three to five years. What strategies will be adopted to attract and retain qualified franchise professionals? Provide a description of the company's external management team (attorney, accountant, etc.).

Exhibits

Include exhibits in the presentation copies of the franchisor's trademarks, marketing brochures, press coverage, as well as in sample franchise agreements and area development agreements.

Private Placements: Legal and Strategic Issues

Growing franchisors are increasingly turning to private placements of their securities as a viable method of raising equity capital. In general terms, a private placement may be used as a vehicle for capital formation anytime a particular security or transaction is exempt from federal registration requirements under the Securities Act of 1933. In order to determine whether a private placement is a sensible strategy for raising capital, it is imperative that franchisors (1) have a fundamental understanding of the federal and state securities laws affecting private placements, (2) be familiar with the basic procedural steps that must be taken before such an alternative is pursued, and (3) have a team of qualified legal and accounting professionals who are familiar with the securities laws to assist in the offering.

The private placement generally offers reduced transactional and ongoing costs because of its exemption from many of the extensive registration and reporting requirements imposed by federal and state securities laws. This is especially true for franchisors, who already have disclosed many of the key items required in a private placement memorandum in their franchise offering circulars. There is much overlap between the two documents, which will further reduce the costs of preparation. The private placement usually also offers the ability to structure a more complex and confidential transaction, because the offeree will typically be a small number of sophisticated investors. In addition, a private placement permits a more rapid penetration into the capital markets than would a public offering of securities requiring registration with the Securities and Exchange Commission (SEC).

An Overview of Regulation D

The most common exemptions from registration that are relied upon by franchisors in connection with a private placement are contained in the Securities and Exchange Commission's Regulation D. The SEC promulgated Regulation D in 1982 in order to facilitate capital formation by smaller companies. Since its inception, Regulation D has been an extremely successful vehicle for raising capital, with billions of dollars being raised each year by small and growing businesses. Regulation D offers a menu of three transaction exemptions, which are discussed below.

Rule 504. The first exemption created by Regulation D is a Rule 504 offering, which permits offers and sales of not more than $1,000,000 in securities (provided that no more than $500,000 is offered and sold without registration under state securities laws) during any twelve-month period by any issuer that is not subject to the reporting requirements of the Securities Exchange Act of 1934 and that is not an investment company. Rule 504 places virtually no limit on the number or the type of investors that participate in the offering. Even though no formal disclosure document needs to be registered and delivered to the offeree under Rule 504, many procedures must still be understood and followed. In particular, because most states do not include an exemption similar to 504, it will nevertheless be necessary to prepare a formal private placement memorandum.

Rule 505. This second exemption under Regulation D allows for the sale of the franchisor's securities to an unlimited number of "accredited investors" and up to thirty-five unaccredited investors regardless of their net worth, income, or sophistication, in an amount not to exceed $5 million in a twelve-month period. Many franchisors select Rule 505 over Rule 504 because its requirements are consistent with many state securities laws and because it establishes a higher ceiling with respect to the total amount of money that may be raised. An accredited investor is any person who falls within one or more of the eight categories set out in Rule 501(a) of Regulation D. Included in these categories are officers and directors of the entity who have "policy-making" functions, as well as outside investors who earned $200,000 per year for the last two years (or $300,000 for each of the last two years in conjunction with a spouse) or whose net worth exceeds $1 million. The issuer should keep in mind, however, that if one or more of the purchasers is not an accredited investor, then a full private placement memorandum must be prepared and delivered to all purchasers. There is an absolute prohibition on advertising and general solicitation for offerings that fall within Rule 505 or 506.

Rule 506. This exemption is most attractive to growing franchisors requiring large amounts of capital because it has no maximum dollar limitation. Similar to provisions in Rule 505, the issuer may sell its securities to an unlimited number of accredited investors and up to thirty-five nonaccredited investors. The primary variation under Rule 506 is that any nonaccredited investor must be a "sophisticated" investor. In this context, a sophisticated investor is one who does not fall within any of the eight categories specified by Rule 501(a) but is believed by the issuer to ". . . have knowledge and experience in financial and business matters that render him capable of evaluating the merits and understanding the risks posed by the transaction, either acting alone or in conjunction with his purchaser representative." Rule 506 does eliminate the need to prepare and deliver disclosure documents in any specified format if only accredited investors participate in the transaction. The same absolute prohibition on advertising and general solicitation imposed by Rule 505 applies to Rule 506 offerings.

The Relationship Between Regulation D and State Securities Laws

Full compliance with the federal securities laws is only one level of regulation that must be taken into account when a franchisor is developing plans and strategies to raise capital through an offering of securities. Whether or not the offering is exempt under federal laws, registration may still be required in the states where the securities are to be sold under applicable blue-sky laws. This often creates expensive and timely compliance burdens for growing franchisors and their counsel, who must contend with this bifurcated scheme of regulation. Generally speaking, there are a wide variety of standards of review among the states, ranging from very tough "merit" reviews (designed to ensure that all offerings of securities are fair and equitable) to very lenient "notice only" filings (designed primarily to promote full disclosure). The securities laws of each state where an offer or sale will be made should be checked very carefully prior to the distribution of the offering documents.

Subscription Materials

A private offering under Regulation D also requires the preparation of certain subscription documents. The two principal documents are the subscription agreement and the offeree questionnaire. The subscription agreement represents the contractual obligation on the part of the investor to buy, and on the part of the issuer, to sell, the securities that are the subject of the offering. The subscription agreement should also contain certain representations and warranties by the investor that serve as evidence of the franchisor's compliance with the applicable federal and state securities laws exemptions. The subscription agreement may also contain relevant disclosure issues addressing investment risks and may also contain operative clauses that will enable the franchisor to execute documents and effect certain transactions after the closing of the offering.

Offeree and Purchaser Questionnaires

Offeree questionnaires are developed in order to obtain certain information from prospective offerees which then serves as evidence of the required sophistication level and the ability to fend for themselves in a private offering. Generally, questionnaires will contain personal information relating to the prospective investor's name, home and business address, telephone numbers, age, social security number, education, employment history, as well as investment and business experience. The requested financial information will include the prospective investor's tax bracket, income, and net worth. The offeror must exercise reasonable care and diligence in confirming the truthfulness of the information provided in the questionnaire; however, the offeree should be required to attest to the accuracy of the data provided.

Venture Capital as a Source of Growth Financing for the Franchisor

A rapidly growing franchisor should strongly consider venture capital as a source of equity financing when it needs additional capital to bring its business plans to fruition but lacks the collateral or current ability to meet debt-service payments that are typically required to qualify for traditional debt financing from a commercial bank. This is especially true for franchisors, whose capital needs are often "soft costs" such as personnel and marketing, for which debt financing may be very difficult to obtain. As franchising as a method of expanding a business matures, a growing number of private investors and venture capitalists have been willing to consider a commitment of capital to an emerging franchisor.

The term *venture capital* has been defined in many ways, but refers generally to the early-stage financing of young emerging growth companies at a relatively high risk usually attributable to the newness of the company itself or even the entire industry. The professional venture capitalist is usually a highly trained finance professional who manages a pool of venture funds for investment in growing companies on behalf of a group of passive investors. Another major source of venture capital for growing franchisors is the Small Business Investment Company (SBIC). An SBIC is a privately organized investment firm that is specially licensed under the Small Business Investment Act of 1958 to borrow funds through the Small Business Administration for subsequent investment in the small business community. Finally, some private corporations and state governments also manage venture funds for investment in growth companies.

There have been some recent trends within the venture capital industry which may increase the chances for early-stage franchisors to obtain venture capital. For example, many venture capital firms have recently expressed an interest in smaller transactions in more traditional industries, with less risk and more moderate (but stable) returns. Many franchisors, which do operate in basic industries (e.g., food, hospitality, entertainment, personal services), can meet these investment criteria. There has been a definite shift away from high tech deals, which are largely dependent on a single patent or the completion of successful research and development, and toward investments in more traditional industries even if they result in less dynamic returns.

Negotiating and Structuring the Venture Capital Investment

Assuming that the franchisor's business plan is favorably received by the venture capitalist, the franchisor must then assemble a management team capable of negotiating the transaction. The negotiation and structuring of most venture capital transactions revolves around the need to strike a balance between the concerns of the founders of the company, such as dilution of ownership and loss of control, and the concerns of the venture capitalist, such as return on investment and mitigating the risk of business failure. The typical end result of these discussions is a *term sheet* that sets forth the key financial and legal terms of the transaction, which will then serve as a basis for the negotiation and preparation of the definitive legal documentation. Franchisors should ensure that legal counsel is familiar with the many traps and restrictions typically found in venture capital financing documents. Franchisors should also ensure that the venture capitalist understands the dynamics of franchising, especially since most venture capitalists will want to play a strong role in the management and control of the company. The term sheet may also contain certain rights and obligations of the parties, which may include an obligation to maintain an agreed valuation of the company, an obligation to be responsible for certain costs and expenses in the event the proposed transaction does not take place, or an obligation to secure commitments for financing from additional sources prior to closing. Often these obligations are also included as part of the "conditions precedent" section of the formal investment agreement.

Negotiation regarding the *structure* of the transaction between the franchisor and the venture capitalist usually center upon the types of securities to be used and the principal terms, conditions, and benefits offered by the securities. The type of securities ultimately selected and the structure of the transaction usually fall within one of the following categories:

- *Preferred stock.* This is the most typical form of security issued in connection with a venture capital financing to an emerging growth company, because of the many advantages preferred stock can be structured to offer to an investor, such as convertability into common stock, dividend and liquidation preferences over the common stock, antidilution protection, mandatory or optional redemption schedules, and special voting rights and preferences.

- *Convertible debentures.* This type of security is basically a debt instrument (secured or unsecured) that may be converted into equity securities upon specified terms and conditions. Until converted, it offers the venture capitalist a fixed rate of return and offers tax advantages (e.g., deductibility of interest payments) to the franchisor. A venture capitalist often prefers a convertible debenture in connection with higher-risk transactions because he or she is able to enjoy the elevated position of a creditor until the risk of the company's failure has been mitigated. Sometimes these instruments are used in connection with bridge financing, pursuant to which the venture capitalist expects to convert the debt to equity when the subsequent rounds of capital are raised. Finally, if the debentures are subordinated, commercial lenders often treat them as the equivalent of an equity security for balance sheet purposes, which enables the franchisor to obtain institutional debt financing.

- *Debt securities with warrants.* A venture capitalist prefers debentures or notes in connection with warrants often for the same reasons that convertible debt is used, namely the ability to protect downside by enjoying the elevated position of a creditor and the ability to protect upside by including warrants to purchase common stock at favorable prices and terms. The use of a warrant enables the investor to buy common stock without sacrificing the position as a creditor, as would be the case if only convertible debt were used in the financing.

• *Common stock.* Venture capitalists rarely prefer to purchase common stock from the franchisor, especially at early stages of development. This is true because "straight" common stock offers the investor no special rights or preferences, no fixed return on investment, no special ability to exercise control over management, and no liquidity to protect against downside risks. One of the few times that common stock might be selected occurs when the franchisor wishes to preserve its Subchapter S status under the Internal Revenue Code which would be jeopardized if a class of preferred stock were to be authorized.

Once the type of security is selected by the franchisor and the venture capitalist, steps must be taken to ensure that the authorization and issuance of the security is properly effectuated under applicable state corporate laws. For example, if the franchisor's charter does not provide for a class of preferred stock, then articles of amendment must be prepared, approved by the board of directors and shareholders, and filed with the appropriate state corporation authorities. These articles of amendment will be the focus of negotiation between the franchisor and the venture capitalist in terms of voting rights, dividend rates and preferences, mandatory redemption provisions, antidilution protection ("ratchet clauses"), and related special rights and features. If debentures are selected, then negotiations will typically focus on term, interest rate and payment schedule, conversion rights and rates, extent of subordination, remedies for default, acceleration and prepayment rights, and underlying security for the instrument, as well as the terms and conditions of any warrants granted along with the debentures. The legal documents involved in a venture capital financing must reflect the end result of the negotiation process between the franchisor and the venture capitalist. These documents contain all of the legal rights and obligations of the parties, striking a balance between the needs and concerns of the franchisor as well as the investment objectives and necessary controls of the venture capitalist.

The Use of Initial Public Offerings by Growing Franchisors

An initial public offering (IPO) is a process whereby a growing enterprise opts to register its securities with the Securities and Exchange Commission (SEC) for sale to the general investing public for the first time. Many growing franchisors view the process of "going public" as the epitome of financial success and reward. And many national franchisors have successful completed public offerings over the past decade, including Shoney's (family restaurants), Wendy's International (fast food), TCBY Enterprises (frozen yogurt), Snelling & Snelling (personnel placement), McDonald's Corp. (fast food), Medicine Shoppes International (pharmacy stores), Ponderosa (steak houses), and Postal Instant Press (printing centers). However, the decision to go public requires considerable strategic planning and analysis from both a legal and a business perspective. The planning and analysis process involves (1) a weighing of the costs and benefits of being a public company, (2) an understanding of the process and costs of becoming a public company, and (3) an understanding of the obligations of the company, its advisors, and its shareholders once the franchisor has successfully completed its public offering.

Costs and Benefits of the IPO

For the rapidly expanding privately held franchisor, the process of going public presents a number of benefits, including (1) significantly greater access to capital; (2) increased liquidity for the franchisor's shares; (3) greater prestige in the financial markets; (4) enhancement of the franchisor's public image (which may have the effect of increasing franchise sales); (5) opportunities for employee ownership and participation; (6) broader growth opportunities including the potential for merger, acquisition, and further rounds of financing; and (7) an immediate increase in the wealth of the company's founders.

However, the many benefits of being a public company are not without their corresponding costs, and the latter must be seriously considered in the strategic planning process. Among these costs are (1) the dilution in the founders' control of the entity, (2) the pressure to meet market and shareholder expectations regarding growth and dividends, (3) changes in management styles and employee expectations, (4) compliance with complex regulations imposed by federal and state securities laws, (5) stock resale restrictions for company insiders, (6) vulnerability to shifts in the stock market, and (7) the sharing of the franchisor's financial success with hundreds, even thousands of other shareholders.

Note that many franchisors have not been intimidated by the disadvantages of being publicly held, primarily because they (1) are already operating in a disclosure-oriented business, (2) are already compelled to provide audited financial statements, and (3) feel that being publicly held will increase credibility, which generally increases franchise sales.

Preparing the Registration Statement

If after weighing the costs and benefits of an IPO, a franchisor selects this financing route, then the franchisor should locate experienced securities counsel (which is also sensitive to the special issues raised by franchising) to assist in the preparation and filing of the registration statement. The registration statement to be filed with the SEC by the franchisor's counsel consists of two distinct parts: The first part is the offering prospectus, which is the document that is widely distributed to underwriters and prospective investors to assist them in analyzing the franchisor and the securities being offered. The second part includes the exhibits and additional information that are provided directly to the SEC as part of the disclosure and registration regulations. The SEC has also established special provisions for small offerings by companies that are not already subject to the reporting requirements of the 1934 Act. This is Form S-18, available for offerings that will not exceed $7.5 million over a twelve-month period. Form S-18 is somewhat less detailed than a disclosure and requires less detailed financial statements.

An Overview of the Registration Process

Once the registration statement has been prepared and is finally ready for filing with the SEC, franchisor's counsel has two choices: Either file the document with the transmittal letter and required fees or schedule a prefiling conference with an SEC staff member to discuss any anticipated questions or problems regarding the registration. Once the registration statement is officially received by the SEC, it is then assigned to an examining group composed usually of attorneys, accountants, and financial analysts, within a specific industry department of the Division of Corporate Finance. The length of time and depth of the review afforded by the examining group to any given registration statement depends on the history of the franchisor and the nature of the securities offered.

In addition to individual state and SEC regulations discussed previously, a franchisor offering its securities to the public must also meet the requirements of the National Association of Securities Dealers (NASD) and state securities laws. The NASD will analyze all elements of the proposed compensation package for the underwriter in order to determine reasonableness.

Once the final underwriting agreement is signed and the final pricing amendment is filed with the SEC, the registration statement will be declared effective and the selling process may begin. To facilitate the mechanics of the offering process, it is recommended that a franchisor retain the services of a registrar and transfer agent, who will be responsible for issuing stock certificates upon closing, maintaining stockholder ownership records, and processing the transfer of shares from one investor to another.

In addition to the obligations discussed previously, the issuer is usually required to file a Form SR, which is a report on the franchisor's use of the proceeds raised from the sale of the securities. An initial Form SR must be filed within ninety days after the registration statement becomes effective and then once every six months thereafter until the completion of the offering and the application of the proceeds toward their intended use.

Ongoing Reporting and Disclosure Requirements of Publicly Held Companies

Section 13 of the Securities Exchange Act of 1934 grants broad powers to the SEC to develop documents and reports to be filed by companies that register their securities for sale to the general public. The three primary reports required by Section 15(d) of the Exchange Act are Form 10-K, Form 10-Q, and Form 8-K, which are described below.

1. *Form 10-K.* This is the annual report that must be filed ninety days after the close of the fiscal year covered by the report. Form 10-K must include a report of all significant activities of the franchisor during its fourth quarter, an analysis and discussion of financial condition, a description of current officers and directors, and a schedule of certain exhibits.

2. *Form 10-Q.* This is the quarterly report that must be filed no later than forty-five days after the end of each of the first three fiscal quarters of each fiscal year. This quarterly filing includes copies of the financial statements for the quarter (accompanied by a discussion and analysis of the franchisor's financial condition by its management) as well as a report of any pending litigation.

3. *Form 8-K.* This is a periodic report designed to ensure that *all material information* pertaining to events significant to the franchisor are disclosed to the investing public as soon as they are available, but not later than fifteen days after the occurrence of the particular event that triggers the need to file the Form 8-K. The duty to disclose "material information" to the general public, whether as part of a form 8-K filing or otherwise, is an ongoing obligation that continues for as long as the franchisor's securities are publicly traded.

Debt Financing Alternatives for the Growing Franchisor

Early-stage franchisors have not had much luck with commercial banks over the past two decades because most lenders prefer to see "hard collateral" on the balance sheet of a borrower, which is often lacking with start-up franchisors who have only their intellectual property, a projected royalty stream, and a business plan to pledge. A second problem is that most lenders prefer to see proceeds allocated primarily to the purchase of "hard assets" (to further serve as collateral), which is the opposite of what many franchisors want to do with their capital. Most early-stage franchisors need capital for "soft costs," such as the development of manuals, advertising materials, and recruitment fees. Often these banks are more interested in providing financing to the franchisees rather than directly to the franchisor. Certainly these intangible assets can be pledged; however, they are likely to be given far less weight than are equipment, inventory, and real estate. By the time the franchise system has matured to the point that a lender is willing to extend capital based upon the franchisor's balance sheet, royalty stream, and track record, no capital is likely to be required.

Despite these problems, it is likely that the optimal capital structure of a growing franchisor will include a certain amount of debt on the balance sheet. The use of debt in the capital structure, commonly known as "leverage," will affect both the valuation of the company and its overall cost of capital. The maximum debt capacity that a growing franchisor will ultimately be able to handle usually involves a balancing of the costs and risks of a default of a debt obligation *against* the desire of the owners and managers to maintain control of the enterprise by protecting against the dilution that an equity offering would cause. Many franchisors prefer preservation of control over the affairs of their company in exchange for the higher level of risk inherent in taking on additional debt obligations. The ability to meet debt-service payments must be carefully considered in the company's financial projections.

If a pro forma analysis reveals that the ability to meet debt-service obligations will put a strain on the franchisor's cash flow, or that insufficient collateral is available (as is often the case for early-stage franchisors who lack significant tangible assets), then equity alternatives should be explored. It is simply not worth driving the company into voluntary or involuntary bankruptcy solely to maintain a maximum level of control. Overleveraged franchisors typically spend so much of their cash servicing the debt that capital is unavailable to develop new programs and provide support to the franchisees, which will trigger the decline and deterioration of the franchise system. In addition, the level of debt financing selected by the franchisor should be compared against key business ratios in its particular industry, such as those published by Robert Morris Associates or Dun & Bradstreet. Once the optimum debt to equity ratio is determined, owners and managers should be aware of the *various sources* of debt financing as well as the *business and legal issues* involved in borrowing funds from a commercial lender.

Sources of Debt Financing

Although most franchisors turn to traditional forms of financing such as term loans and operating lines of credit from commercial banks, there exists a wide variety of alternative sources of debt financing. Some of these alternatives include:

- *Trade credit.* The use of credit with key suppliers is often a practical means of survival for rapidly growing corporate franchisors. When a franchisor has established a good credit rating with its suppliers but as a result of rapid growth tends to require resources faster than it is able to pay for them, trade credit becomes the only way that growth can be sustained. A key supplier has a strong economic incentive for helping a growing franchisor continue to prosper and may therefore be more willing to negotiate credit terms that are acceptable to both parties.

- *Equipment leasing.* Most rapidly growing franchisors are desperately in need of the *use* but not necessarily the *ownership* of certain vital resources to fuel and maintain growth. Therefore, equipment leasing offers an alternative to ownership of the asset. Monthly lease payments are made in lieu of debt-service payments. The "effective rate" in a leasing transaction is usually much less than the comparable interest rate in a loan.

- *Factoring.* Under the traditional factoring arrangement, a company sells its accounts receivables (or some other income stream such as royalty payments in the case of franchising) to a third party in exchange for immediate cash. The third party or "factor" assumes the risk of collection in exchange for the ability to purchase the accounts receivable at a discount determined by the comparative level of risk. Once notice has been provided to debtors of their obligation to pay the factor directly, the seller of the accounts receivable is no longer liable to the factor in the event of a default, although the factor will retain a holdback amount to partially offset these losses.

- *Miscellaneous sources of nonbank debt financing.* Debt securities such as bonds, notes, and debentures may be offered to venture capitalists, private investors, friends, family, employees, insurance companies, and related financial institutions. Many smaller businesses will turn to traditional sources of consumer credit, such as home equity loans, credit cards, and commercial finance companies to finance the growth of their business. In addition to the Small Business Administration (SBA) loan programs, many state and local governments have created direct loan programs for small businesses.

Although all available alternative sources of debt financing should be actively considered, traditional bank loans from commercial lenders are the most common source of capital for franchisors. Franchisors should take the time to learn the lending policies of the institution, as well as the terms and conditions of the traditional types of loans such as term loans, operating lines of credit, real estate loans, and long-term financing.

Negotiating With Commercial Lenders

Negotiating the financing documents that will be executed by the franchisor in a typical commercial bank loan requires a delicate balancing between the requirements of the lender and the needs of the borrower. The lender will want to have all rights, remedies, and protection available to mitigate the risk of loan default. On the other hand, the franchisor as borrower will want to minimize both the amount of collateral given to secure the debt and the level of control exercised by the lender under the affirmative and negative covenants of the loan agreement while achieving a return on its assets that greatly exceeds its debt-service payments.

Before examining each document involved in a typical debt financing, you should understand some general rules of loan negotiation:

- *Interest rates.* A banker will generally calculate the rate of interest in accordance with prevailing market rates, the degree of risk inherent in the proposed transaction, the extent of any pre-existing relationship with the lender, and the cost of administering the loan.
- *Collateral.* The commercial lender may request that certain collateral be pledged that has a value equal to or greater than the proceeds of the loan. When collateral is requested, franchisors should attempt to keep certain key assets of the

business outside of the pledge agreement so that they are available to serve as security in the event that additional capital is needed at a later time. Beyond the traditional forms of tangible assets that may be offered to the lender as collateral, borrowers should also consider intangibles such as assignment of lease rights, key-man insurance policies, intellectual property, and goodwill. Naturally, loss of these assets could be very costly to the franchisor in the event of default and should be pledged only as a last resort.

• *Prepayment rights.* Regardless of the actual term of the loan, the borrower should negotiate a right to prepay the principal of the loan without penalty or special repayment charges. Many commercial lenders seek to attach prepayment charges to term loans that have a fixed rate of interest, in order to ensure that a minimum rate of return is earned over the projected life of the loan.

• *Hidden costs and fees.* Many commercial banks attempt to charge the borrower with a variety of direct and indirect costs and fees in connection with the debt financing. Included in this category are closing costs, processing fees, filing fees, late charges, attorneys' fees, out-of-pocket expense reimbursement (courier, travel, photocopying, etc.), court costs, and auditing or inspection fees.

• *Commitment fees.* Many lenders also charge a fee for issuing a firm commitment to make the loan, after conducting its credit review and obtaining credit committee approval to make the loan. Typically, all or some of this is reimbursable if the borrower actually draws the loan.

• *Restrictive covenants.* The typical loan agreement will include a variety of affirmative and negative restrictive covenants designed to protect the interests of the lender. Franchisors should carefully renew these covenants to ensure that the implementation of the company's business plan will not be unduly impeded.

13

Special Issues in Mergers and Acquisitions

Franchisors are no less susceptible to the pressures of competition, shifts in demand and demographics, or the need to respond to changes in law or technology than is a company that has selected an alternative form of distribution and growth. Mergers and acquisitions of other competing or complementary franchise systems represent a viable strategy for responding to these pressures. Some of the most common reasons why franchisors consider a merger or acquisition with another franchisor include:

- The franchisor may wish to add new products or services to its existing line and does not want to incur the expense and uncertainty of internal research and development.
- The franchisor may want to expand its geographic or customer base without the expense of attracting new franchisees into these locations or developing a new advertising and marketing program.
- Small to medium-size franchisors may want to merge to meet the competition of an "industry giant" or eliminate the threat of a smaller competitor.
- The franchisor may want to achieve market efficiencies through the acquisition of suppliers (backward integration) or existing franchisees or distributors (forward integration).

- The franchisor may want to strengthen or expand its management personnel and marketing capabilities.

Franchisors must be aware of the legal requirements, ramifications, and potential barriers to a proposed merger or acquisition. Franchisors must be especially aware of the unique relationship between franchisor and franchisee and analyze the ways in which the proposed merger or acquisition may affect the franchisor-franchisee relationship.

Analysis of Target Companies

A franchisor must begin the process with an acquisition plan identifying the specific objectives of the transaction and the criteria to be applied in analyzing a potential target company operating within the targeted industry.

Once acquisition objectives have been identified, the next logical step is to narrow the field of candidates. The transaction should achieve one or more of the acquisition objectives developed and the target company should meet many, if not all, of the criteria identified. A candidate under serious consideration should possess most or all of the following criteria:

- The target operates in an industry that demonstrates growth potential.

- The target has taken steps to protect any proprietary aspects of its products and services.

- The target company has developed a well-defined and established market position.

- The target company has strong franchise agreements with its franchisees with minimal amendments or "special deals."

- The target company should be involved in a minimal amount of litigation (especially if the litigation is with key customers, distributors, franchisees, or suppliers).

- The target company should be in a position to readily obtain key third-party consents from lessors, bankers, credi-

(Text continues on page 288.)

Figure 13-1. Alternative structures for the acquisition of a franchisor.

The focus of this chapter is on an acquisition or merger transaction between two competing or complementary franchisors.

However, there are a wide range of structural alternatives in the acquisition of a franchisor. Consider the following:

Type of Transaction	Example
(1) Franchisor Acquires a Competing Franchisor	International chain of Dunkin Donuts acquires its largest competitor, Mister Donut, in 1989; Marriott Corp. sells its 600-unit chain of Roy Rogers to competitor Hardee's Food Systems, Inc. on April 16, 1990; 500-unit Precision Tune of Sterling, Virginia, acquires 87-unit National 60-Minute Tune, Inc., which operates in Oregon and Washington, in early 1990.
(2) Franchisor Acquires a Complementary Franchisor	H & R Block (tax services) acquires Hyatt Legal Services and Personnel Pool of America in the 1980s; Service Master (office cleaning/franchisor with over 1,000 units) acquires 370-unit Merry Maids (housecleaning) in 1989.
(3) Franchisor Acquired by Domestic Venture Capital Investment Group	California-based Supercuts, Inc., a 541-unit hair care chain, is acquired by Knightsbridge Partners.
(4) Franchisor Acquired by Group of Overseas Investors	Southland Corporation, which owns the 7-Eleven chain of 7,000 convenience stores, sells, subject to certain debt restructuring by

	Southland, 75 percent of its stock to Ito-Yokado Co., Ltd., the second-largest chain of supermarkets in Japan; Grand Metropolitan PLC, a British conglomerate, acquires Burger King from Pillsbury. In July of 1990, the French hotel company Accor purchases the Motel 6 franchise chain for $1.3 billion.
(5) Franchisor Acquired by its Own Managers (Backed by Group of Passive Investors)	At the request of a group of franchisees, executive Vice-President, Stephen Danneman acquires the 126-unit World Bazaar furniture chain in 1988 from its original owner, Munford, Inc., backed by a group of investors.
(6) Franchisor Acquired by Group of Franchisees	Franchisees have acquired the ownership of national and regional franchisors such as Straw Hat (pizza), Arthur Treacher's (fast food), Eastern Onion (singing telegrams), Dial One (home care referrals), and Bob's Big Boy (family restaurants).
(7) Franchisor Acquired by a Multinational Conglomerate	A number of multinational conglomerates have acquired franchisors over the past decade, such as Pillsbury Corporation's ownership of Burger King and Pepsico's ownership of the Taco Bell, Pizza Hut, and Kentucky Fried Chicken franchise systems. In February of 1990, Bass PLC, a British conglomerate, paid $2.23 billion for the Holiday Inn franchise network, leaving the Hampton Inn and Embassy Suites

Figure 13-1. continued

	franchise chains to its reorganized U.S. company, Promus Companies, Inc., based in Memphis, Tennessee. Promus went on to organize a financing affiliate to fund new construction by its franchisees, Hospitality Capital Group, which is two-thirds owned by two Japanese conglomerates.
(8) Franchisor Acquires a Competing Nonfranchised Business	Blockbuster Video acquires one of its largest nationwide competitors, Erol's in October of 1990. Erol's had announced plans to begin franchising in August of 1990.

tors, suppliers, and investors (where required; failure to obtain necessary consents to the assignment of key contracts may serve as a substantial impediment to the completion of the transaction).

■ The target company should be positioned for a sale in order to ensure that negotiations focus on the terms of the sale, *not* whether to sell in the first place.

In addition to the general business issues discussed above, the following specific franchising issues should be examined when you study the feasibility of the acquisition of a franchisor:

■ The strength and registration status of the target franchisor's intellectual property
■ The strength of the target franchisor's agreements and relationships with its network of franchisees

- The status of any litigation or regulatory inquiries involving the franchisor
- Compliance by the franchisees of the target franchisor with the terms of the franchise agreements and overall quality control standards
- The strength of the franchisor's management team and sales staff
- The quality of the franchisor-franchisee relationship
- Industry and economic trends that may affect the growth of the target's franchise system
- The regularity of the franchisor's cash flow (e.g., compliance by the franchisees with their royalty obligations)
- The strength of the franchisor's training, operations, and field support programs; manuals; and personnel
- The existence of a franchisee association (and its hostile or advisory status and relationship with the franchisor)
- The strength and performance of the franchisor's company-owned units (where applicable)
- The target franchisor's relative market penetration, growth plans, and sales history
- The target franchisor's relationship with suppliers key to the franchise network

Effective rating and analysis of the field of acquisition candidates will depend, in part, on the data gathered during the preacquisition review.

The Preacquisition Review

The preacquisition review is the preliminary analysis conducted on the two or three finalists that most closely meet the franchisor's acquisition objectives. The key areas of inquiry at this stage in the transaction are the target's management team, financial performance to date and projected performance, the

strength of the target's intellectual property, areas of potential
liability to the franchisor as a successor company, identification of any legal or business impediments to the transaction,
confirmation of any facts underlying the terms of the proposed
valuation and bid, and the terms of the target's existing franchise and area development agreements. This information can
come from meetings and requests for information from the target's management team or from external sources, such as trade
associations, customers and suppliers of the target, industry
publications, franchise regulatory agencies, chambers of commerce, securities law filings, or private data sources such as
Dun & Bradstreet, Standard & Poor's, and Moody's.

In analyzing the target franchisor, a wide variety of legal
documents and records, where applicable, should be carefully
reviewed and analyzed by the acquiring entity and its legal
counsel. Inasmuch as the two key assets being acquired are the
trademark rights and the obligations of the franchisee under
the franchise agreement (e.g., royalty system), these two areas
should be especially carefully examined.

During the preacquisition review, the acquiring entity and
its legal counsel should be gathering data necessary to answer
the following types of preliminary legal and strategic questions relevant to the transaction:

- What legal steps will need to be taken to effectuate the
  transaction (e.g., director and stockholder approval,
  share transfer restrictions, restrictive covenants in loan
  documentation, etc.)?
- What antitrust problems, if any, are raised by the transaction? Will filing be necessary under the premerger notification provisions of the Hart-Scott-Rodino Act?
- Will the transaction be exempt from registration under
  applicable federal and state securities loans under the
  "sale of business" doctrine?
- What potential adverse tax consequences to the buyer,
  seller, and their respective stockholders may be triggered by the transaction?
- What are the potential postclosing risks and obligations

of the buyer? To what extent should the seller be held liable for such potential liability? What steps, if any, can be taken to reduce these potential risks or liabilities? What will it cost to implement these steps?

- What are the impediments to the assignability of key tangible and intangible assets of the target company which are desired by the buyer, such as real estate, intellectual property, favorable contracts or leases, human resources, or plant and equipment?
- What are the obligations and responsibilities of the buyer and seller under applicable environmental and hazardous waste laws, such as the Comprehensive Environmental Response Compensation and Liability Act (CERCLA)?
- What are the obligations and responsibilities of buyer and seller to the creditors of the target (e.g., bulk transfer laws under the applicable state's commercial code)?
- What are the obligations and responsibilities of buyer and seller under applicable federal and state labor and employment laws (e.g., will the buyer be subject to successor liability under federal labor laws and as a result be obligated to recognize the presence of organized labor and therefore be obligated to negotiate existing collective bargaining agreements?)?
- To what extent will employment, consulting, confidentiality, or noncompetition agreements need to be created or modified in connection with the proposed transaction?
- Does the target franchisor fit into the long-range growth plans of the acquiring franchisor?
- What are the target franchisor's strong points and weaknesses? How does management of the acquiring franchisor plan to eliminate those weaknesses?
- Has the acquiring franchisor's management team developed a comprehensive plan to integrate the resources of the target?
- What is the target franchisor's ratio of company-owned outlets to franchisees?

- Are the target's products and services competitive in terms of price, quality, style, and marketability?
- Does the target franchisor manufacture its own products? What proportions are purchased from outside sellers?
- Is the target franchisor's trademark secure and without restrictions on use or transfer?
- What are the terms of the target's agreements with its existing franchisees? Are these agreements assignable? Do they contain clauses giving the franchisor discretion to change the system or ownership? Could any of these terms cause problems for the acquiring franchisor at a later date?
- Is the target currently involved in litigation with franchisees, creditors, competitors, or suppliers? Threatened litigation? Potential litigation? What is the risk of exposure to the acquiring franchisor?
- What is the target's past and current financial condition? What about future projections? Are they realistic?
- Have the target's registration and disclosure documents been properly filed and updated?
- What is the target franchisor's sales history? Has there been a steady flow of franchise sales and royalty payments?
- What is the target franchisor's attrition rate? Have there been many recent terminations or transfers? Have any of these been contested by franchisees as lacking good cause?

The Role of the Franchisee in a Proposed Merger or Acquisition

Unlike other types of growing companies involved in mergers and acquisitions, franchisors have existing contractual vertical distribution systems in place through their franchisees. The interests of these franchisees ought to be taken into account when the franchisor's counsel analyzes the legal consequences and potential costs of the proposed merger or acquisition. These franchisees are clearly "interested parties," whose contractual and other legal and equitable rights must be considered. Although there is no statutory or legal basis for disclosing the intent to engage in a merger or acquisition, nor is there typically a contractual requirement to obtain their approval, good "franchisee relations" practice would dictate their involvement in some fashion. The cooperation level of the franchisee networks of both buyer and seller can either greatly facilitate the transaction or virtually kill the deal, depending on how this communication problem is handled.

For example, if the franchisor acquires another franchisor in a competitive or parallel line of business, careful merger planning and negotiation will be necessary to ensure a smooth integration of the target's franchise system into the buyer's existing operations (assuming that only one system will survive after the transaction) and to avoid potential litigation or costly settlement with affected franchisees of either system. In addition, if conversion or change is planned as a result of the merger or acquisition, franchisors should expect to involve franchisees, at least to a certain extent, in the decision-making process. The acquiring franchisor should not automatically assume that franchisees in the acquired system will be willing to convert to the buyer's existing system. When change or conversion is contemplated, some attrition and/or franchisee resistance should be expected in both systems, and the impact and costs of this attrition and resistance will typically be reflected in the purchase price of the target franchisor.

On one hand, the franchisee is typically neither a shareholder, creditor, investor, officer, or director of the franchisor and would technically be governed only by the terms of franchise agreements, which usually gives broad latitude to the franchisor to assign rights or modify the franchise system. Yet to ignore the fact that the franchisee is clearly an interested and affected party in any change in the franchisor's organizational structure or system is unrealistic and could result in very costly litigation that might even outweigh any anticipated benefits to the proposed merger or acquisition.

Figure 13-2. Legitimate concerns of the franchisee network in a merger or acquisition.

Clearly, the franchisee will have some legitimate questions and concerns when it first learns of the proposed transaction. The savvy franchisor will anticipate these concerns and integrate the proposed solutions into its acquisition plan and communications with the franchisees and/or the franchisee association:

(1) What are the acquiring franchisor's plans for the acquired system? Consolidation and conversion? At whose cost? Liquidation? Growth?

(2) What is the reputation and management philosophy of the acquiring franchisor? What are its attitudes toward field support and ongoing training?

(3) Will the acquiring franchisor be sensitive to the rights and concerns of the franchisees? Or will the franchisees adopt a "we'd rather fight than switch" mentality toward the new buyer in anticipation of hostile negotiations?

(4) What is the financial strength of the acquiring franchisor? Will the acquiring franchisor open up new opportunities for the franchisees, such as access to new product lines, financing programs for growth and expansion, produce purchasing, and cooperative advertising programs?

(5) If the target franchisor owns real property that is leased to franchisees, will the terms and conditions of the current leases be honored by the acquiring franchisor? What about other contractual obligations? Are there any special relationships with third-party vendors that will be affected or damaged by the transaction?

Special Problems to Consider in the Acquisition of a Franchisor

There are many potential areas of dispute between the acquiring or acquired franchisor and its franchisees that may arise as a result of a merger or acquisition. Naturally, the anticipated costs of these post-transactional problems should be factored into the price and terms of the merger or acquisition. Whether or not these issues will arise will of course depend on a variety of factors, including the nature of the businesses of the merging franchisors (products, services), the territories in which they operate, the terms of the contracts with existing franchisees, the size and market power of the merging franchisors, the competitors (or lack of) of each of the franchisors, and most importantly, the postmerger plans of the entities. In adopting strategies to resolve problem areas, both companies should be cognizant of their implied obligation to act in good faith and in a commercially reasonable manner, a covenant recognized by many state courts in their interpretation of the franchise relationship. Among the issues to which both franchisors should pay special attention:

- To what extent has territorial exclusivity been granted to the franchisees of each system? Is the exclusivity given only for a certain trademark or line of business? Is the territorial exclusivity conditioned on the performance of the franchisees? Will substantially similar franchisees violate this exclusivity? How else might the postacquisition structure affect these covenants?
- Will all existing franchisees of both systems be maintained, or will a consolidated distribution system result in termination of some franchisees?
- Will the existing franchisees of the acquired system be converted to the business format of the acquirer? Vice versa? Who will pay the costs of building conversion, new training, products, and services? Will the franchisor finance all or part of the conversion costs?

Figure 13-3. Special incentives to offer franchisees to facilitate system conversion.

If the proposed merger or acquisition will involve a system conversion by either the franchisees of the acquiror or acquiree, then the buyer should expect some resistance. The timetable, costs, and legal issues surrounding the conversion should all be considered. There are a number of incentives (or "sweeteners") that could be offered to the franchisees in order to ease the burden of conversion and to facilitate a rapid and smooth conversion, rather than a proposed conversion fraught with delay and litigation. These sweeteners may include:

(1) Royalty moratorium or reduction in royalty rates
(2) Modification of existing performance quotas
(3) Expansion of the franchisee's protected territory
(4) Price cuts on required (and optional) inventory and supplies
(5) Reduction of required advertising fund contributions
(6) The formation of special product purchasing cooperatives
(7) Credits and cash allowances toward the cost of system conversion
(8) Offering of new signs, uniforms, displays, products, and business forms required for system conversion at no or low cost
(9) Access to low-rate financing for expansion
(10) The offer of additional franchise or area development rights at reduced costs
(11) The extension of the term of each franchisee's franchise agreement
(12) The offer of a seat on the board of directors by a representative of the franchisee association
(13) An increase in the franchisee's role in the management and allocation of advertising contributions
(14) Eligibility and participation in group insurance plans

(15) Additional training and field support at no extra charge
(16) Temporary reductions in minimum monthly fees
(17) Opening of a second location within the franchisee's own territory at a reduced cost
(18) Temporary abatement of royalty fees, minimum monthly fees, and/or advertising contributions
(19) Additional supervision or management consulting services by franchisor at no charge or at a reduced rate
(20) Additional or enhanced advertising that can be prepared for the franchisee's use, advertising novelties, and related promotional campaigns
(21) Additional or refresher training courses, workshops, or seminars that may be offered at no charge to franchisees, their managers, etc.
(22) Thirty-day supply of forms, records, office materials, accounting and reporting documents

---

- Will existing franchisees of each system be forced to add the products and services of the other? Will this present tying or full-line forcing problems?
- Does the acquiring franchisor have sufficient support staff to adequately service the new franchisees, or will the acquiring company's existing franchisees be ignored in order to develop and market the new acquisitions? What rights do the existing franchisees have to challenge this lack of attention?
- Will a new, third type of system combining the products and services of the acquiring and acquired franchisors be offered to prospective franchisees of the surviving entity? Will existing franchisees of either system be eligible to convert to this new system?
- Can the acquiring franchisor legitimately enforce an interm covenant against competition when the franchisor

itself has acquired and is operating what is arguably a competitive system?

- Do the franchisees of either franchisor have a Franchisee Association or Franchisee Advisory Council? Must these groups be consulted? What duty does the franchisor have to involve these groups in merger planning? What about regional and multiple franchisees holding development rights?
- Does either franchisor have company-owned outlets in its distribution system? What will be the status of these outlets after the merger or acquisition?
- To what extent will royalty payments, renewal fees, costs of inventory, performance quotas, and advertising contributions be affected by the contemplated merger or acquisition? On what grounds could franchisees challenge these changes as unreasonable, breaches of contract, or violations of antitrust laws? How and when will these changes be phased into the system? Will the franchisees be given a chance to opt in or opt out? (mandatory v. optional changes?)
- Will the proposed transaction result in the termination of some of the franchisees of either system due to over-saturation of the market, territorial overlap, or under-performance? What legal and statutory rights of the franchisee are triggered?

The difficult legal and strategic issues that are triggered in a merger or acquisition by and among franchisors can be resolved, and litigation avoided, with careful planning by the acquiring and acquired franchisors, which will necessarily include communication with the franchisees of both systems in the negotiations and implementation of the merger or acquisition.

Part Five

Alternatives to Franchising

14

Licensing, Joint Ventures, and Other Alternatives to Franchising

A wide variety of successful companies for one reason or another do not necessarily meet the foundational requirements needed to develop a business format franchising program. This does not mean, however, that the benefits of a contractual growth-oriented marketing strategy cannot be obtained through the use of licensing, joint ventures, distributorships, sales agencies, multilevel marketing plans, and other commonly adopted alternatives to franchising. This chapter examines many of these alternatives, with an emphasis on systems that provide a viable alternative to the capital and management costs of internal growth.

Licensing Proprietary Products, Services, and Technology

Licensing is a contractual method of developing and exploiting intellectual property by transferring rights of use to third parties *without* the transfer of ownership. Virtually any proprietary product or service may be the subject of a license agreement, ranging from the licensing of the Mickey Mouse character by Walt Disney Studios in the 1930s to modern-day licensing of computer software and high technology. From a legal perspective, licensing involves complex issues of contract, tax, antitrust, international, tort, and intellectual property law. From a business perspective, licensing involves a weighing of the advantages of licensing against the disadvantages in comparison to alternative types of vertical distribution systems.

Many of the benefits of licensing to be enjoyed by a growing company closely parallel the advantages of franchising, namely:

- Spreading the risk and cost of development and distribution
- Achieving more rapid market penetration
- Earning initial license fees and ongoing royalty income
- Enhancing consumer loyalty and goodwill
- Preserving the capital that would otherwise be required for internal growth and expansion
- Testing new applications for existing and proven technology
- Avoiding or settling litigation regarding a dispute over ownership of the technology

The disadvantages of licensing are also similar to the risks inherent in franchising, such as:

- A somewhat diminished ability to enforce quality control standards and specifications
- A greater risk of another party infringing upon the licensor's intellectual property
- A dependence on the skills, abilities, and resources of the licensee as a source of revenue
- Difficulty in recruiting, motivating, and retaining qualified and competent licensees
- The risk that the licensor's entire reputation and goodwill may be damaged or destroyed by the act or omission of a single licensee

- The administrative burden of monitoring and supporting the operations of the network of licensees

Failure to consider all of the costs and benefits of licensing could easily result in a regretful strategic decision or the
terms of an unprofitable license agreement due to either an
underestimation of the licensee's need for technical assistance
and support or an overestimation of the market demand for
the licensor's products and services. In order to avoid such
problems, a certain amount of due diligence should be conducted by the licensor prior to any serious negotiations with a
prospective licensee. This preliminary investigation generally
includes market research, legal steps to fully protect intellectual property, and an internal financial analysis of the technology with respect to pricing, profit margins, and costs of
production and distribution. It will also include a more specific analysis of the prospective licensee with respect to its
financial strength, research and manufacturing capabilities,
and reputation in the industry. Once the decision to enter into
more formal negotiations has been made, the terms and conditions of the license agreement should be discussed. Naturally, these provisions will vary, depending on whether the
license is for merchandising an entertainment property, exploiting a given technology, or distributing a particular product to an original equipment manufacturer (OEM) or value-
added reseller (VAR).

Chapter 15 provides an overview of the two most common
forms of licensing arrangements: merchandise licensing and
technology transfer and licensing.

Distributorships, Dealerships, and Sales Representatives

Many growing product-oriented companies choose to bring
their wares to the marketplace through independent third-
party distributors and dealerships. These dealers are generally

more difficult to control than is a licensee or franchisee and as a result the agreement between the manufacturer and the distributor is much more informal than a franchise or license agreement. This type of arrangement is commonly used by manufacturers of electronic and stereo equipment, computer hardware and software, sporting goods, medical equipment, and automobile parts and accessories.

In developing distributor and dealership agreements, growing companies must be careful to avoid being included within the broad definition of a franchise under FTC Rule 436, which would require the preparation of a disclosure document. To avoid such a classification, the agreement should impose minimal controls over the dealer, and the sale of products must be at bona fide wholesale prices. In addition, the manufacturer must offer no more than minimal assistance in the marketing or management of the dealer's business. A well-drafted distributorship agreement should address the key issues outlined in Figure 14-1.

Distributors are often confused with sales representatives, but there are many critical differences. Typically, a distributor buys the product from the manufacturer, at wholesale prices, with title passing to the distributor when payment is received. There is usually no actual fee paid by the distributor for the grant of the distributorship, and the distributor will typically be permitted to carry competitive products. The distributor is expected to maintain some retail location or showroom where the manufacturer's products are displayed. The distributor must maintain its own inventory storage and warehousing capabilities. The distributor looks to the manufacturer for technical support; advertising contributions; supportive repair, maintenance, and service policies; new product training; volume discounts; favorable payment and return policies; and brand name recognition. The manufacturer looks to the distributor for in-store and local promotion, adequate inventory controls, financial stability, preferred display and stocking, prompt payment, and qualified sales personnel. Although the distributorship network offers a viable alternative to franchising, it is not a panacea. The management and control of the

Figure 14-1. Elements of distributorship agreement.

1. What is the scope of the appointment? Which products is the dealer authorized to distribute and under what conditions? What is the scope, if any, of the exclusive territory to be granted to the distributor? To what extent will product, vendor, customer, or geographic restrictions be applicable?

2. What activities will the distributor be expected to perform in terms of manufacturing, sales, marketing, display, billing, market research, maintenance of books and records, storage, training, installation, support, and servicing?

3. What obligations will the distributor have to preserve and protect the intellectual property of the manufacturer?

4. What right, if any, will the distributor have to modify or enhance the manufacturer's warranties, terms of sale, credit policies, or refund procedures?

5. What advertising literature, technical and marketing support, training seminars, or special promotions will be provided by the manufacturer to enhance the performance of the distributor?

6. What sales or performance quotas will be imposed on the dealer as a condition to its right to continue to distribute the manufacturer's products or services? What are the rights and remedies of the manufacturer if the dealers fails to meet these performance standards?

7. What is the term of the agreement and under what conditions can it be terminated? How will post-termination transactions be handled?

distributors may be even more difficult than that involved in franchising (especially without the benefit of a comprehensive franchise agreement) and the termination of these relationships is regulated by many state antitermination statutes.

The sales representative or sales agent is an independent marketing resource for the manufacturer. The sales representative, unlike the distributor, does not typically take title to the merchandise, maintain inventories or retail locations, or engage in any special price promotions unless these are instigated by the manufacturer.

Joint Ventures

Another major alternative to committing the capital and management resources necessary for internal expansion is joint venturing or, as it has come to be known more recently, "strategic partnering." It is estimated that strategic partnering and other related commercial alliances will be responsible for 19 percent of all financing over the next five years. Joint venturing and other commercial alliances often function in many respects as an alternative to a merger. Under a standard joint venture agreement, two companies join together either through a partnership-type agreement or through joint ownership of a specially created corporation in order to achieve greater efficiency and certain economies of scale. In the course of analyzing a target's suitability for a partnering arrangement, a growing company should look closely not only at the products and services being offered but also at the competence of the management team. There are numerous preliminary questions that need to be addressed by growing businesses interested in undertaking a joint venture or partnership arrangement. The following is a summary of some of the more salient points:

- Exactly what type of tangible and intangible assets will be contributed to the joint venture by each party? Who will have ownership rights in the property contributed during the term of the joint venture and thereafter? Who will own property developed as a result of joint development efforts?
- What covenants of nondisclosure or noncompetition will be expected of each joint venturer during the term of the agreement and thereafter?

- What timetables or performance quotas for completion of the projects contemplated by the joint venture will be included in the agreement? What are the rights and remedies of each party if these performance standards are not met?
- How will issues of management and control be addressed in the agreement? What will be the respective voting rights of each party? What are the procedures in the event of a major disagreement or deadlock? What is the fallback plan?

Once these preliminary issues have been discussed by the parties, a formal joint venture agreement, partnership agreement, or corporate shareholders agreement should be prepared. If the proposed relationship includes an acquisition of stock or assets by one party in the enterprise of the other party, it will be necessary to scrutinize the transaction for potential antitrust violations. Any liaison that substantially increases the influence of one or the other parties in a particular market section should be reviewed prior to final implementation.

Structuring Joint Ventures

The precise terms of the agreement between the parties depend upon the nature and the structure of the arrangement. At a minimum, however, the following topics should be addressed in as much detail as possible:

- *Nature, purpose, and trade name for the joint venture.* The parties should set forth the legal nature of the relationship between themselves along with a clear statement of purpose to prevent future disputes as to the scope of the arrangement. If a new trade name is established for the venture, provisions should be made as to the use of the name and any other trade or service marks registered by the venture upon termination of the entity or project.

- *Status of the respective joint venturers.* The agreement should clearly indicate whether each party is a partner, shareholder, agent, independent contractor, or any combination thereof. Agent status, whether actual or imputed, can greatly affect liability between the venturers and with regard to third parties.
- *Representations and warranties of each joint venturer.* Standard representations and warranties will include obligations of due care and due diligence as well as mutual covenants governing confidentiality and anticompetition restrictions.
- *Capital and property contributions of each joint venturer.* A clear schedule should be established of all contributions, whether in the form of cash, shares, real estate, or intellectual property. Detailed descriptions will be particularly important if the distribution of profits and losses is to be based upon overall contribution. The specifics of allocation and distribution of profits and losses among the venturers should also be clearly defined.
- *Management, control, and voting rights of each joint venturer.* If the proposed venture envisions joint management, it will be necessary to specifically address the keeping of books, records, and bank accounts; the nature and frequency of inspections and audits; insurance and cross-indemnification obligations; as well as responsibility for administrative and overhead expenses.
- *Rights in joint venture property.* Growing companies should be especially mindful of intellectual property rights and should clearly address the issues of ownership use and licensing entitlements not only for the venturers' presently existing property rights, but also for future use of rights (or products or services) developed in the name of the venture itself.
- *Restrictions on transferability of ownership interest in the joint venture.* Stringent conditions should be placed on the ability of the venturers to transfer interests in the venture to third parties.

- *Default, dissolution, and termination of the joint venture.* The obligations of the venturers and the distribution assets should be clearly defined along with procedures in the event of bankruptcy and grounds for default.
- *Dispute resolution procedures.* The parties may wish to consider arbitration as an alternative dispute resolution mechanism.
- *Miscellaneous.* Provisions should also be made indicating (1) the governing law, (2) remedies under force majeure situations, (3) procedures for notice and consent, and (4) the ability to modify or waive certain provisions.

Cooperatives

Cooperatives have been formed as associations of member companies in the same or similar industries in order to achieve operating, advertising, and purchasing efficiencies and economies of scale. Typically the cooperative is owned and controlled by its members. Cooperatives have been especially effective in certain inventory-intense industries, such as hardware, automobile parts and accessories, pharmacies, and grocery stores. There is typically a common trade identity that each independent business may use in its advertising and promotion; however, ownership of the actual trademarks rests with the cooperative itself. Retail cooperatives, if properly structured, are exempt from FTC Rule 436 and from some state franchise laws. The organization and ongoing operation of the cooperative should be periodically reviewed by counsel in order to ensure that certain federal and state antitrust and unfair competition laws are not violated.

Consulting and Training Services

Many veterans of a particular industry choose to share their expertise with others by charging fixed or hourly fees for consulting or training services. Instead of being licensed, this information is essentially sold to the client or seminar attendee at a fixed price. If support is needed by the client, then additional time may be purchased. This alternative creates competitors without the benefit of an ongoing royalty fee and should only be considered if the expertise to be conveyed falls short of what would be needed in a business format franchise or even in a licensing situation.

Employee Ownership and Profit Sharing

Many growth companies initially turn to franchising as an expansion alternative because of the need to develop "motivated managers" at each site. The theory is that this owner/operator has a better feel for the local market and as an owner will be more motivated to promote the franchisor's products and services. But there are many ways to motivate managers and make them feel like owners, such as employee stock ownership plans, executive stock option arrangements, and profit-sharing plans. As an alternative to franchising, each unit could be separately incorporated, with a minority stock interest granted to the key individuals responsible for the operations of that unit. Such an arrangement could be done on a "per store" or regional basis. Although this results in some dilution of the ownership and control of the store or region, the managers would be expected to execute a shareholders' agreement that would place certain stock transfer restrictions as well as predetermined buy-out arrangements on the ownership of the stock. Naturally, the terms of these stock ownership and profit-sharing arrangements should be structured with the assistance of a tax accountant and securities law counsel.

Multilevel Marketing Plans

Multilevel marketing (MLM) is a method of direct selling of products or services according to which distributors or sales representatives sell products to the consumer outside of a retail store context and often in a one-to-one setting. In some cases, the distributors purchase the manufacturer's products at wholesale and profit by selling the product to the consumer at retail price. In other instances, distributors sponsor other sales representatives or distributors and receive commissions on the sales made by the sponsored representative or any further representative sponsored in a continuous "down-line sales organization." Leading merchandisers who use this form of marketing include Shaklee Corporation, Amway Corporation, and Mary Kay Cosmetics.

MLM companies are regulated by numerous overlapping laws that vary from state to state. MLM programs are affected by a combination of pyramid statutes, business opportunity statutes, multilevel distribution laws, franchise and securities laws, various state lottery laws, referral sales laws, the federal postal laws, and Section 5 of the Federal Trade Commission Act.

Recently, many MLM plans have been targeted for prosecution and litigation based on the above laws. To date, enforcement of statutes and regulations has been selective and arbitrary and many regulatory officials have developed negative attitudes toward the legality of any one MLM program. Therefore, from a legal standpoint, MLM is an uncertain and speculative activity and there is no assurance that even the most legitimate MLM program will be immune from regulatory inquiry.

Multilevel Marketing Statutes

Six states have laws specifically regulating companies that adopt multilevel marketing programs: Georgia, Louisiana, Maryland, Massachusetts, New Mexico, and Wyoming. Any MLM company operating in any of these states typically must file an annual registration statement giving notice of its operations in that state and must appoint that state's secretary of state as its agent for service of process.

A "multilevel marketing company" is typically defined by these states as an entity that "sells, distributes, or supplies, for valuable consideration, goods or services, through independent agents or distributors at different levels and in which participants may recruit other participants in which commissions or bonuses are paid as a result of the sale of the goods or services or the recruitment of additional participants."

In addition to imposing the annual registration requirement, several states have placed additional regulations governing the activities of the MLM companies such as:

- Requiring that MLM companies allow their independent representatives or distributors to cancel their agreements with the company, and upon such cancellation the company must repurchase unsold products at a price not less than 90 percent of the distributor's original net cost
- Prohibiting MLM companies from representing that distributors have or will earn stated dollar amounts
- Prohibiting MLM companies from requiring distributors to purchase certain minimum initial inventories (except in reasonable quantities)
- Prohibiting that compensation be paid solely for recruiting other participants

Business Opportunity Laws

A "business opportunity" is typically defined as the sale or lease of products or services to a purchaser for the purpose of enabling the purchaser to start a business and in which the seller represents that:

- The seller will provide locations or assist the purchaser in finding locations for the use of vending machines
- The seller will purchase products made by the purchaser using the supplies or services sold to the purchaser
- The seller guarantees the purchaser will derive income from the business opportunity which exceeds the price paid for the business opportunity or that the seller will

      refund all or part of the price paid for the business op-
      portunity if the purchaser is unsatisfied with the busi-
      ness opportunity

- Upon the payment by the purchaser of a certain sum of
  money (usually between $25 and $500), the seller will
  provide a sales program or marketing program that will
  enable the purchaser to derive income from the business opportunity which exceeds the price paid for the
  business opportunity

This definition (or some variation thereof) can be found in over twenty state statutes nationwide. While the first two elements do not apply to MLM companies, the third and fourth elements would in all probability relate to MLM companies that offer to repurchase sales kits and unsold inventory if a distributor discontinues selling and its sales kits exceed the amounts specified in the various state statutes. It is interesting to note that the very requirement imposed on MLM companies by many of the MLM statutes (e.g., requiring the company to buy back unused products) is an element of a business opportunity.

Business opportunity offerers are required to file a registration statement with the appropriate state agency (usually the Securities Division or Consumer Protection Agency) and a disclosure statement (similar to that required of franchisors) that would then be provided to each prospective offeree.

MLM companies are, however, often exempt from the coverage of the business opportunity laws by virtue of "sales kit exemptions" in the statutes. This type of exemption excludes from the calculation of "required payment" monies paid for sales demonstration equipment or materials sold to the purchaser at the company's cost.

Of additional interest to MLM companies is the typical exemption in the business opportunity laws for the sale of an ongoing business. This allows the sale of a distributorship or business opportunity to another without triggering the business opportunity laws. The following states have adopted business opportunity statutes:

California	Nebraska
Connecticut	New Hampshire
Florida	North Carolina
Georgia	Ohio
Iowa	South Carolina
Kentucky	Texas
Louisiana	Utah
Maine	Virginia
Maryland	Washington
Minnesota	

Pyramid Laws

Consumers often confuse legitimate *multilevel marketing programs* (which are generally valid methods for distributing products and services to the public) with *pyramid schemes* (which are generally unlawful schemes subject to criminal prosecution in many states).

Numerous laws and regulations have been enacted in the United States to prohibit pyramid schemes. Some of the state laws enacted declare unlawful "pyramid sales schemes," "chain distributions," "referral selling," "endless chains," and the like. Pyramid distribution plans have also been declared unlawful as lotteries, unregistered securities, violations of mail fraud laws, or violations of the Federal Trade Commission Act.

Broadly speaking, a pyramid distribution plan is a means of distributing a company's products or services to consumers. Pyramid schemes generally consist of several distribution levels through which the products or services are resold until they reach the ultimate consumer. A pyramid differs from a valid multilevel marketing company in that in its elemental form a pyramid is merely a variation on a chain letter and almost always involves large numbers of people at the lowest level who pay money to a few people at the utmost level. New participants pay a sum of money merely for the chance to join the program and advance to the top level, where they will profit from the initial payments made by later participants.

One of the most common elements of pyramid schemes is an intensive campaign to attract new participants who serve to fund the program by providing the payoff to earlier participants. Some schemes use high-pressure sales techniques such as "go go chants" and "money hums" to increase crowd enthusiasm. Often meetings are held in distant locations with everyone traveling to them by bus as a captive audience. These bus rides and meetings may include an emotional "pep rally" type recruiting approach. In one New Jersey case, prospective recruits who did not sign up at the initial meeting were taken on a charter plane trip to the company's home office, during which flight, known as a go tour, they were subjected to intense pressure to sign contracts before the plane landed. On the plane, references were made to the success of others, large amounts of money were displayed amid talk of success, and at times piles of cash and contracts were dropped into the laps of prospects. The format of the meetings is often completely scripted and prepared strictly in accordance with the company's guidelines and policies. These scripts invariably make reference to the financial success awaiting those who participate. In the New Jersey case, recruits were told that they could easily become millionaires.

A pyramid scheme *always* involves a certain degree of failure by its participants. A pyramid plan can only work if there are unlimited numbers of participants. At some point the pyramid will fail to attract new participants, and those individuals who joined later will not receive any money because there will be no new bottom level of participants to support the plan.

In order to avoid prosecution, the promoters of pyramid schemes often attempt to make their plans resemble multilevel marketing companies. Pyramid schemes, therefore, often claim to be in the business of selling products or services to consumers. The products or services, however, are often of little or no value, and there is no true effort to sell them because emphasis remains almost solely on signing up new participants who are needed to "feed the machine."

There are several ways to distinguish a legitimate multilevel marketing program from unlawful pyramid schemes:

1. *Initial payment.* Typically the initial payment required of a distributor of products and services of a multilevel marketing program is minimal; often the distributor is required to buy only a sales kit that is sold at cost. Because pyramid plans are supported by the payments made by the new recruits, participants in a pyramid plan are often required to pay substantial sums of money just to participate in the scheme.
2. *Inventory loading.* Pyramid schemes typically require participants to purchase large amounts of nonrefundable inventory in order to participate in the program. Legitimate multilevel marketing companies usually repurchase any such inventory if the distributor decides to leave the business. Many state laws require the company to repurchase any resalable goods for at least 90 percent of the original cost.
3. *Head-Hunting.* Pyramid plans generally make more money by recruiting new prospects ("head-hunting") than by actually selling the products. Multilevel marketing programs, on the other hand, make money by the sale of legitimate and bona fide products to consumers.

More than twenty-five states have laws prohibiting pyramid schemes whether as "endless chains," "chain distribution schemes," or "pyramids." Programs with the following three elements are prohibited:

1. An entry fee or investment that must be paid by the participant in order to join
2. Ongoing recruitment of new prospects
3. The payment of bonuses, commissions, or some other valuable to participants who recruit new participants

Generally, the purchase by a participant of a sales kit (at cost) is not deemed to be an entry fee or investment.

The following is a summary of other laws used to prosecute pyramid plans (the same laws are often used to regulate multilevel marketing companies):

- *Referral sales statutes.* More than ten states prohibit referral sales programs, which are generally defined to include the payment of some compensation to a buyer in return for furnishing to the seller the names of prospective recruits. Thus, any scheme in which the buyer is told that he or she can receive a return of the money paid if he or she provides a list of names to the seller is an unlawful referral sale.

- *Lottery statutes.* Many states prohibit pyramid programs as lotteries on the basis that financial success in the program is not based upon skill and judgment but upon the element of chance, e.g., that an endless stream of new participants will join the program, causing the original participant to receive a return higher than the initial entry fee paid to join.

- *Securities laws.* The sale of a security that is not registered is a violation of state and federal law. The Securities and Exchange Commission (SEC) has taken the position that the money paid by a prospect to participate in a scheme (with the expectation of profit based primarily on the activities of other parties) will be considered to be an investment contract or security that must be registered with the SEC.

- *Mail fraud laws.* Pyramid programs have been prosecuted under mail fraud laws that prohibit endless chain schemes involving the exchange of money or other things of value through use of the U.S. mail.

- *Federal Trade Commission Act.* Section 5 of the FTC Act prohibits unfair methods of competition in commerce and unfair or deceptive practices. This broad provision has been used to justify action by the FTC against pyramid programs. In one of its most famous cases, the FTC argued that Amway Corporation was an illegal pyramid program. The FTC ultimately determined that Amway is *not* a pyramid scheme because the only required "investment" was a sales kit sold to distributors at cost, Amway guaranteed it would repurchase unsold inventory, and the *sponsoring distributor received nothing from the mere act of sponsoring* but rather began to earn money only when the newly recruited distributor sold products to consumers.

Multilevel marketing is a method of distributing goods or services not through retail stores but rather through the efforts of independent distributors or sales agents. These distributors have a great deal of flexibility in training their own salespeople and will earn money arising out of products sold by these salespeople (i.e., the down-line sales organization) as well as sales arising out of their own efforts. Because the initial cost is often minimal, multilevel marketing is increasing in popularity and is attractive to individuals interested in starting a business without a substantial capital investment.

15

Structuring Licensing Programs and Agreements

Licensing programs offer many of the same benefits of franchising, such as more rapid market penetration through shifting the capital costs of expansion, and share many of the same risks inherent in franchising, such as the possible loss of quality control and a dependence on the skills and resources of the licensee.

The two principal types of licensing occur at two different levels in the marketplace: (1) technology licensing, where the strategy is to find a licensee for exploitation of industrial and technological developments; and (2) merchandise and character licensing, where the strategy is to license a recognized trademark or copyright to a manufacturer of consumer goods in markets not currently served by the licensor.

Technology Transfer and Licensing Agreements

The principal purpose behind technology transfer and licensing agreements is to join the technology proprietor, as licensor, and the organization that possesses the resources to properly develop and market the technology, as licensee. This marriage, made between companies and inventors of all shapes and

Figure 15-1. Why growing companies develop technology licensing programs.

(1) To match promising technology with the resources necessary to bring it to the marketplace

(2) To raise capital and earn royalty income (e.g., there are many enterpreneurs who have had doors slammed in their face by commercial banks and venture capitalists who have ultimately obtained growth capital and cash flow from licensees)

(3) As a defensive strategy; this can occur from one of two perspectives: (1) The licensor may want to have its competitors as licensees instead of watching as they eventually develop their own technology or (2) the licensee may want to pre-empt a competitor or gain access to its confidential information by approaching the competitor to obtain a license. (*WARNING:* Some competitors will acquire an exclusive license to technology merely to "sit on it" so that it never enters the marketplace. Be prepared to negotiate certain performance standards or limits to exclusivity in the agreement in order to avoid such a trap.)

(4) To shift (or share) the product liability risk inherent in the production or marketing of hazardous or dangerous products with the licensee

(5) To reach new geographic markets unfamiliar to the technology proprietor, such as overseas, where the technology may need to be adapted or otherwise modified to meet local market conditions

(6) To make the widest possible use of the technology by licensing other applications or by-products of the technology that may be outside the licensor's expertise or targeted markets

(7) To avoid or settle actual or pending litigation (many litigants in intellectual property infringement or misappropriation cases windup settling the case using some form of a cross-license in lieu of costly attorney's fees and litigation expenses).

sizes, occurs often between an entrepreneur with the technology but without the resources to adequately penetrate the marketplace, as licensor, and the larger company, which has sufficient research and development, production, human resources, and marketing capability to make the best use of the technology. The industrial and technological revolution has witnessed a long line of very successful entrepreneurs who have relied on the resources of larger organizations to bring their products to market, such as Chester Carlson (xerography), Edwin Land (Polaroid cameras), Robert Goddard (rockets), and Willis Carrier (air-conditioning). As the base for technological development becomes broader, large companies look not only to entrepreneurs and small businesses for new ideas and technologies, but also to each other, foreign countries, universities, and federal and state governments to serve as licensors of technology.

In the typical licensing arrangement, the proprietor of intellectual property rights (patents, trade secrets, trademarks, and know-how) permits a third party to make use of these rights according to a set of specified conditions and circumstances set forth in a license agreement. Licensing agreements can be limited to a very narrow component of the proprietor's intellectual property rights, such as one specific application of a single patent, or be much broader in context, such as in a classic "technology transfer" agreement, where an entire bundle of intellectual property rights are transferred to the licensee typically in exchange for initial fees and royalties. The classic technology transfer arrangement is actually more akin to a "sale" of the intellectual property rights, with a right by the licensor to get the intellectual property back if the licensee fails to meet its obligations under the agreement.

Key Elements of a Technology Licensing Agreement

Once the decision to enter into more formal negotiations has been made, the terms and conditions of the license agreement should be discussed. Naturally these provisions vary, depending on whether the license is for merchandising an entertainment property, exploiting a given technology, or distributing a particular product to an original equipment manufacturer (OEM) or value-added reseller (VAR). As a general rule, any well-drafted license agreement should address the following topics:

- *Scope of the grant.* The exact scope and subject matter of the license must be initially addressed and carefully defined in the license agreement. Any restrictions on the geographic scope, rights of use, permissible channels of trade, restrictions on sublicensing, limitations on assignability, or exclusion of improvements to the technology (or expansion of the character line) covered by the agreement should be clearly set forth in this section.

- *Term and renewal.* The commencement date, duration, renewals and extensions, conditions to renewal, procedures for providing notice of intent to renew, grounds for termination, obligations upon termination, and licensor's reversionary rights in the technology should all be included in this section.

- *Performance standards and quotas.* To the extent that the licensor's consideration will depend on royalty income that will be calculated from the licensee's gross or net revenues, the licensor may want to impose certain minimum levels of performance in terms of sales, advertising, and promotional expenditures and human resources to be devoted to the exploitation of the technology. Naturally, the licensee will argue for a "best efforts" provision that is free from performance standards and quotas. In such cases, the licensor may want to insist on a minimum royalty level that will be paid regardless of the licensee's actual performance.

- *Payments to the licensor.* Virtually every type of license agreement includes some form of initial payment and ongoing royalty to the licensor. Royalty formulas vary widely, however, and may be based upon gross sales, net sales, net profits, fixed sum per product sold, or a minimum payment to be made to

Figure 15-2. Tips for the prospective licensor.

1. *Finding the Right Dance Partner*—The quest for the appropriate licensee should be approached with the same zeal and diligence that one would adopt in the search for a marriage partner. No stone should remain unturned either in narrowing the field of prospective licensees and in the due diligence process applied to a particular proposed licensee. The goals and objectives of each party, the financial strength of the licensee, the licensee's past licensing practices, the qualifications of licensee's jurisdiction (other states, other countries), and the skills of the licensee's sales and marketing team *should all be examined prior to the commencement of the negotiation of the license agreement.* Access to the licensor's intellectual property should be severely restricted unless and until these criteria have been examined and met to the satisfaction of the licensor.

2. *Avoiding the Inferiority Complex*—Although a small company or entrepreneur, looking to license its technology to a larger business, often faces an uphill battle, this is not sufficient reason to merely "roll over" in the licensing negotiations. There are too many horror stories of entrepreneurs who were impressed and intimidated by the larger company's resources and lawyers and as a result "sold their soul" at far below the current or eventual market value of the technology.

3. *Don't Go in Naked; Don't Be a Motor Mouth*—Many prospective licensors make the mistake of telling too little or saying way too much in the initial meetings and negotiations with the prospective licensee. Finding the right balance of disclosure to pique the interest of the licensee without "giving away the farm" is never easy; however, there is a commonly accepted solution, the *licensing memorandum.* The licensing memorandum, when used in tandem with confidentiality agreements, can provide the prospective licensee with the information it needs to conduct the preliminary analysis without jeopardizing the rights of the licensor. The memorandum should contain a

Figure 15-2. continued

___

discussion of the technology and the portfolio of intellectual property rights that protect the technology, the background of the proprietor, the projected markets and applications of the technology, the proposed terms and financial issues between licensor and licensee, and a dicussion of existing competitive technology and technological trends that could affect the future value of the license.

4. *Things Can and Will Change—Be Prepared*—Like marriages, most licensing agreements are intended to continue over a long period of time. As a result, it is difficult to predict technological, social, economic and political trends that will affect the rights and obligations of the licensor and licensee during the term of the agreement. Licensing agreements, like all legal documents, require a certain degree of precision to be enforceable and workable for the parties; however, the inevitability of change should result in a framework of trust and flexibility. Not every detail will be addressed nor every change in the external environment anticipated. Technologies become obsolete, governments get overthrown, rock stars lose popularity, movie sequels flop, and a corporation's personnel may be restructured, but the licensing agreement must be flexible enough to handle all of these unforeseen changes.

___

the licensor over a given period of time or may include a sliding scale in order to provide some incentive to the licensee as a reward for performance.

• *Quality control assurance and protection.* Quality control standards and specifications for the production, marketing, and distribution of the products and services covered by the license must be set forth by the licensor. In addition, procedures should be included in the agreement which allow the licensor an opportunity to *enforce* these standards and specifications, such as a right to inspect the licensee's premises; a right to review, approve, or reject samples produced by the licensee; and a right to review and approve any packaging, labeling, or advertising materials to be used in connection with the exploitation of the products and services that are within the scope of the license.

- *Insurance and indemnification.* The licensor should take all necessary and reasonable steps to ensure that the licensee has an obligation to protect and indemnify the licensor against any claims or liabilities resulting from the licensee's exploitation of the products and services covered by the license.

- *Accounting, reports, and audits.* The licensor must impose certain reporting and record-keeping procedures on the licensee in order to ensure an accurate accounting for periodic royalty payments. Further, the licensor should reserve the right to audit the records of the licensor in the event of a dispute or discrepancy, along with provisions as to who will be responsible for the cost of the audit in the event of an understatement.

- *Duties to preserve and protect intellectual property.* The obligations of the licensee, its agents, and employees to preserve and protect the confidential nature and acknowledge the ownership of the intellectual property being disclosed in connection with the license agreement must be carefully defined. Any required notices or legends that must be included on products or materials distributed in connection with the license agreement (such as the status of the relationship between licensee and licensor or identification of actual owner of the intellectual property) are also described in this section.

- *Technical assistance, training, and support.* Any obligation of the licensor to assist the licensee in the development or exploitation of the subject matter being licensed is included in this section of the agreement. The assistance may take the form of personal services or documents and records. Either way, any fees due to the licensor for such support services which are over and above the initial license and ongoing royalty fee must also be addressed.

- *Warranties of the licensor.* A prospective licensee may demand that the licensor provide certain representations and warranties in the license agreement. These may include warranties regarding the ownership of the intellectual property, such as absence of any known infringements of the intellectual property or restrictions on the ability to license the intellectual property, or warranties pledging that the technology has the features, capabilities, and characteristics previously represented in the negotiations.

- *Infringements.* The license agreement should contain procedures under which the licensee must notify the licensor of any known or suspected direct or indirect infringements of the subject matter being licensed. The responsibilities for the cost of protecting and defending the technology should also be specified in this section.

Special Issues in Negotiating and Drafting Technology Licensing Agreements

There are a wide variety of special contractual issues that must be addressed in the preparation of a technology license agreement. These include:

Defined Terms. What many entrepreneurs may initially view as "legal boilerplate" is often the most hotly contested component of the license agreement. This initial section of the license agreement is intended to do much more than make the document "easier to read," but rather defines some of the key aspects of the relationship with respect to the specific field of the technology licensed, the territory to be covered, the milestones and objectives that must be met, the specific patents or trademarks that will be included within the scope of the license, and the nature of the compensation to be paid to the licensor.

Reports to the Licensor, Record Keeping by the Licensee. In all licensing agreements, adequate reporting and record keeping by the licensee is critical to ensure that the licensor receives all royalty payments when due. In a technology licensing agreement, additional reports should be prepared monthly or quarterly that disclose the licensee's actual use of the technology; research studies or market tests that have directly or indirectly used the technology; the marketing, advertising, or public relations strategies planned or implemented that involve the technology; progress reports regarding the meeting of established performance objectives and timetables; reports of any threatened or actual infringement or misappropriation of the licensor's technology; and any requests for sublicenses or cross-licenses that have been made by third parties to the licensee.

Exclusivity of the License Granted. The term *exclusive* in the context of a licensing agreement negotiation is often misunderstood. Exclusivity could apply to a territory, an application of the technology, or a method of production of the products that result from the technology. Exclusivity may or may not include the licensor itself and may or may not permit the granting of sublicenses or cross-licenses to future third parties who are not bound by the original license agreement. Exclusivity may or may not be conditioned on the licensee meeting certain predetermined performance standards. Exclusivity may be conditional for a limited time period on the continued employment of certain key technical staff of the licensee. All of these issues, surrounding what on its fact appears to be a "simple" term, must be discussed in the negotiations and ultimately addressed in the license agreement.

Technical Support and Assistance, Dependence on Key Personnel. The proper development and exploitation of the technology often depends on the availability of the proprietor and the licensor's technical team to provide support and assistance to the licensee. The conditions under which this team will be available to the licensee should be included in the technology license agreement. Provisions should be drafted to deal with scheduling conflicts, the payment of travel expenses, the impact of disability or death of the inventor, the availability of written or videotaped data in lieu of the inventor's physical attendance, the regularity and length of periodic technical support meetings, and the protection of confidential information.

Merchandise and Character Licensing Agreements

The use of commonly recognized trademarks, brand names, sports teams, athletes, universities, television and film characters, musicians, and designers to foster the sale of specific products and services is at the heart of today's merchandise and character licensing environment. Manufacturers and distributors of products and services license these words, images and symbols for products that range from clothing to housewares to toys and posters. Certain brand names and characters have withstood the test of time, while others fall prey to fads, consumer shifts, and stiff competition. For example, Pierre Cardin, the designer, has issued over 500 licenses to companies that use his name on goods manufactured according to his quality control specifications. Mr. Cardin continues to be a symbol of good quality and respect. On the other hand, the popularity of the Izod Lacoste alligator logo has waned since the early 1980s, yielding to stronger competitors such as Ralph Lauren's Polo logo. At the time this book is being written, manufacturers of consumer goods are competing fiercely for the rights to license the cartoon image of Bart Simpson (of the Fox Network television show "The Simpsons") and the four characters that make up the Teenage Mutant Ninja Turtles, also of television fame. Whether or not these characters will be in such demand by the time this book is published remains to be seen.

The trademark and copyright owners of these properties and character images are motivated to license for a variety of reasons. Aside from the obvious desire to earn royalty fees and profits, many manufacturers view this licensing strategy as a form of merchandising *to promote the underlying product or service.* The licensing of a trademark for application on a line of clothing helps to establish and reinforce brand awareness at the consumer level. For example, when R. J. Reynolds Tobacco Company licenses a leisure apparel manufacturer to produce a line of Camel wear, the hope is to sell more cigarettes, appeal to the life-style of its targeted consumers, maintain consumer awareness, *and* enjoy the royalty income from the sale of the clothing line. Similar strategies have been adopted by manufacturers in order to revive a mature brand or failing product. In certain instances, the spin-off product that has been licensed was almost as financially successful as the underlying product it was intended to promote.

Brand name owners, celebrities, and academic institutions must be very careful not to grant too many licenses too quickly. The financial rewards of a flow of royalty income from hundreds of different manufacturers can be quite seductive but must be weighed against the possible loss of quality control and dilution of the name, logo, or character. The loyalty of the licensee network is also threatened when too many licenses are granted in closely competing products. Retailers also become cautious when purchasing licensed goods from a licensee if there is a fear that quality control has suffered or that the popularity of the licensed character, celebrity, or image will be short-lived. This may result in smaller orders and an overall unwillingness to carry inventory, especially in the toy industry, where purchasing decisions are being made by (or at least influenced by) the whims of a five-year-old child who may strongly identify with a character image one week and then turn away to a totally different character image the next week. It is incumbent on the manufacturers and licensees to develop advertising and media campaigns to hold the consumer's attention for an extended period of time. Only then will the retailer be convinced of the potential longevity of the product line. This requires a balancing of the risks and rewards between licensor and licensee in the character-licensing agreement in the areas of compensation to the licensor, advertising expenditures by the licensee, scope of the exclusivity, and quality control standards and specifications.

In the merchandise licensing community, the name, logo,

symbol, or character is typically referred to as the Property, and the specific product or product line (e.g., the T-shirts, mugs, posters, etc.) is referred to as the Licensed Product. This area of licensing offers opportunities and benefits to both the owners of the properties and the manufacturers of the licensed products. For the owner of the property, brand recognition, goodwill, and royalty income are strengthened and expanded. For the manufacturer of the licensed products, there is an opportunity to leverage the goodwill of the property to improve sales of the licensed products. The manufacturer has an opportunity to "hit the ground running" in the sale of merchandise by gaining access to and use of an already established brand name or character image.

Naturally, each party should conduct due diligence on the other. From the perspective of the owner of the property, the manufacturer of the licensed product should demonstrate an ability to meet and maintain quality control standards, possess financial stability, and offer an aggressive and well-planned marketing and promotional strategy. From the perspective of the manufacturer of the licensed property, the owner of the property should display a certain level of integrity and commitment to quality, disclose its future plans for the promotion of the property, and be willing to participate and assist in the overall marketing of the licensed products. For example, if a star basketball player were to be unwilling to appear for promotional events designed to sell his own specially licensed line of basketball shoes, this would present a major problem and is likely to lead to a premature termination of the licensing relationship.

Special Issues in Negotiating and Preparing Merchandise and Character Licensing Agreements

There are several key areas that must be addressed in the preparation and negotiation of a merchandise licensing agreement. These include (1) scope of the territorial and product exclusivity; (2) assignability and sublicensing rights; (3) the definition of the property and the licensed products; (4) quality control and approval; (5) ownership of artwork and designs; (6) term renewal rights and termination of the relationship; (7) initial license and ongoing royalty fees; (8) performance criteria for the licensee; (9) liability insurance; (10) indemnification; (11) duty to pursue trademark and copyright infringement; (12) minimum advertising and promotional requirements; (13) accounting and record keeping of the licensee; (14) inspection and audit rights of the licensor; (15) rights of first refusal for expanded or revised characters and images; (16) limitations on licensee's distribution to related or affiliated entities; (17) representations and warranties of the licensor with respect to its rights to the property; (18) the availability of the licensor for technical and promotional assistance; and (19) miscellaneous provisions, such as law to govern, inurement of goodwill, nature of the relationship, notice, and force majeure.

Let's take a look at a few of these provisions in greater detail.

Definition of Key Terms. The definition of the property and the licensed products is usually accomplished with the use of schedules, illustrations, and exhibits. For example, suppose a manufacturer of children's sportswear wanted to license the likeness of basketball star Michael Jordan for a new line of clothing. Will the property consist of unlimited use of the name and likeness of Mr. Jordan, or will it be only for a specific drawing or caricature of his face? Similarly, will the licensed products be defined as virtually any style or size of children's sportswear or will they be limited to "children's short-sleeved T-shirts up to size 20 and matching children's short pants?" Naturally, there is room for much variation and negotiation in these defined terms. In order to avoid claims and litigation over unauthorized use of the property, the licensor and licensee should clearly communicate their intent to counsel before preparation of the merchandise licensing agreement.

Term and Termination. As discussed earlier, the world of merchandise licensing is subject to short-lived fads, the performance of celebrities, and the whims of the fickle consumers. Just as the licensor will want to reserve the right to terminate the agreement if the licensee is not properly performing, so too will the licensee want a right to terminate if the property quickly loses its charm (and therefore its ability to generate revenues). The events triggering termination, the obligation to give notice and opportunity to cure, and the obligations of each party following the termination must be addressed.

Royalty Payments. The key economic issue in the agreement is the section dealing with royalty payments that must be paid to the licensor by the licensee in exchange for the use of the property over a period of time. The royalty obligation is usually stated as a fixed percentage of the licensee's sales of the licensed products or as a lump sum per unit of the licensed product. Royalty rates are based purely on market forces and the negotiation skills of the parties and their counsel. This section must also address the basis for the calculation of the royalty payment (e.g., the definition of *gross revenues, net sales,* etc.), any minimum royalty payments that must be paid quarterly or annually by the licensee to the licensor, any adjustments to the royalty rate (which is tied to performance, inflation, a change in market conditions, etc.), royalties on noncash sales, and the licensee's obligation to prepare reports and statements to support the calculation of the royalty payment.

Index